Forensic Photography Techniques for Examining Skeletal Remains

Based on over 30 years of the author's expertise in the field of forensic photography, this book offers invaluable skills to successfully take good-quality photographs.

This book addresses the reality that forensic photographers often work with varying levels of equipment quality—from professional cameras to basic personal devices—yet must produce consistently high-quality, legally admissible evidence. Across 18 chapters, Alain Wittmann demonstrates techniques to produce a composition that not only is of high quality but also fulfils the purpose of drawing attention to the subject matter as the primary focal point. When composing a photograph, it is necessary to consider both evidentiaryly important and non-essential elements to ensure that the image accurately documents the subject while maintaining focus on the subject of interest. Whether you are working with minimal material or even a complex case, this manual emphasizes fundamental photography principles, including proper exposure, framing, and preparation techniques that can produce clear, unambiguous images without requiring expensive equipment or post-processing software. The book also includes a quiz, useful resources, and a glossary of key phrases used within the field so that you can better engage with the material and test your knowledge.

Forensic Photography Techniques for Examining Skeletal Remains will be valuable to forensic photographers, medical professionals, and anyone working with human remains who needs to create accurate photographic documentation that can withstand legal scrutiny and effectively communicate findings to courts and investigators.

Forensic Photography Techniques for Examining Skeletal Remains

Alain Wittmann

CRC Press
Taylor & Francis Group
Boca Raton London New York

CRC Press is an imprint of the
Taylor & Francis Group, an **informa** business

Cover image created and designed by Alain Wittmann

First edition published 2027
by CRC Press
2385 NW Executive Center Drive, Suite 320, Boca Raton FL 33431

and by CRC Press
4 Park Square, Milton Park, Abingdon, Oxon, OX14 4RN

CRC Press is an imprint of Taylor & Francis Group, LLC

ISBN: 9781041292760 (hbk)
ISBN: 9781041292777 (pbk)
ISBN: 9781003768838 (ebk)

DOI: 10.4324/9781003768838

Typeset in Minion
by Deanta Global Publishing Services, Chennai, India

Author's Note

The methods, photographs, and explanations that are included in this manual are derived from my 30 years of experience and will be of assistance to you in the process of taking photographs with a good quality. When making a decision about what to include, it is necessary to take into account both the things that are essential and the things that are not significant. In order to achieve the purpose of this attempt, which is to draw attention to the subject matter as the primary focus point, that is the objective of this manual. This manual will assist you in enhancing your images in a manner that is both instructive and free of any potential ambiguity, regardless of whether you are working with a small amount of material or even a complicated situation. To fully understand what constitutes adequate preparation, you will find in this manual numerous examples used in various situations. The final section of this manual contains a basic guideline that can be used in cases involving skeletal remains.

Contents

A Foreword by Duarte Nuno Vieira, Professor at the University of Coimbra

Photographic documentation of injuries and sequelae today constitutes a fundamental element within the scope of correct medical-legal and anthropological forensic expert interventions, in accordance with the expert *leges artis*. Photography makes it possible to fully highlight what was observed, reinforcing the expert interpretation carried out, facilitating the analysis and issuing of opinions by other experts, as well as an easier apprehension and understanding of expert findings and results by the judicial decision-maker, in the certainty that similar traumatic contexts can provide sometimes quite different aspects.

While it is true that photographic documentation does not dispense with the need for the expert report to incorporate a detailed, complete, and appropriate description of what was observed, the truth is also that this description, however complete and exhaustive it may be, does not dispense with (should not dispense with) its complementation by the image of what was observed, described, and expertly interpreted.

It is precisely from this perspective that all the most relevant international protocols in the field of medical-legal and anthropological forensic expertise today (see, for example, the Istanbul and Minnesota protocols) give a very particular emphasis on the need to photographically document all expert elements, being today absolutely clear and indisputable that a medical-legal or anthropological forensic expert report will only reach its maximum quality if it involves and incorporates the images of the expert elements that served as its basis, to the interpretation and conclusions it presents.

Unfortunately, in many expert interventions, substantial deficiencies and insufficiencies continue to be found in relation to what should be properly completed photographic documentation. Many medico-legal and forensic experts have not received adequate training on how to properly document, through images, the evidence and the various pathologies, natural and traumatic, found during the examinations they carry out. On the other hand, while scientific literature and bibliographical support are now abundant in multiple areas of forensic intervention, the truth is that books and other biographical sources dedicated to the issue of forensic photographic documentation within this area of medico-legal interventions and forensic anthropology continue to be scarce. It is also true that the number of highly qualified experts with international experience in the field of photographic expert documentation is small and that the number of those with the desire and ability to transmit their knowledge and experience in writing is even smaller.

I met Alain Wittmann many years ago. We were both involved in the extensive medico-legal and anthropological forensic operation carried out in Kosovo at the beginning of the 21st century, after the armed conflict that devastated that region. I then had the opportunity to see the extraordinary work he carried out daily in documenting the multiple traumatic pathologies that were being observed in the context of the thousands of medico-legal and forensic anthropology examinations carried out at the time. The images he obtained were fundamental for the interpretation and expert discussion of the cases observed and for their subsequent presentation and defense in legal proceedings. They simultaneously constituted a documentary collection of enormous relevance so that future professionals can contact and learn about the multiple aspects of forensic pathology and anthropology. Alain is today one of the biggest international references in the field of forensic photographic documentation, with intense expert experience. But, above all, he is a conscientious and determined professional, with enormous dedication to his work, committed to providing others with the fruits of his work, his reflections, and his experience, as well as the innovations and technical improvements that he was able to introduce into the context of his professional field.

This is a book written in simple and clear language, but always rigorous and scientifically based, which highlights a competent, serious professional, concerned with justice and the training of those who contribute to it, with the sharing and transmission of experiences and knowledge. It is a book that provides fundamental guidelines for all those who, in the context of their expert intervention, are faced with the need to photographically document what they observed and must interpret, addressing the best that can currently be provided in terms of technical, scientific, and expert information in the context of photographic documentation in forensic pathology and anthropology examinations. It provides us with the theoretical and practical foundations for knowledge, understanding, and adequate production of this photographic documentation. It provides us with the basis for rigorous and adequate photographic documentation, which will provide greater solidity to the forensic reports that incorporate it.

It is, therefore, a fundamental book for all forensic pathologists and forensic anthropologists, whether for those taking the first steps in discovering the fascinating forensic universe, or for professionals who already explore it, as reading and analyzing it will also result in an expansion and consolidation of knowledge and perspectives. And it is equally relevant for all those who, directly or indirectly, resort to or are confronted with medical-legal forensic anthropology expertise, namely magistrates, lawyers, or researchers. With this book, it will be possible to obtain more relevant expert results, which will result in more appropriate and scientifically based judicial decisions. I am sure that it will become an element of mandatory consultation and reference and that it will undoubtedly represent a starting point for new journeys, for the awakening of new vocations, and for the opening of other professional horizons for some of its readers.

I am therefore pleased to strongly recommend its reading, not only to all those who are interested in forensic sciences, but also to all those who, directly or indirectly, are interested in the problems of this expert field. I am sure that readers will derive the greatest satisfaction and benefit from it and that they will also find new stimuli for reflection and for an increasingly qualified expert practice, carried out with sensitivity and common sense, in a correct, effective, and humanized way.

I warmly congratulate the author for this contribution he makes to medical-legal and anthropology expertise, thanking him deeply for the enormous honor he gave me by inviting me to write a foreword to it.

Duarte Nuno Vieira

Full Professor at the University of Coimbra, President of the Portuguese National Academy of Medicine, and Chairman of the Forensic Advisory Board of the Prosecutor of the International Criminal Court. Past President of the International Academy of Legal Medicine, the International Association of Forensic Sciences, the World Association of Police Medical Officers, the Mediterranean Academy of Forensic Sciences, the European Council of Legal Medicine, the Ibero-American Network of Forensic Medicine and Forensic Science Institutions, and the Latin American Association of Medical Law.

A Foreword by Jose Pablo Baraybar, PhD, Forensic Anthropologist

It is both an honor and a profound responsibility to introduce this indispensable manual, *Forensic Photography Techniques for Examining Skeletal Remains*, penned by Alain Wittmann. Having collaborated with Alain across some of the most complex forensic investigations of our time, I can attest not only to his technical mastery but also to his unwavering commitment to clarity, precision, and ethical rigor.

Alain's career spans nearly three decades, a journey marked by contributions to forensic science from the mass graves of the Balkans to the archaeological sites of Peru; his lens has captured evidence that speaks when words fail. His tenure with institutions such as the International Criminal Tribunal for the Former Yugoslavia (ICTY), the United Nations Mission in Kosovo, and the Peruvian Forensic Anthropology Team (EPAF) underscores a legacy built on meticulous attention to detail and an unyielding pursuit of accountability. This manual distills that legacy into a pragmatic, accessible guide—one that transcends borders, budgets, and bureaucratic constraints.

What sets this work apart is its grounding in real-world challenges. Alain understands that forensic photographers often operate in resource-limited environments, where improvisation is as critical as technical knowledge. Whether documenting bullet trajectories in skeletal remains or recovering faded tattoos through infrared imaging, he demystifies complex processes without compromising rigor. The chapters on exposure, sensor dynamics, and file formats are not mere technical primers; they are lifelines for practitioners navigating the delicate balance between speed and accuracy. His insistence on RAW files, for instance, is not dogma but a hard-earned lesson from courtrooms where image integrity meant the difference between justice and obscurity.

Yet this manual is more than a technical guide. It is a testimony of Alain's philosophy that forensic photography is both science and storytelling. Every image must "speak" with unambiguous clarity—a principle echoed in his meticulous frameworks for autopsies, reconstructions, and evidence logging. The inclusion of case studies, such as reconstructing gunshot trajectories with colored rods or revealing hidden identifiers on mummified remains, transforms theory into tangible practice. Even the quiz at the end serves a deeper purpose: to sharpen the reader's instinct for problem-solving.

Those familiar with Alain's work will recognize his signature blend of humility and authority. His anecdotes—like the comparison of 4-megapixel and 36-megapixel cameras—remind us that equipment is a tool, not a crutch. The true "sensor" is the photographer's eye, disciplined by preparation and ethical responsibility.

To newcomers and seasoned experts alike, this manual offers more than techniques—it offers a worldview. In Alain's hands, the camera becomes an instrument of justice, a means to illuminate truths that might otherwise remain buried. As forensic science evolves, this text will endure as a foundational resource, bridging the gap between protocol and practice, between seeing and understanding.

It is my sincere hope that readers will carry forward Alain's ethos: that every photograph, no matter how challenging the circumstances, must serve as an unassailable witness to the facts. In doing so, we honor not only the victims whose stories these images tell but also the integrity of the profession itself.

Jose Pablo Baraybar, PhD
Forensic Anthropologist

A Foreword by Alan Robinson, Senior Forensic Scientist

When Alain Wittmann asked me if I would write the Foreword to his book, I was deeply honored and warmly welcomed the opportunity. I am well placed to write it, as everything I know about Forensic Photography I learned from him.

I began working with Alain almost 20 years ago at the UN Office on Missing Persons and Forensics in Kosovo, and later in the Department of Forensic Medicine for the EULEX Rule of Law mission, also in Kosovo. There he was the Forensic Photographer for exhumations, skeletal analyses, autopsies, death scene investigation, clinical forensics, and evidence collection and handling.

Well before and since then, he has been building local and international forensic capacity, having trained dozens of people on behalf of the United Nations, the European External Action Service, the International Committee of the Red Cross, and several non-government organizations, including the Peruvian Forensic Anthropology Team.

I have always been supremely impressed by his diligence, attention to detail, technological awareness, and most of all, by his ability to listen and understand the needs of forensic specialists to best illustrate their findings.

I will not define Forensic Photography, as the reader can best learn that from the author himself, and I won't remind everyone that "an image is worth 1000 words"; rather, I prefer to share how forensic photography, in the hands of Alain, has impacted my own work to establish the Forensic Truth.

With over 25 years of experience and several court appearances as an expert witness for cases of international crimes (Genocide, Crimes Against Humanity, Crimes Against the Civilian Population, among others), successfully explaining complex topics to judges, prosecutors, and defenders would not have been possible, or even feasible, without the forensic photography techniques used by Alain.

Accurate, well-lit, correctly exposed, and adequately composed images that tell a factual story without the need for elaborate, highly technical, and potentially tedious statements have, without fail, succinctly delivered the message across to wide-ranging audiences linked to the pursuit of justice.

Most importantly, on the many occasions in which families of victims have asked me to see images related to the cases affecting their loved ones, the author's images proved invaluable to comply with my duty to enable the relatives' Right to Know, in a compassionate but scientifically rigorous manner.

So, dear reader, whether you are a judge, a prosecutor, an investigator, a forensic expert, a forensic student, or indeed a professional forensic photographer, you would do well to learn about the importance of the work and wealth of experience here shared with you by Alain Wittmann.

Alan Robinson
Senior Forensic Scientist
Former Head, Forensic Science Unit (FSU)
UNITAD—United Nations

About the Author

Alain Wittmann is a professional forensic photographer with over 30 years of experience. Before he became an international consultant, he worked for the International Criminal Tribunal for the Former Yugoslavia (ICTY), the United Nations Mission in Kosovo (UNMIK) at the Office of Missing Persons and Forensics (OMPF), and the European Union Rule of Law Mission in Kosovo (EULEX) at the Department of Forensic Medicine (DFM). Over the course of his career, he has participated in international forensic investigation teams that have conducted exhumations, crime scenes, autopsies, forensic examinations, and identifications in over 18 countries.In Peru, he collaborated with the Peruvian Forensic Anthropology Team (EPAF), the Truth and Reconciliation Commission (CVR), the National Criminal Court, the Human Rights Association, the Prosecutor's Office, and the Inter-American Court.His images have featured in several forensic and anthropology books.

Acknowledgments

In my 30-year career, I have had the opportunity to collaborate with a wide variety of professionals, including pathologists, archaeologists, anthropologists, odontologists, radiologists, police officers, and crime scene investigators. I would like to take this opportunity to express my gratitude to each one of them. Because of them, I have been able to learn a significant amount about each of their areas of specialty, which in turn has allowed me to successfully innovate and enhance my photographic practice.

Introduction

Introduction

A good forensic investigation requires a certain level of discipline and skill. Among the specialized methods that are used in the evidence collection process, whether criminal or civil, is forensic photography.

My observations have shown that the budget allocated to photography varies from one country to another, from one department to another, or from one institution to another

Unfortunately, in our profession, some photographers work with the latest generation equipment, while others use basic or even personal equipment, all of which affect the product. Yet the task is the same regardless of whether the photographer is using a camera with an interchangeable lens, a compact camera, or a phone. What you need to know is that the quality of the photography will be determined by the exposure, framing, preparation, and one's ability to photograph.

No matter whether you are working with minimal material or even on a complex case, this manual will assist you in improving your photography in a manner that is both didactic and clear of any potential ambiguity.

Based on my 30 years of expertise, the methods, examples, and explanations that are provided in this manual will be of great assistance. You will learn how to select a good exposure, how to choose a good frame, how to prepare your image, and how to make and operate your equipment without the need to invest in professional or the latest equipment. You will also be able to produce a good photograph, free of ambiguity, without having to resort to Photoshop or Lightroom for retouching light, sharpening, cropping, and other related aspects of photography.

Before shooting, you should take into consideration that exposure, framing, and preparation are crucial. So too are what you will include, as well as what is significant and what is not significant. The objective is to produce a composition that is of good quality and draws direct attention to the subject matter.

When forensic photography is used in a case, you must know what to photograph and how to photograph it. During a situation that involves Skeletal remains, which can involve bone reconstruction, bullet trajectory, injury, or other evidence, interpretation will be important to obtain a clear image that is free from any potential ambiguity.

The strategies I have used in my work, which in numerous instances have featured as evidence in both national and international courts, can help to accomplish these objectives.

Because it captures the essence of forensic photography, the proverb "a good picture is worth a thousand words" is one that I use regularly in my workshops. After finishing this manual, I have high expectations that the reader will have a better understanding of the true significance of this idiom.

DOI: 10.4324/9781003768838-1

Photographers or other professionals who work with skeletal remains, be it in forensic cases or not, are the target audience for whom this manual can be a very useful resource.

What the human eye sees is faithfully reproduced in the form of a picture by the camera. Yet photos can record details with a degree of clarity that the human eye may not always be able to achieve. This is one of the advantages of photography.

To illustrate this point, I will now discuss La Photographie Judiciaire, which was written in 1890 by the Frenchman Alphonse Bertillon, who was one of the early pioneers of the use of photography in court procedures in France. It is the third chapter of this manual that I would like to draw attention to.

The Use of Photography as a Recording Device

In addition, judicial photography is utilized in all criminal and civil trials when it is essential to maintain an exact, comprehensive, and impartial image of the location, the goods, and the individuals involved. Even though these details may have been overlooked or forgotten by the entire world, their meticulous preservation through photography can be of extreme importance.

Forensic Photography

Since the 19th century, photography has been used as a form of evidence in legal proceedings. Because photography is an essential component of this process, it is always included in forensic investigation. As digital photography is constantly evolving, the possibilities for taking photographs are expanding with it.

With the invention of a prototype in 1975, Steven Sasson marked the beginning of the history of the digital camera. On the other hand, the first digital camera that was accessible for purchase was released in the year 1988. In accordance with protocols that differ from nation to nation, these digital cameras have been gradually acknowledged by the judicial system since the late 1990s.

Fundamentally, photography is the art of reproducing an exact image of something. This fundamental principle also holds true for forensic photography. We can capture information that cannot be kept indefinitely pertaining to the likes of crime scenes, injuries discovered during an autopsy, or forensic medical examinations, to facilitate the investigation of cases involving living people who have been the victims of physical violence, torture, or other crimes. This is because we can record the information.

More specifically, photography is an essential component of the method that forensic investigators use to create a visual record of the evidence that they have obtained during their investigations. Ever since the incorporation of photography into the legal system, forensic images can be offered in court as a valid piece of evidence.

The term "crime scene" often goes together with the popular conception of this field of photography. But what is frequently overlooked is that forensic photography is also utilized during clinical examinations, autopsies, analysis of human remains, and various other fields of medical investigation that are conducted as part of civil and criminal cases.

Yet while it is essential to differentiate between images taken at the scene of a crime and those taken for a medico-legal investigation, the fact that these two tasks are carried out in very different ways does not change the reality that they are complementary to one another and that they both contribute to the accomplishment of the same objective.

DOI: 10.4324/9781003768838-2

Some Roles

As a member of a legal team consisting of forensic professionals, the photographer will attempt to recreate events and establish the facts within the context of judicial investigations.

A forensic photographer is required to do everything possible to document any information that could contribute to the identification of individuals or the collection of evidence.

A detailed documentation of the forensic photography technique is the responsibility of the photographer, who is the one who is accountable for it. To make a visual record that is accurate, exhaustive, and objective of the evidence and the scene, it is necessary to take photographs of all the evidence in its natural context. This must be done before the evidence is treated or manipulated in any manner.

This includes documentation of all steps, where applicable, before, during, and after an assessment, exhumation, crime scene investigation, autopsy, medical examination, human skeleton, and other comparable procedures, including general and detailed photographs.

Ensure that the documentation of all relevant information is carried out by working closely with other forensics in a strong manner.

To guarantee that each photograph contains both the case number and a ruler that may be utilized to determine the size of the subject that is being photographed.

DOI: 10.4324/9781003768838-3

Camera

1

Camera

Images can be captured with digital photography in a quick and simple manner utilizing equipment such as digital single-lens reflex cameras (DSLRs), compact cameras, bridge cameras, mirrorless cameras, and smartphones. The resolution can reach over 100 megapixels, depending on the device that is being used.

A camera can also be used to record video, which offers further possibilities.

In this manual, I will write exclusively about reflex cameras, which include both full-frame and APS cameras, because these are currently the most frequently used in the field. But keep in mind that the method will be the same no matter what the camera uses.

Even though it is generally acknowledged that having a higher number of megapixels will result in a higher quality of image, it is ultimately up to the photographer to select the appropriate settings in order to achieve good photography. These settings include shutter speed, aperture, ISO, and framing.

I have made numerous significant changes to my apparatus over the course of my professional career, as technology has evolved. My first device was a 35mm film camera; then I started using my first digital camera, a Kodak, in 1999. Currently, I use three Nikon cameras: a D800, a D5300, and a D200, which is equipped with an infrared sensor.

Presented here are a total of six photographs that I took over the course of my career. The resolution of these photographs ranges from 4 to 36 megapixels, and each was captured using a different camera operated in a different setting: Canon Power Shot G2, with 4 megapixels, Nikon Coolpix 5700 with 5 megapixels, Fujifilm FinePix S9100 with 9 megapixels, Nikon D200 with 10 megapixels, Nikon D90 with 12 megapixels, and Nikon D800 with 36 megapixels.

By carefully examining Figures 1.1 through 1.6, can you identify which camera was used to capture each photograph?

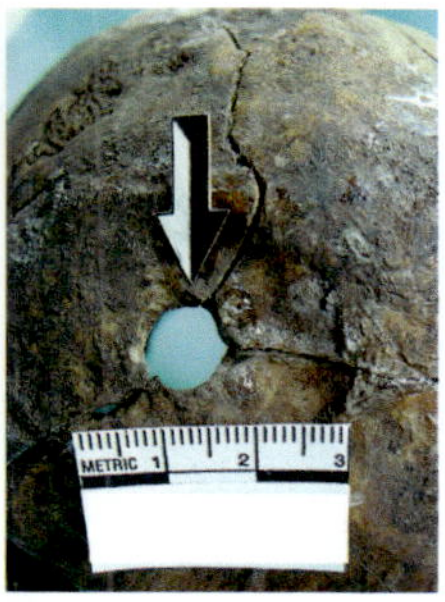

Figure 1.1 Skull occipital, bullet entrance.

Source: Photograph by the author.

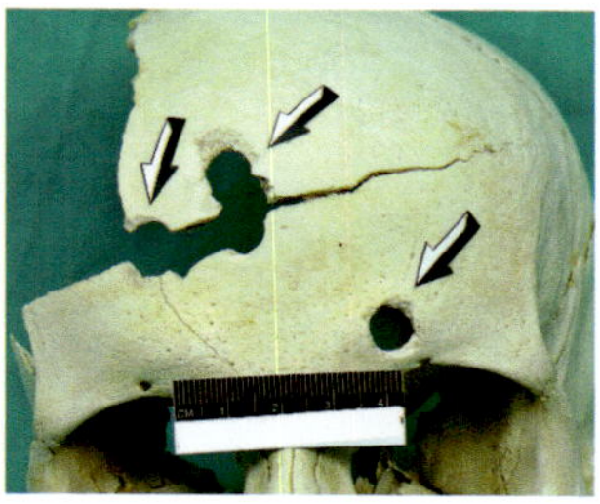

Figure 1.2 Skull frontal bone, bullet's entrance.

Source: Photograph by the author.

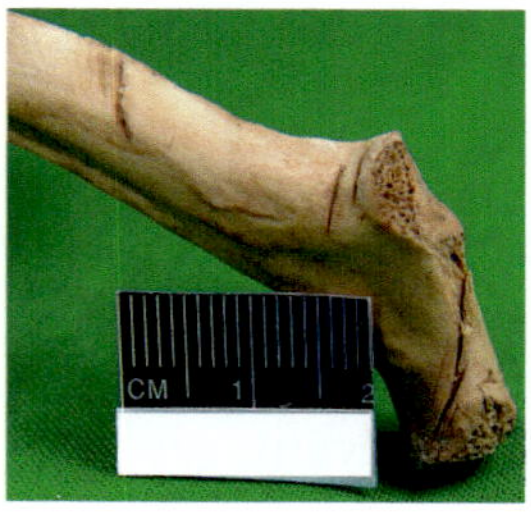

Figure 1.3 Animal rib with cuts.

Source: Photograph by the author.

DOI: 10.4324/9781003768838-4

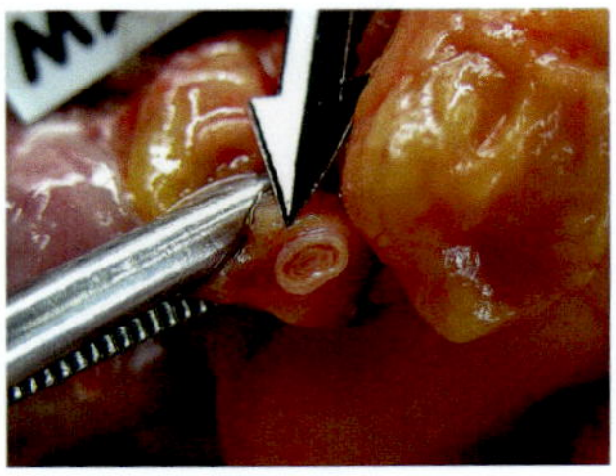

Figure 1.4 Heart obstructed coronary artery.

Source: Photograph by the author.

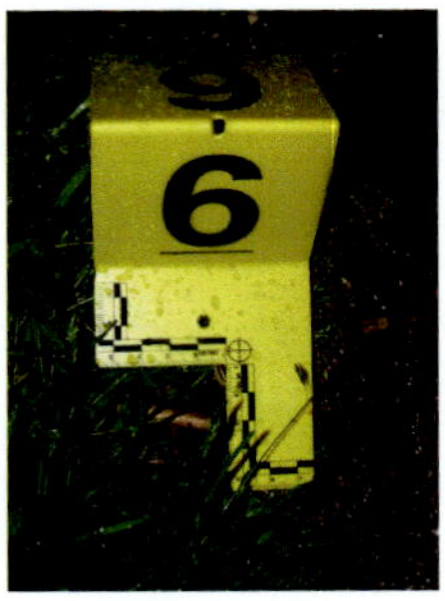

Figure 1.5 Shell case from crime scene.

Source: Photograph by the author.

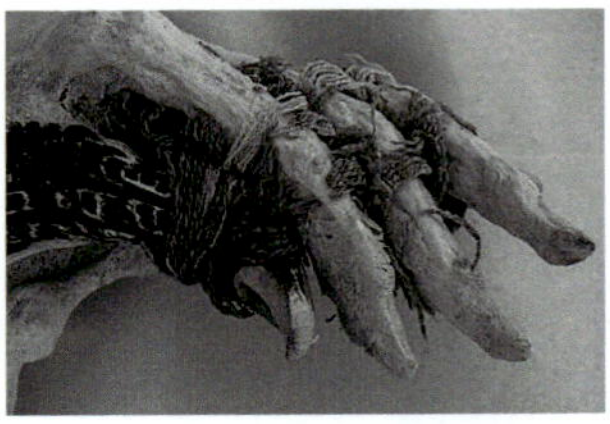

Figure 1.6 Pachacamac Museum—Mummy's hand with tattoo.

Source: Photograph by the author.

You will find the answer at the end of this manual.

Basic Recommendations

- Before buying a digital camera and considering what different models offer, you should think about your needs and how you intend to use the device.
- Check the official website of your camera to see if there are any new firmware updates available.
- Although digital photography has advantages, there are also some disadvantages to consider. Here are some examples of both. Note that they are based on my opinions, because each photographer will have different opinions depending on their own needs and the brand of camera they use.

Some advantages

- The memory card can hold many photos.
- The photo immediately appears on the screen.
- The ISO can be changed on each shot.
- The ability to create a video.
- Connection to a printer, depending on the model.
- Wi-Fi and GPS, depending on the model.
- EXIF data.
- Two card slots, depending on the model.
- Articulated LCD screen, depending on the model.

Some disadvantages

- Risk of memory card failure.
- Light sensitivity.
- Photos can be enhanced.

- Battery consumption can be heavy.
- A powerful computer is needed if it uses high-resolution images.
- Regular backup is necessary.

Basic Knowledge of a Digital Camera

Digital cameras offer numerous options, but many of them are not useful in our case. Remember what I said about considering what you need.

In this manual, we will talk about digital cameras whose lenses can be changed. Because it is essential to have at least some level of familiarity with the fundamentals of photography before you start using your camera, this chapter will cover some basic but essential topics.

Basic Principles

- The light enters the lens, bounces off the mirror, passes through the pentaprism, and reaches the viewfinder, allowing the photographer to see the scene before taking the photograph. As illustrated in Figure 1.7.

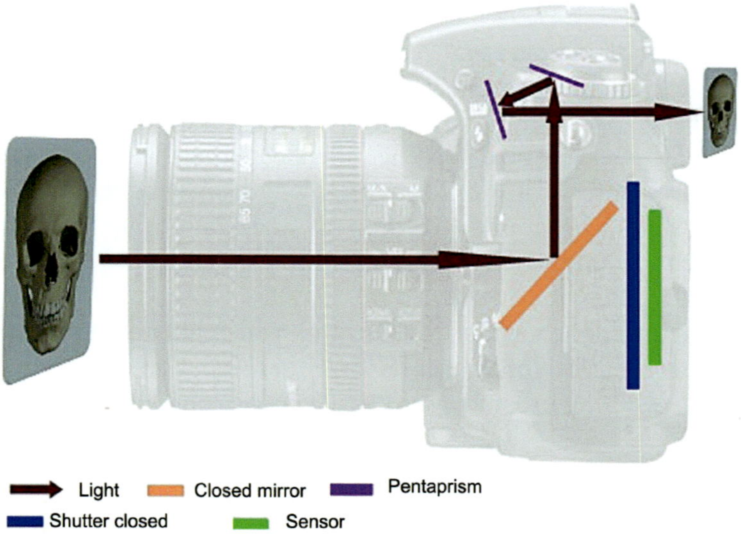

Figure 1.7 Camera operation before shooting.

Source: Photograph by the author.

- When you take a picture, the mirror moves so it faces up, the shutter opens so light can reach the sensor, then the shutter and mirror close so the image is captured and visible on the screen.

As illustrated in Figure 1.8

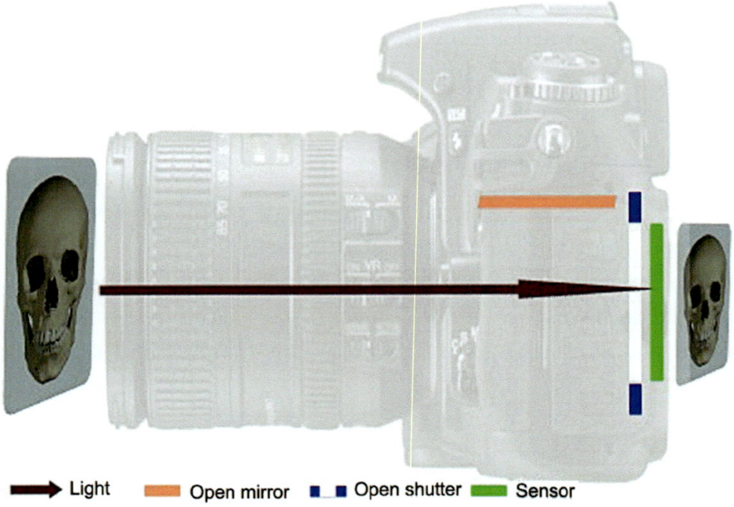

Figure 1.8 Camera operation during shooting.

Source: Photograph by the author.

Sensor

The two main types of digital interchangeable-lens cameras generally used are full-frame cameras and APS-format cameras. The primary difference between these two formats lies in the size of their image sensor. Because sensor size affects the field of view produced by a given lens, the effective framing of a scene differs between the two formats, as demonstrated in Figure 1.9. Consequently, different focal lengths may be required to achieve the same angle of view on full-frame and APS cameras. The relationship between these sensor formats and their corresponding focal-length equivalencies is shown in Table 1.1.

- The first is the full frame format (24 × 36 mm), which has no multiplier factor.
- The second incorporates a multiplier factor (either APS, Foveon, or 4/3, depending on the brand), resulting in a narrower viewing angle compared to the 24 × 36 mm format.

Table 1.1 The following table provides examples of the focal-length equivalencies of an 18–200 mm lens when used with different camera formats and sensor sizes

Camera brand	Sensor format (mm)	Type	Multiplier factor	Lens 18–200 mm equivalent to (mm)
Canon, Nikon, Sony	24 × 36	Full frame	1	18–200
Canon	28.77 × 18.70	APS	1.3	23.40–260
Nikon, Pentax, Sony	23.60 × 15.80	APS	1.5	27–300
Canon	22 × 15	APS	1.6	28.80–320
Sigma	20.70 × 13.80	APS	1.7	30.60–340
Olympus	4/3	APS	2	36–400

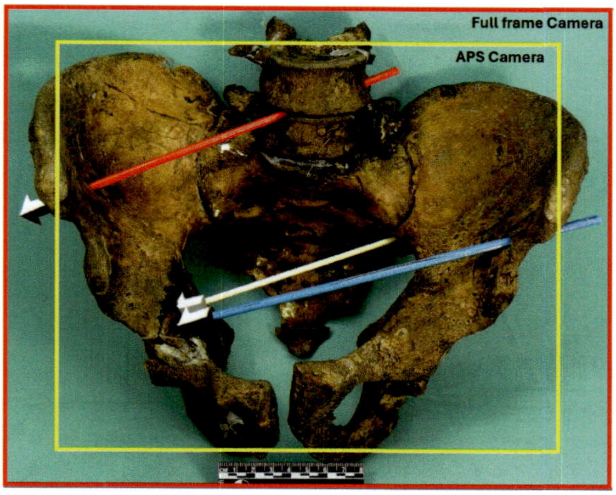

Figure 1.9 This illustration gives you an approximate view of what the angle of view of a photo might look like if taken from the same position with the same lens but using a camera with a full-frame sensor or an APS sensor. This results in a narrower viewing angle.

Source: Photograph by the author.

Exposure Mode (Auto, P, S, A, M)

To get a properly exposed photograph, the shutter speed, aperture, and ISO settings will be determined by the various exposure modes that are available on the camera: auto, programmed, shutter priority, aperture priority, and manual. The mode that is chosen will influence the amount of control that the photographer will have over the camera to take a satisfactory shot.

Auto

Every aspect of the system is under the control of the camera, including the shutter speed, aperture, and sensitivity settings, as well as the flash. The photographer does not have the ability to alter any of these components.

Programmed (P)

The shutter speed and aperture are both pre-set to ensure that optimum exposure is achieved.

Shutter Priority (S)

The photographer is responsible for selecting the shutter speed, and the camera will automatically calculate and adjust the aperture to achieve the desired exposure.

Aperture Priority (A)

The photographer is responsible for choosing the aperture, and the camera will automatically calculate and adjust the shutter speed to achieve the desired exposure.

Manual (M)

The photographer must control all aspects of the camera, including the aperture, the speed, the sensitivity, and the flash, to obtain good exposure.

Observations:

Personally, I prefer to use manual mode because it provides me with the greatest level of control over my camera and, as a result, enables me to produce the type of image I'm looking for. Nevertheless, there are times when I am forced to switch to automatic mode to snap images as quickly as possible. For example, when I am at a crime scene or an exhumation.

Autofocus Area Selector (AF)

If the photographer uses the autofocus system incorrectly, the resulting image may appear blurred, as illustrated in Figure 1.10. To achieve proper focus, the camera's autofocus system automatically adjusts the focus when the shutter button is pressed halfway, as illustrated in Figure 1.11.

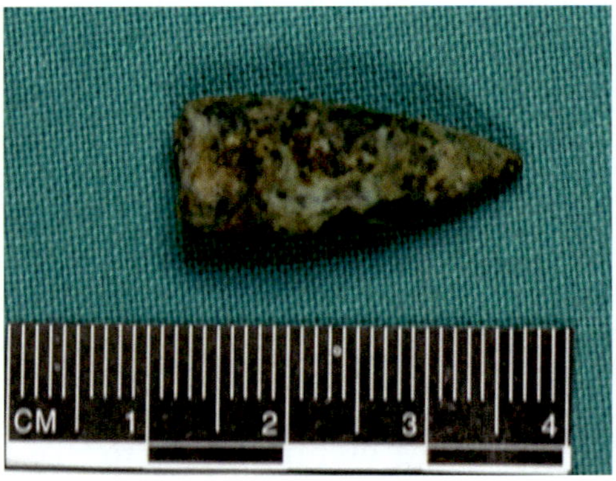

Figure 1.10 The bullet was taken with poor focusing.

Source: Photograph by the author.

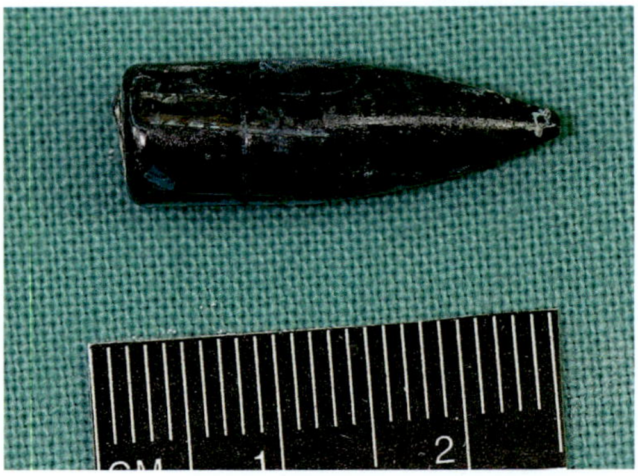

Figure 1.11 The bullet was taken with good focus.

Source: Photograph by the author.

Bringing an object into focus allows different features to be brought out, resulting in a more distinctive image.

The SLR camera has a mode that gives the user the ability to select a specific autofocus setting. Depending on the camera used, the autofocus point will be different.

Examples of how to use single point autofocus are shown in Figures 1.12 to 1.14.

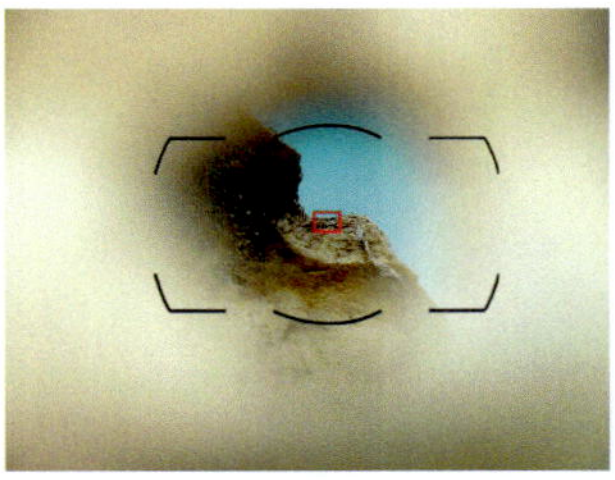

Figure 1.12 Internal view of a skull wound caused by a bullet.

Source: Photograph by the author.

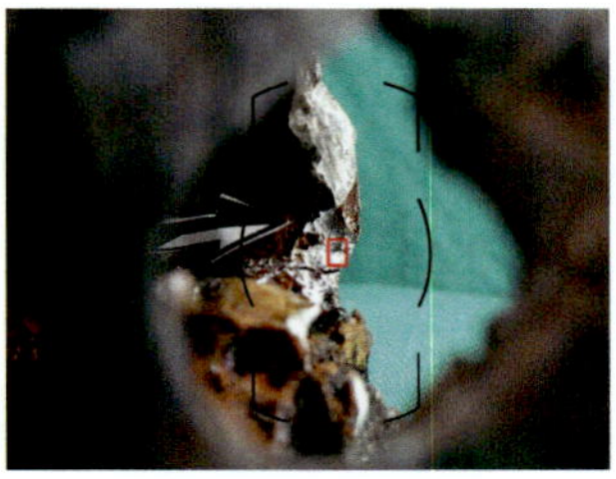

Figure 1.13 Internal view of a skull wound caused by a bullet.

Source: Photograph by the author.

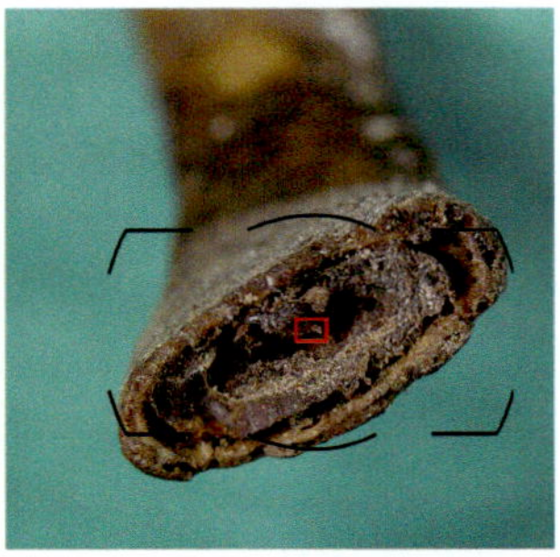

Figure 1.14 A view of a rib sternal end.

Source: Photograph by the author.

Examples of how to use multiple points autofocus are shown in Figures 1.15 to 1.17.

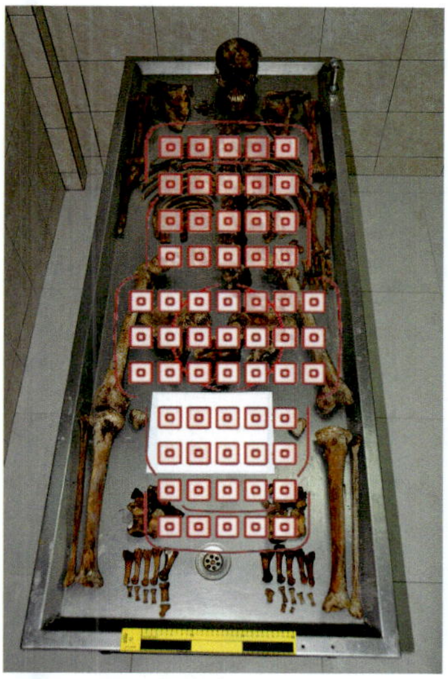

Figure 1.15 General skeletal view in its anatomical position.

Source: Photograph by the author.

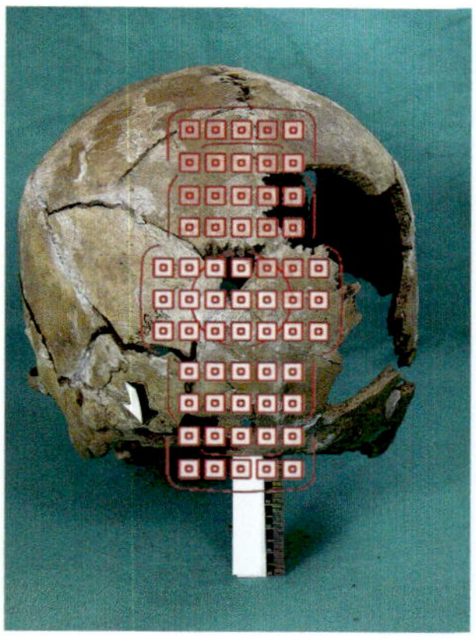

Figure 1.16 General view of the rear part of the skull.

Source: Photograph by the author.

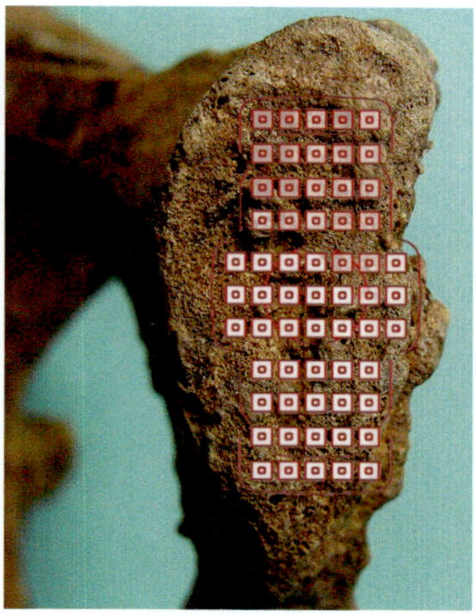

Figure 1.17 View of a pubis symphysis.

Source: Photograph by the author.

Observation
If you choose the wrong autofocus, part of your image may be blurred. This is because the focus does not properly cover the subject. As illustrated in Figures 1.18 and 1.19.

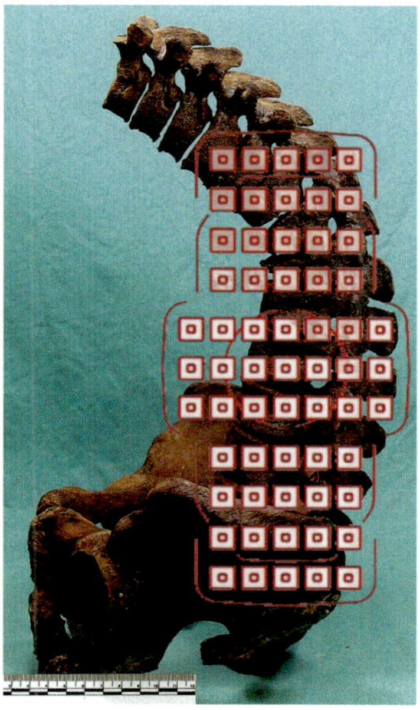

Figure 1.18 An image with good focusing will be crisp.

Source: Photograph by the author.

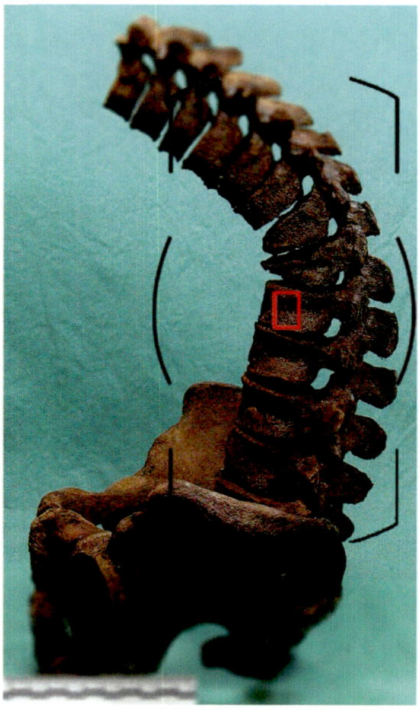

Figure 1.19 Areas of the image are blurry due to poor focus.

Source: Photograph by the author.

Exposure

When we talk about exposure, we are referring to the impact that is produced by a collection of parameters that include the ISO, the speed, and the aperture. It is the responsibility of the photographer to choose the appropriate level of light.

An image is considered well-exposed when it is neither too dark nor too light. A photo that is too light will be considered overexposed, while a photo that is too dark will be considered underexposed. The differences in exposure are seen in Figures 1.20 to 1.22.

Figure 1.20 Underexposed.

Source: Photograph by the author.

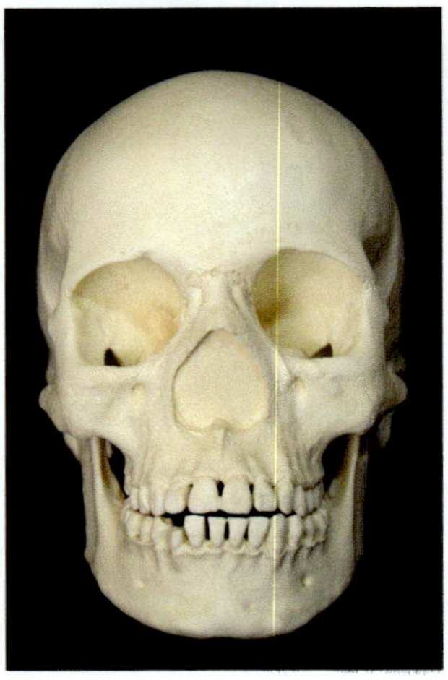

Figure 1.21 Good exposure.

Source: Photograph by the author.

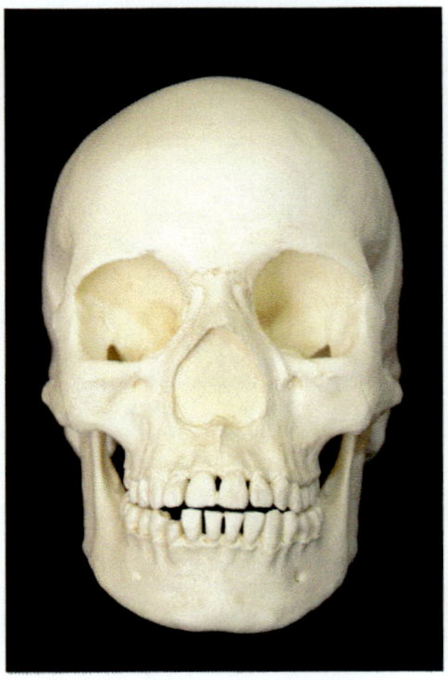

Figure 1.22 Overexposed.

Source: Photograph by the author.

Aperture

The aperture has two functions: it is used to control the amount of light that reaches the sensor, but also describes the distance between the nearest and farthest elements that will be in focus in the image. We refer to this as the depth of field (DOF).

Aperture has a scale that is made up of the letter "f" along with a number: f/1 - f/1.4 - f/1.8 - f/2 - f/2.8 - f/5.6 - f/8 - f/11 - f/16 - f/22 - f/32, and so on, depending on the model of the camera and lens.

Images from left to right show the three different exposure variations (Figure 1.23).

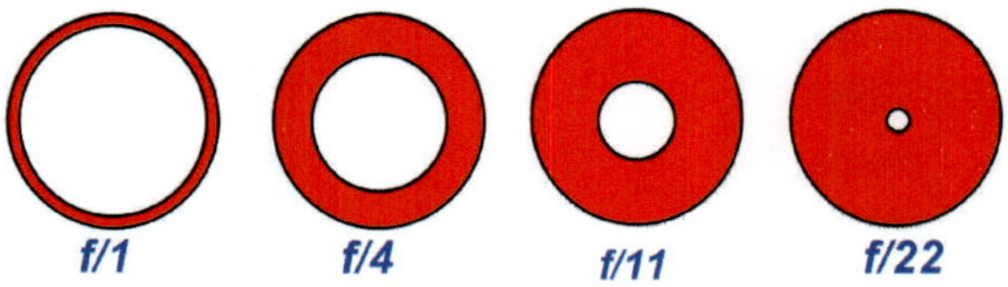

Figure 1.23 Example of different apertures. From left to right: a large aperture f/1 (small DOF) to a small aperture f/22 (large DOF).

Source: Photograph by the author.

1. Depth of field, which describes the distance between the closest and farthest things that are in focus in an image, as demonstrated in Figure 1.24.

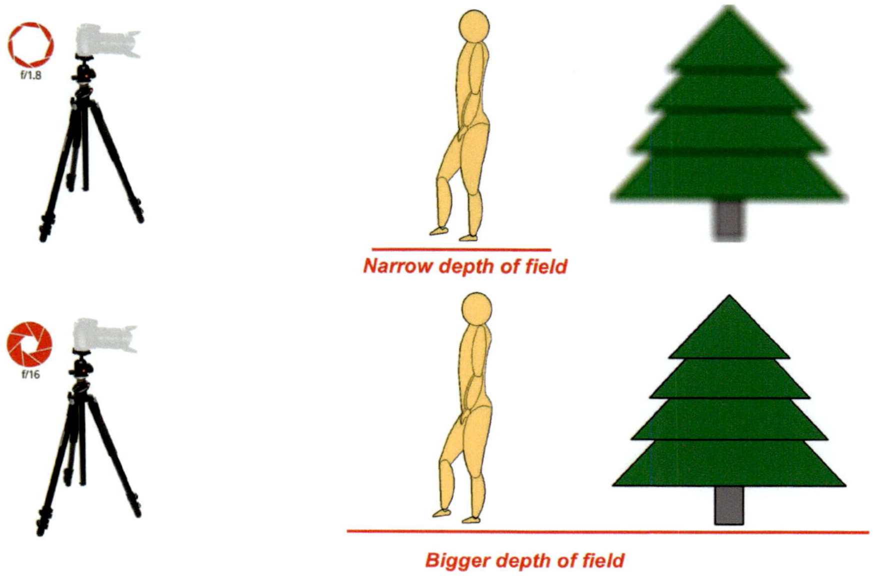

Figure 1.24 An approximate illustration of the difference in depth of field that occurs when using an aperture of f/1.8 and f/16.

Source: Photograph by the author.

Figures 1.25 and 1.26 illustrate an example of how the aperture can be utilized.

When the aperture is wide open (f/2.8 or f/4), only the foreground will be in focus while the elements in the background will be blurred (shallow depth of field).

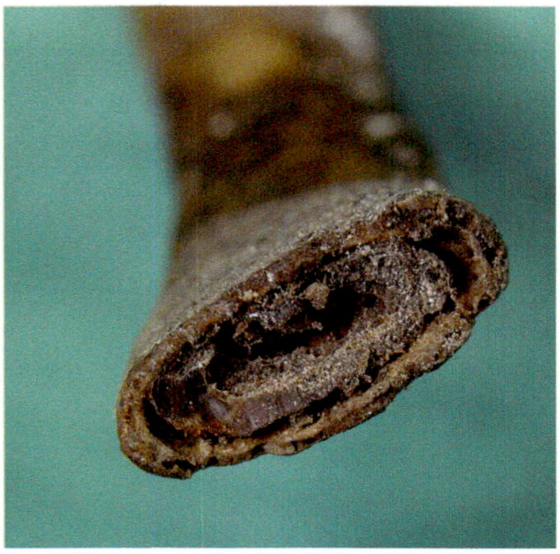

Figure 1.25 Example with a wide aperture.

Source: Photograph by the author.

When the aperture is closed (f/16 or f/22), both the primary subject and the elements surrounding it will be sharp (large depth of field).

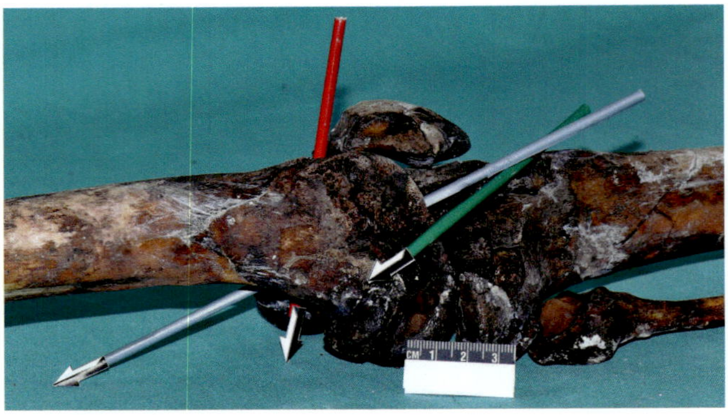

Figure 1.26 Example with a small aperture.

Source: Photograph by the author.

2. The amount of light will be affected depending on whether a large or small aperture is used. Depending on the number selected, the amount of light will be either half or double.

Example: f/4 to f/5.6 will reduce the amount of light, and f/5.6 to f/4 will increase it.

When the aperture is closed (either f/16 or f/22), the resulting image will have a low level of brightness. In contrast, the image that is produced will be extremely bright if the aperture is set to a wide-open setting (f/1.4 or f/2.8)

Figures 1.27 and 1.28 are illustrations of how the appearance of your photograph can change depending on the aperture you use.

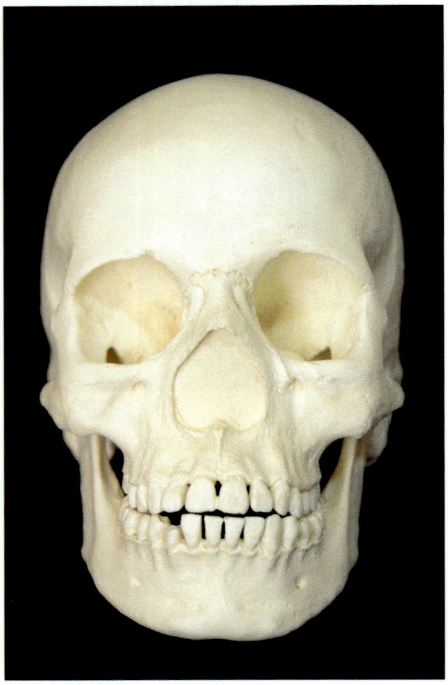

Figure 1.27 With aperture f/1.4.

Source: Photograph by the author.

Figure 1.28 With aperture f/22.

Source: Photograph by the author.

Shutter Speed

As the shutter speed is increased, the subject will be captured with greater clarity, and there will be a decrease in the likelihood of the subject being out of focus. In general, the minimum shutter speed should be equal to the focal length (50, 100, or 200 mm) when you're holding your camera in your hand. However, it is possible to use a slower speed if the lens is equipped with a VR (vibration reduction system).

There are two purposes of adjusting the shutter speed:

1. Adjusting the amount of time between when the shutter is opened and when it is closed. If you have a fast shutter speed, the exposure time will be shorter, while if you have a slow shutter speed, the exposure time will be longer.

Either seconds or fractions of a second are used to measure the shutter speed. This scale ranges from 1/30th to 1/8000th of a second, depending on the brand of the camera, because shutter speeds differ from camera to camera.

Figures 1.29 and 1.30 illustrate the distinction between low speed and high speed.

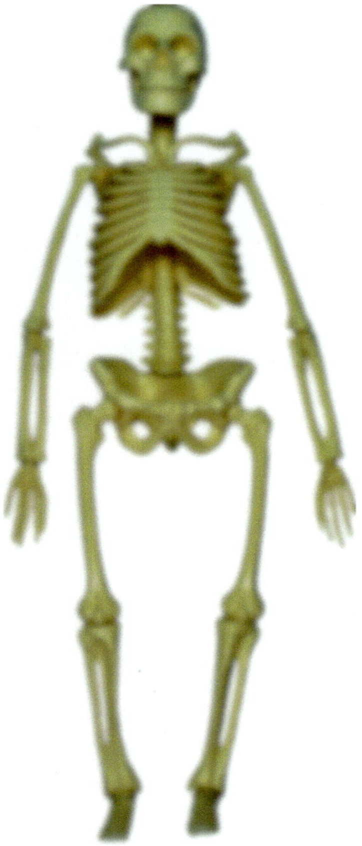

Figure 1.29 1/301/30 second blurry photo.

Source: Photograph by the author.

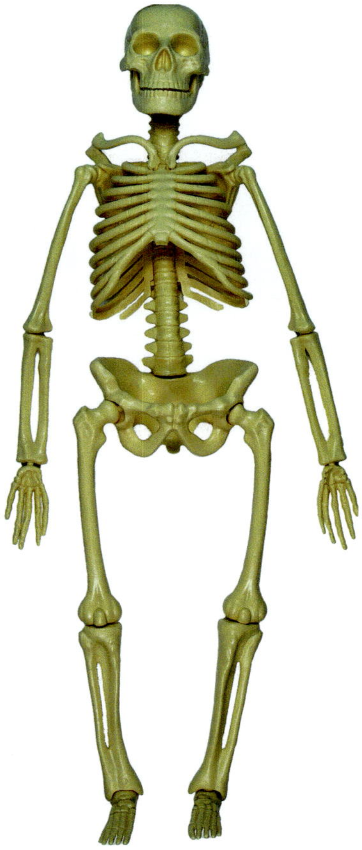

Figure 1.30 1/1251/125 second clear photo.

Source: Photograph by the author.

2. Adjusting the amount of light that is allowed to reach the sensor. The amount of light produced by each successive number is both increased and decreased by a factor of two:

1/30s to 1/60s reduced amount of light—1/30s to 1/15s a greater amount of illumination

Sensitivity (ISO)

The ISO setting is used to compensate for the lack of light, but the quality of the photograph will be either good or poor, depending on the ISO setting that is used. Depending on the model, cameras can have an ISO range of 50 to 25600 or even higher.

A high ISO, such as 1600 or more, is recommended for use in darker environments.

Figures 1.31 to 1.33 show examples of images taken in an autopsy room without additional lighting, using different ISO settings ranging from 400 to 1600.

Figure 1.31 With an ISO400.

Source: Photograph by the author.

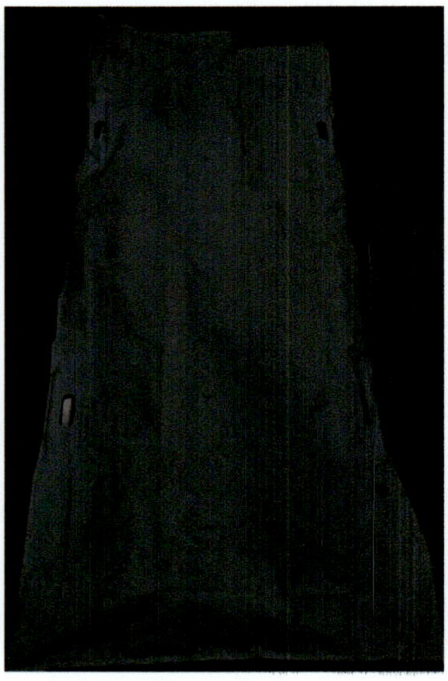

Figure 1.32 With an ISO800.

Source: Photograph by the author.

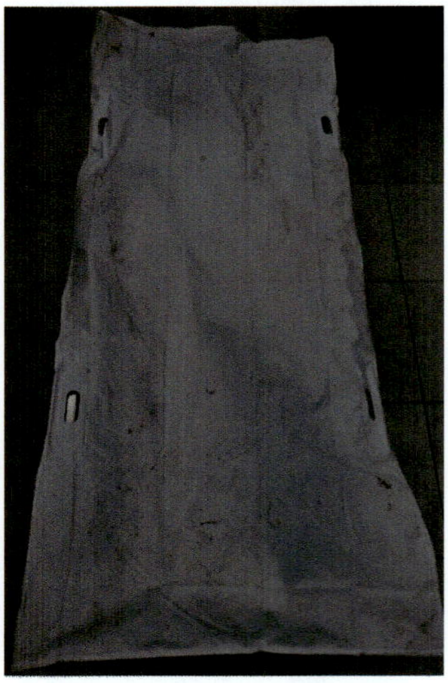

Figure 1.33 With an ISO1600.

Source: Photograph by the author.

A low ISO, such as 25, 50, or 100, is appropriate for use in bright circumstances and results in good image quality.

When taking a photo, you should always choose a low ISO level if possible, as increasing your ISO can have negative consequences. The amount of noise that is evident in the image will vary depending on the type of camera that was used; nonetheless, the intensity of the noise will increase in proportion to the ISO setting.

Figures 1.34 and 1.35 illustrate a comparison between an image captured at a low ISO setting and an image captured at a high ISO setting.

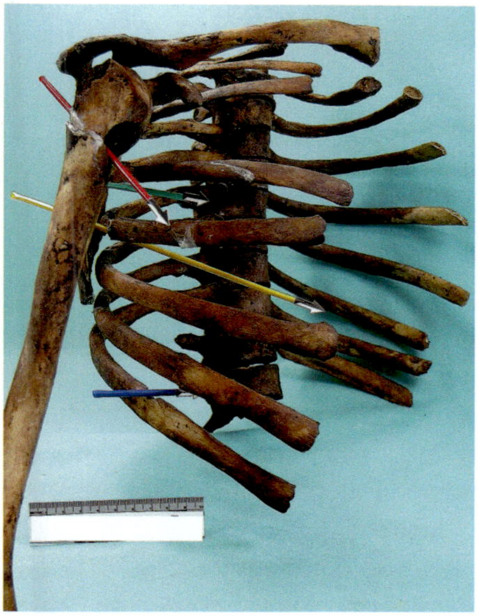

Figure 1.34 Photograph taken with an ISO of 100.

Source: Photograph by the author.

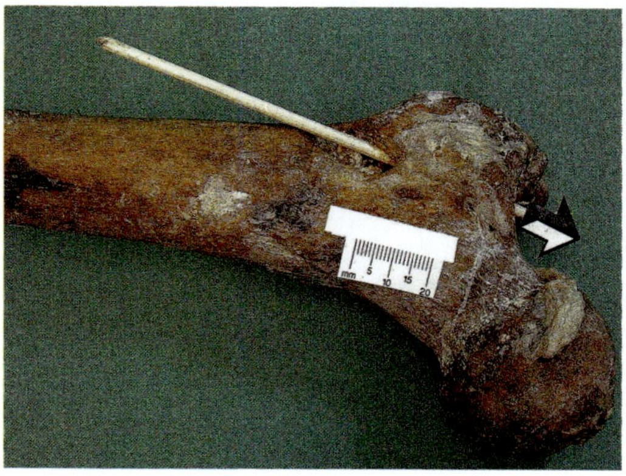

Figure 1.35 Photograph taken with an ISO of 1600.

Source: Photograph by the author.

Exposure Triangle

To successfully gather light for photographic purposes, it is essential to have a fundamental understanding of the exposure triangle.

Aperture, shutter speed, and ISO are the three elements that come together to form the exposure triangle.

These three components coordinate their actions to control the amount of light that enters the camera and produce an image, as illustrated in Figure 1.36.

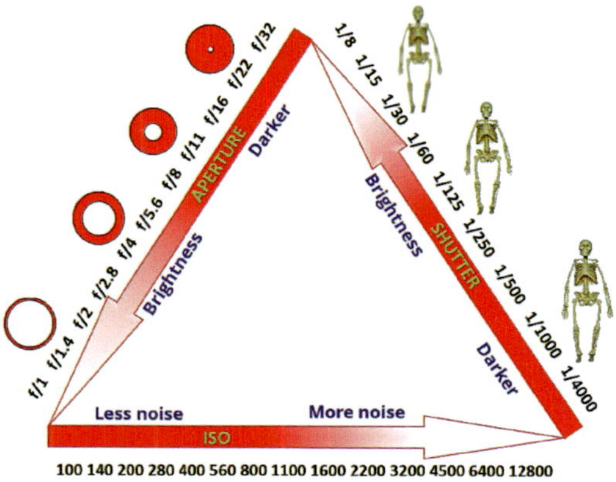

Figure 1.36 An illustration thatdescribes the relationship that exists between shutter speed, ISO, and aperture to obtain a correct exposure.

Source: Photograph by the author.

Aperture
When the aperture is open, you have a shallow depth of field but a lot of light; when the aperture is closed, you have a large depth of field but a small amount of light. The aperture has an "inverse" influence on the depth of field and the amount of light.

Speed
Speed has an "inverse" influence, which means that using a fast speed will result in a small amount of light reaching the sensor, whereas a slow speed will result in a significant amount of light reaching the sensor.

ISO
ISO goes a long way to compensating for a lack of light; however, the higher the sensitivity setting, the greater the amount of noise that will be present.

The reason why these three settings are so important is that they all come together to produce good exposure, which is necessary for a good image to be captured.

This means that these settings should not be considered independently of one another. If you want to change the shutter speed, the aperture, or the ISO, you will need to make a corresponding adjustment to one of the other two elements to compensate.

The following are two examples of the relationships that exist between the three components:

1. You are currently using an aperture setting of f/8, and you would like to switch to f/16. This will result in a decrease in the amount of available light; to compensate, either increase the ISO or slow the shutter speed to have more light.
2. You have an ISO of 200, and you want to switch to ISO 800; this will increase the amount of light; to compensate, close the aperture or increase the speed.

Exposure Compensation

The camera allows you to adjust the exposure, which in turn allows you to control the brightness of your image. This adjustment is typically represented by a plus or minus sign on your camera.

Figures 1.37 to 1.39 show the various compensatory effects that can be applied to an image.

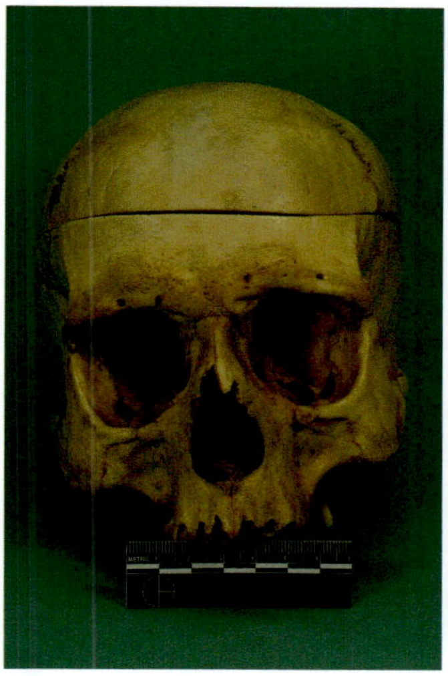

Figure 1.37 Image with compensation of –1EV.

Source: Photograph by the author.

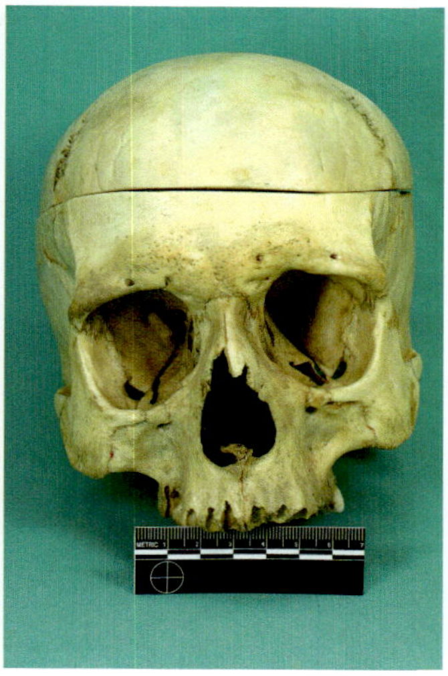

Figure 1.38 Image without compensation.

Source: Photograph by the author.

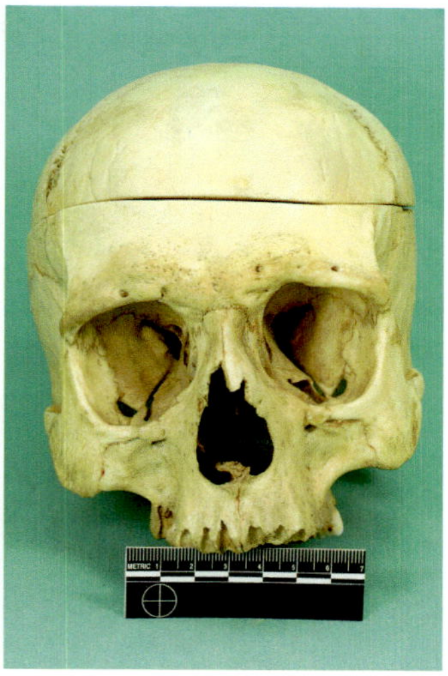

Figure 1.39 Image with compensation of +1 EV.

Source: Photograph by the author.

As can be seen in the photographs that follow, there are instances when it is essential to make use of compensation to highlight particular aspects of the image. As illustrated in Figures 1.40 and 1.41

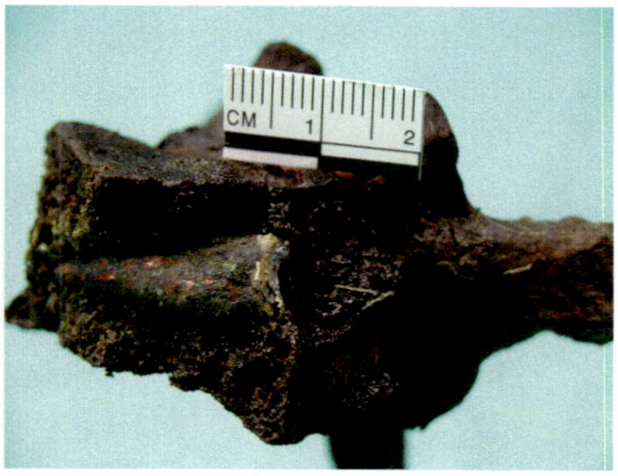

Figure 1.40 Without compensation.

Source: Photograph by the author.

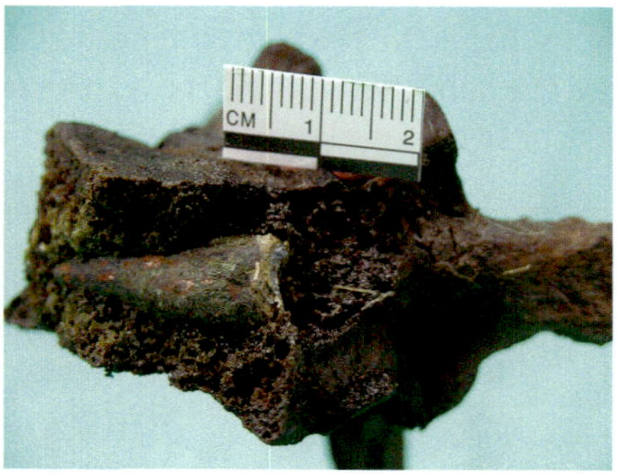

Figure 1.41 With compensation of +1.

Source: Photograph by the author.

White balance and color temperature

When you take a picture of something, a variety of light sources and color temperatures are brought into play to create the final image. This relates to the inherent characteristics of photography. The purpose of the function known as "white balance" is to modify the tonal values of an image to produce colors corresponding to the image. The automatic parameter allows the sensor to adjust the color to the lighting conditions of the scene. But sometimes it is necessary to adjust the white balance because some sensors are more sensitive than others in automatic mode. As illustrated in Figures 1.42 and 1.43.

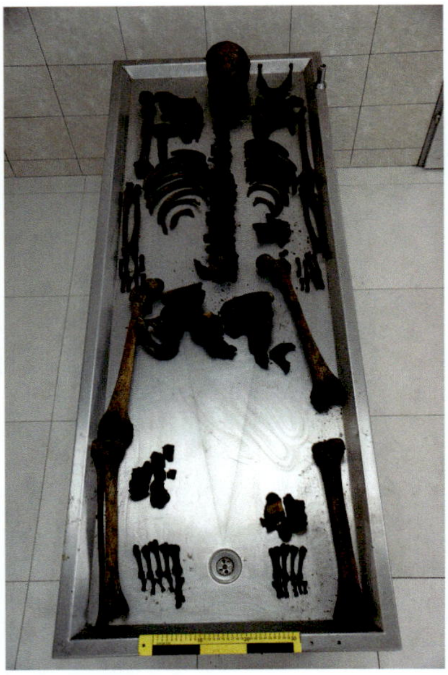

Figure 1.42 Photo taken with a reflex camera (DSLR).

Source: Photograph by the author.

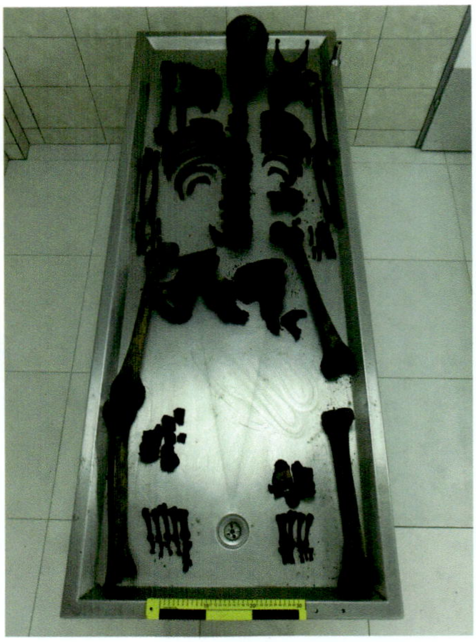

Figure 1.43 Photo taken with a compact camera.

Source: Photograph by the author.

Histogram

The term "histogram" refers to a graphical representation of the light distributed throughout an image. If the curve is on the left side of the graph, the image will be dark; and inversely, if the curve is on the right side of the graph, the image will be clear.

In certain circumstances, as demonstrated in Figure 1.44, the histogram is a valuable tool that helps the photographer adjust the exposure. It is important to note that, depending on the subject and the details to be emphasized, an image may need to be intentionally darker or brighter to reveal specific features more effectively.

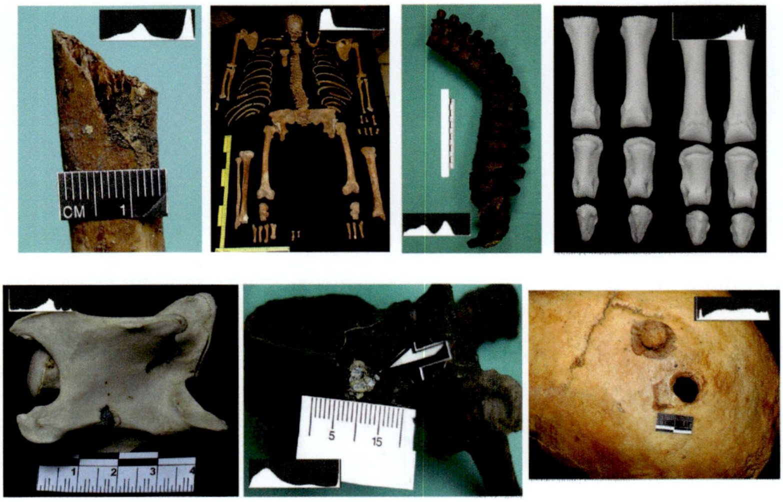

Figure 1.44 The following photographs, along with their corresponding histograms, illustrate how the curve works depending on what you want to capture.

Source: Photograph by the author.

File Format

JPEG, TIFF, and RAW are the three file formats that are used most frequently in photography today. JPEG and RAW are the only two formats that we will discuss.

JPEG

The JPEG file format is one that employs lossy compression on the files that it creates. This means that the quality of an image is diminished because its data is processed and compressed before being saved, resulting in a decrease in image quality. Nonetheless, it is the most used file format because JPEG files are smaller and take up less space on memory cards, are simple to transfer, and can be examined at a much faster rate.

Depending on your brand of camera, you will have the following compression options available in your camera settings:

1. JPEG Fine: Lossy compression.
2. JPEG Normal: Increased compression, reduced file size, and reduced quality versus "fine".
3. JPEG Basic: Greatest compression, lowest file size, lowest quality.

The following are some advantages and disadvantages:

- Faster saving.
- Reduced file size.
- More images are stored on memory cards.
- Faster transfer
- Faster opening on the computer.
- Does not require the installation of special software.
- Loss of image information.
- Files are destructive.
- Easy to alter.

Note

Your selected JPEG compression option may result in color loss, edge aliasing, and noise, all of which will have an impact on the quality of the image. And when you re-edit and re-save your JPEG image, data loss will be compounded.

RAW

A RAW file, otherwise known as a "**digital negative**", is one that has not been compressed or treated in any way. It is a lossless format, which means that it does not compress the image data that it collects and stores a greater amount of detail without compromising the quality of the image. Having said that, each image will take up a considerable amount of storage space on the memory card.

The exact name of the RAW file will vary from one type of camera to another, depending on the brand.

Some examples:

Nikon: NEF; Canon: CR2, CR3, CRW; Sony: ARW, SRF, SR2; Kodak: DCR, KDC; Olympus: ORF, Panasonic RW2.

The following options will be available to you in the camera settings, but again, they may vary depending on the kind of camera you have.

1. Raw
2. Raw + JPEG Fine
3. Raw + JPEG Normal
4. Raw + JPEG Basic

In addition, depending on your model of camera, you may be able to locate the "lossless compression" option on the camera that you are using. This option indicates that the images are compressed to conserve space on the memory card, but that the compression will be reversed, and the image will be restored without any data loss when accessed on a computer.

The following are some advantages and disadvantages of the RAW format:

- Exceptional photography quality.
- Every detail of the image is preserved.
- More details in the image.
- Non-editable file.
- Larger file size.
- Requires additional storage space.
- Post-processing is required.
- Editing software is required.
- Authenticity validation.
- A slower recording speed (depending on the memory card that is being used).

Note:
I use both RAW and JPEG Fine formats for my photographs. In most cases, each image is recorded simultaneously to separate memory cards, with one copy saved in RAW format and the other in JPEG format. This approach provides an additional layer of security in the event of a problem with one of the memory cards. However, depending on the camera being used, I may also save both the RAW and JPEG versions of an image to a single memory card, as shown in Figure 1.45.

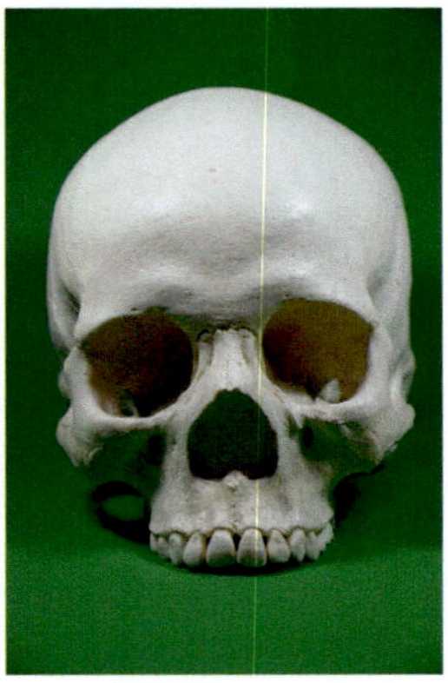

Figure 1.45 An example showing the same photograph saved in different file formats: JPEG (9.47 MB) and RAW (28.2 MB).

Source: Photograph by the author.

Image Size

Image size, which refers to the dimensions of an image, should not be confused with image quality, which is associated with the file type (such as RAW or JPEG) as well as the compression ratio of your camera.

Your camera gives you the ability to select the size of your image, which is measured in width by height. This size will influence the number of pixels that are contained within your image. You will have the option of choosing between large (L), medium (M), and small (S), depending on the brand of your camera.

Figure 1.46 shows the detail indicated by the arrow, which is used in Figures 1.47 and 1.48 to provide an example of a photograph captured using two different image sizes, L and S, selected in the camera settings. The images were then enlarged eight times on a computer screen to facilitate comparison.

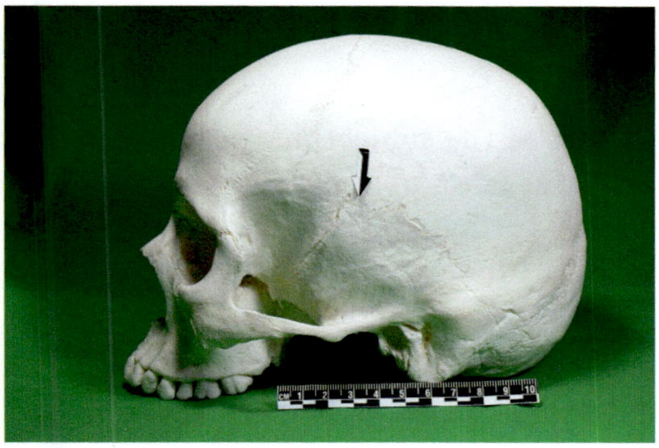

Figure 1.46 Photography used as a reference.

Source: Photograph by the author.

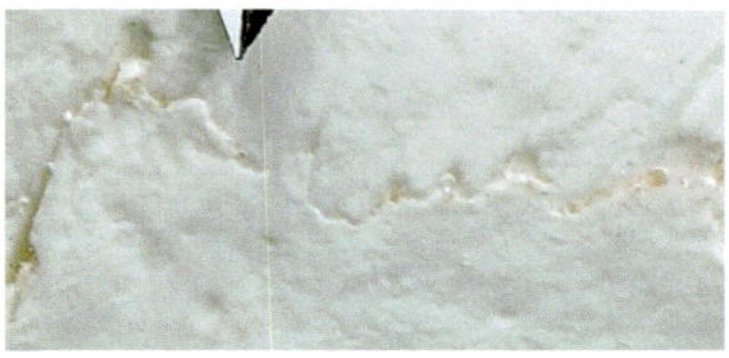

Figure 1.47 With a size L and a magnification of eight times, the details are in focus.

Source: Photograph by the author.

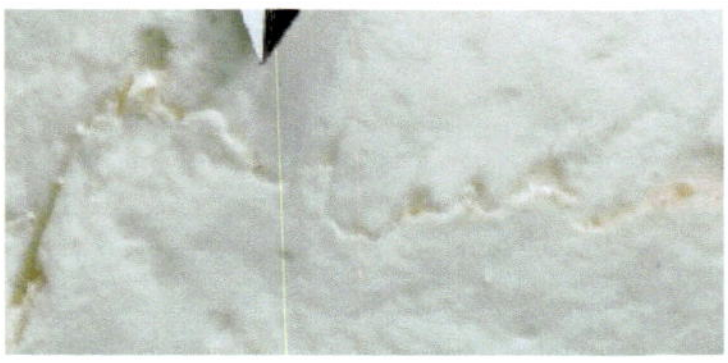

Figure 1.48 With a size S and a magnification of eight times, the details are not in focus.

Source: Photograph by the author.

Pixel-based resolution is the phrase used to describe how an image's resolution is determined by the amount of pixels that comprise it. Image quality and the largest print size that may be produced are both impacted by this resolution. As seen in Table 1.2, a higher resolution generally yields better image quality and enables higher-quality reproductions.

Table 1.2 **The following is an illustration that is approximative of how a photograph might print depending on the settings that you select on your camera, as well as the type of paper, printer, and software that you use.**

Paper size	Camera 16 megapixel	Camera 24 megapixel	Camera 36 megapixel
A2—420 × 594 mm 16.5 × 23.4 in			
A3—297 × 420 mm 11.7 × 16.5 in			
A4—210 × 297 mm 8.3 × 11.7 in			
A5—148 × 210 mm 5.8 × 8.3 in			

Excellent quality and details—Good with poor details.

Recommendation

It is vital to have a comprehensive understanding of the subject matter to effectively set up your camera. If you are not constrained by the amount of memory that you have available, you are advised to shoot images in RAW format and in large sizes. This will guarantee that you will get an extremely high-quality image, which is especially important in forensic photography when it is not always possible to redo certain photographs.

Memory Card

2

When purchasing a memory card, it is essential to take into consideration not only the amount of storage space available on the card but also its speed as well as its class. This is especially important to keep in mind if you are shooting at a high resolution using the RAW file format. The number of photographs that can be stored on a memory card can vary depending on the subject being photographed (that is, the amount of detail in the photo) as well as the settings that are selected on the camera.

On the other hand, a low-end memory card can soon become unreliable due to issues such as file system corruption, bad sectors, or manufacturing defects. This can happen after the card has been used only a few times.

However, it is possible that recording issues will arise as the battery begins to run low.

Figures 2.1 and 2.2 show a problem that may arise with memory cards that have bad sectors.

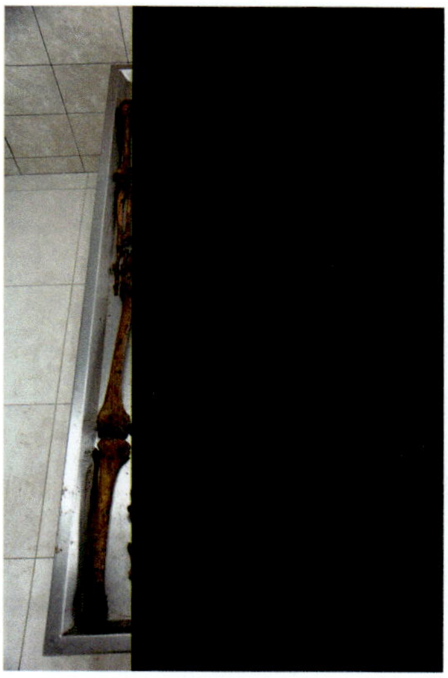

Figure 2.1 Example of a problem during recording.

Source: Photograph by the author.

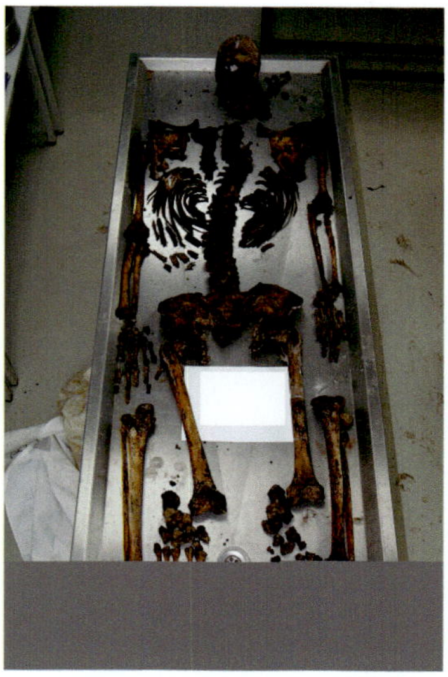

Figure 2.2 Another example of a problem during recording.

Source: Photograph by the author.

A very good quality memory card will usually remain reliable for several years. Both SanDisk Extreme PRO and Lexar Professional are examples of memory card brands that are known for their speed and high levels of quality.

Figure 2.3 and 2.4 show a problem that can occur when transferring data to a hard drive, failing SSD/HDD drives, and bad sectors.

DOI: 10.4324/9781003768838-5

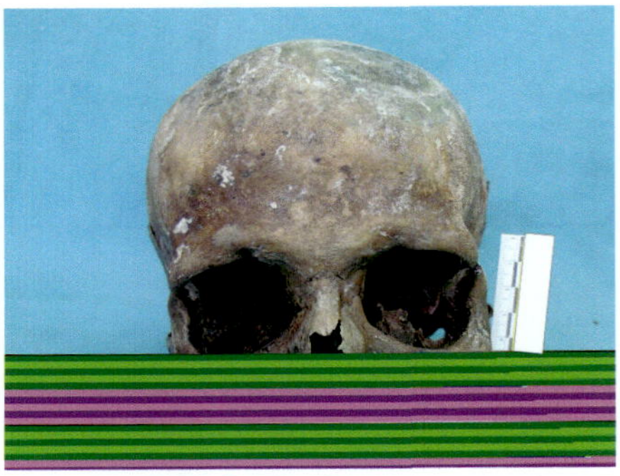

Figure 2.3 Example of an HDD with bad sectors. **Source**: Photograph by the author.

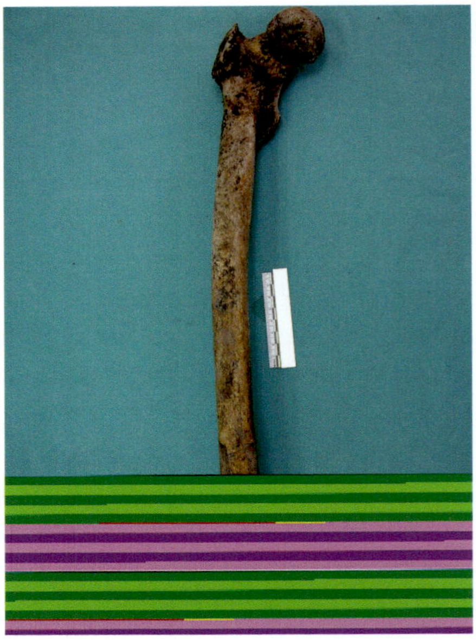

Figure 2.4 Another example of an HDD with bad sectors. **Source**: Photograph by the author.

As seen in Figures 2.5 and 2.6, reproducing the same shot is not always feasible, particularly when the subject cannot be photographed again.

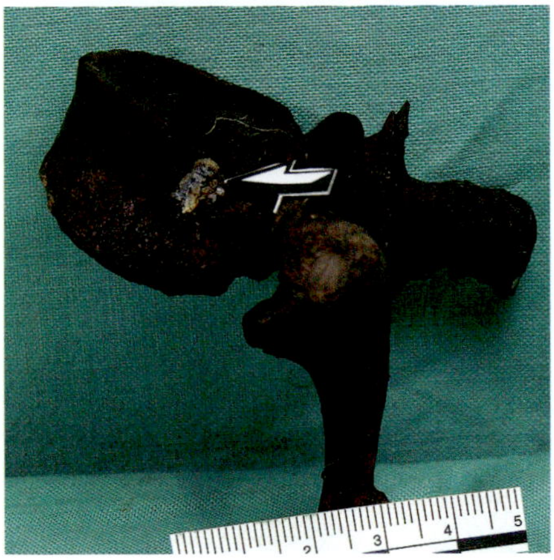

Figure 2.5 Bullet inside the body of the thoracic vertebra. **Source**: Photograph by the author.

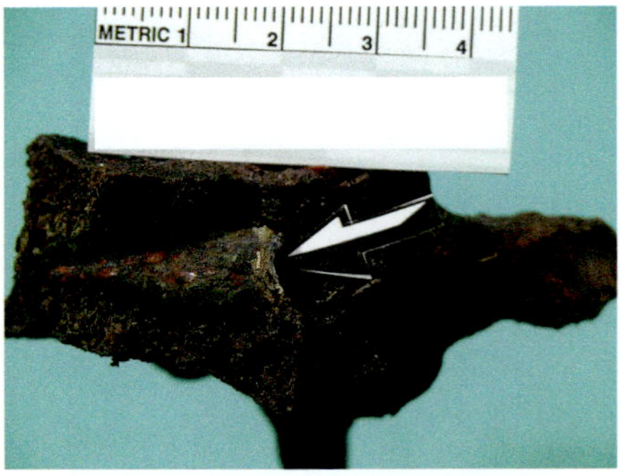

Figure 2.6 It was necessary to shatter the vertebra to make the bullet visible. **Source**: Photograph by the author.

Some recommendations:

- **It is important to keep in mind that anything you photograph will be saved on a card.**
- **Make sure you use a reputable memory card brand, such as Lexar or SanDisk.**
- **You should avoid removing the memory card from the camera if it has not been turned off first.**
- **You should always make sure to keep a copy of your files on an external hard drive in case your internal hard drive fails.**
- **Keep in mind that you will begin to have issues with a memory card of inferior quality after a few formats.**
- **Check the battery regularly to ensure it is always charged.**

Lens

3

There are many kinds of lenses, including fixed focus lenses, zoom lenses, wide-angle lenses, macro lenses, and others, and each type is designed for a specific purpose.

Reminder:

- **It is important to remember that when using a digital camera with an APS sensor, the focal length will be multiplied by 1.5 for Nikon and 1.6 for Canon.**
- **If you are using a lens that is 18 mm with an APS, you will have a focal length of 27 mm with a Nikon and 28.8 mm with a Canon.**

General Photography

It is recommended that a lens with a focal length ranging from 16 to 24 mm be utilized to take a satisfactory photograph of the anatomical position. To ensure that you have a decent vision, it will be quite helpful to use a stepladder.

Figures 3.1 to 3.4 show the results that were obtained both with and without the use of a stepladder.

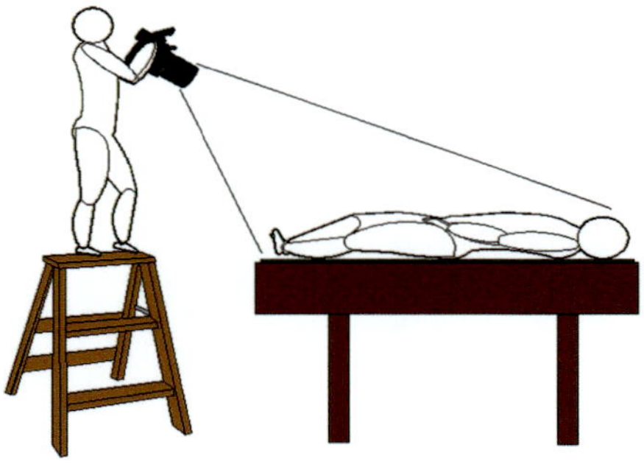

Figure 3.1 Illustrate the approximate position between the photographer and the body using a ladder and a focal length of 18 mm.

Source: Photograph by the author.

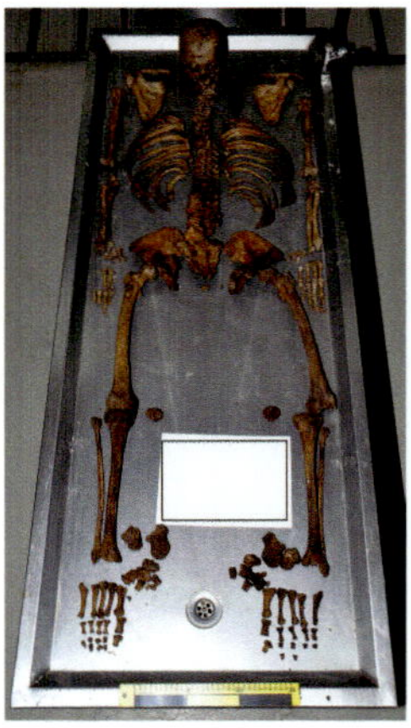

Figure 3.2 Example of how the photo will look.

Source: Photograph by the author.

DOI: 10.4324/9781003768838-6

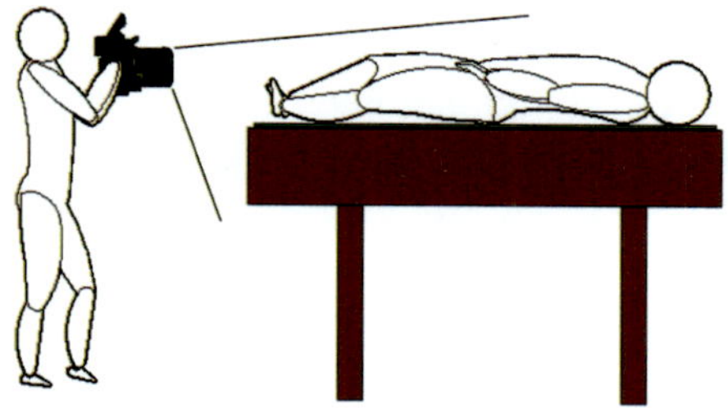

Figure 3.3 Illustrate the approximate position of the photographer without the use of a ladder.

Source: Photograph by the author.

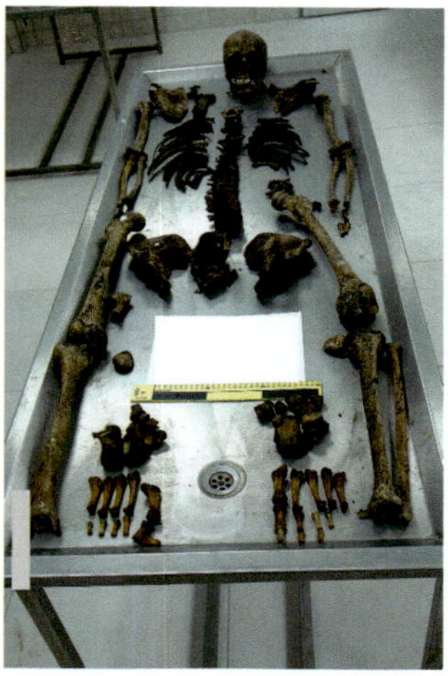

Figure 3.4 Example of how the photo will look.

Source: Photograph by the author.

Detail

General View

Lenses with focal lengths ranging from 16 to 200 mm are generally used. For my own work, I use two lenses: The first has a focal length that ranges from 18 to 200 mm, while the second has a focal length that ranges from 18 to 140 mm. This allows me to take very good photos, both in wide shots and at mid-range.

Macrophotography

In most cases, a macro lens with a focal length ranging from 40 to 105 mm is utilized.

High-magnification close-ups of small subjects are possible with this specialty lens, which was designed to capture details that are unreachable with a zoom lens, and this lens reveals the smallest details of the subjects being photographed.

The unfortunate reality is that these lenses are quite pricey and, depending on one‘s financial situation, may not be within the reach of everyone. Nevertheless, there are other accessories that are cheaper and just as efficient for macro photography. These items are less well-known. There are two additional choices: an extension tube and a macro lens with a universal snap-on mount. Both alternatives will enable you to capture excellent degrees of detail.

To create photographs that are extremely detailed, I make use of these two additional options for macro photography. These options enable me to select the magnification that I want to utilize with my 18–200 mm lens. Several photographs that were taken using these two choices are included in this manual.

Extension tube

The extension tube is a handy accessory that eliminates the need to purchase a macro lens. It allows me to bring the lens closer to the subject, thus achieving greater magnification.

Extension tubes are used in conjunction with interchangeable lenses to shorten the distance that separates the lens from the subject. These tubes are positioned between the camera and the lens.

They are available in three distinct sizes: 12, 20 and 36 mm for Nikon as shown in Figure 3.5 and 13, 21 and 31 mm for Canon. They can be used individually or in pairs, depending on the level of magnification required.

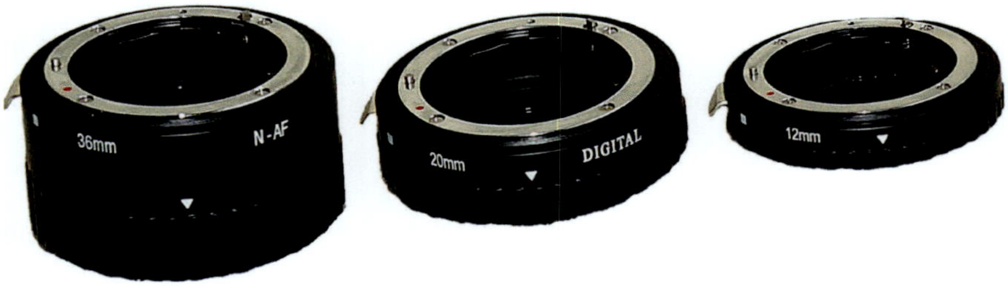

Figure 3.5 Example of extension tube for Nikon 12, 20, and 36 mm.

Source: Photograph by the author.

Figures 3.6 to 3.8 illustrate three examples of magnification obtained with the same focal length, first without an extension ring and then with extension rings of increasing magnification. As the extension ring length increases, the magnification of the subject correspondingly increases.

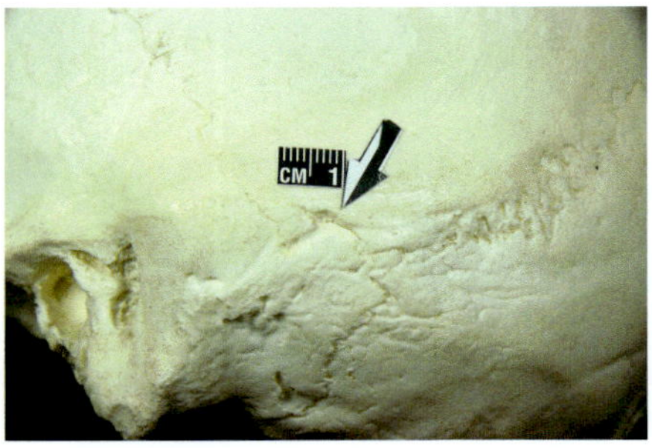

Figure 3.6 This photograph was taken with a focal length of 200 mm without an extension tube.

Source: Photograph by the author.

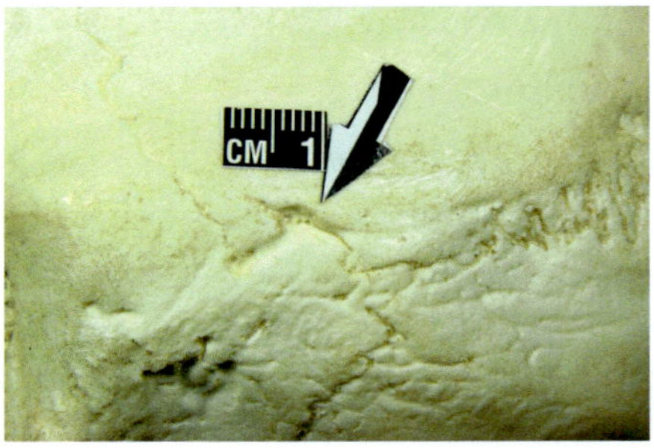

Figure 3.7 This photograph was taken with a focal length of 200 mm using a 12 mm extension.

Source: Photograph by the author.

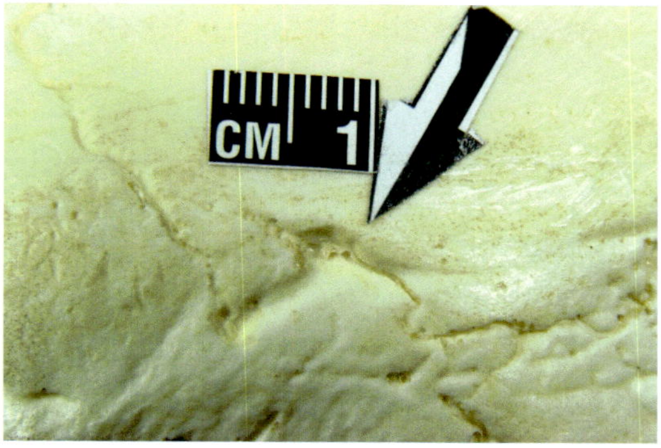

Figure 3.8 This photograph was taken with a focal length of 200 mm using an extension of 36 mm.

Macro Lens with Universal Snap-on Mount

Figure 3.9 illustrates a close-up lens, an accessory that increases magnification by reducing the minimum focusing distance between the lens and the subject. Owing to its universal mounting system, it is attached to the front of the camera lens. This accessory provides particularly good results when paired with a lens featuring a 50 mm filter diameter.

The results will vary, as shown in Figures 3.10 and 3.11, depending on the objective used.

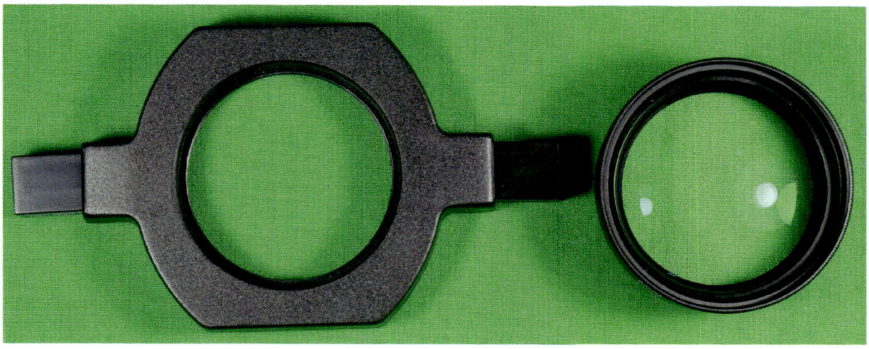

Figure 3.9 Macro lens with universal snap-on mount.

Source: Photograph by the author.

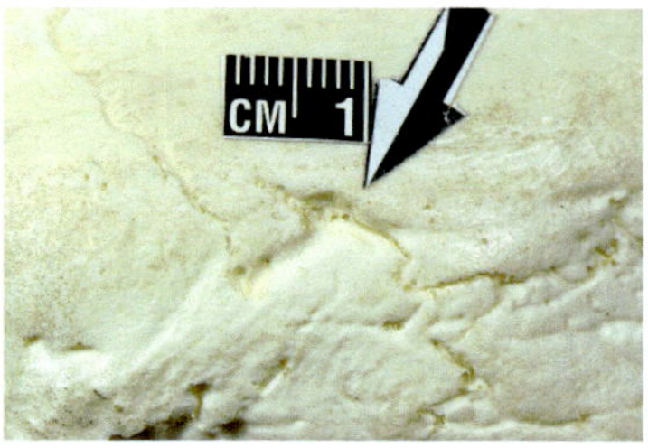

Figure 3.10 This photograph was taken with a 50 mm lens with this macro lens.

Source: Photograph by the author.

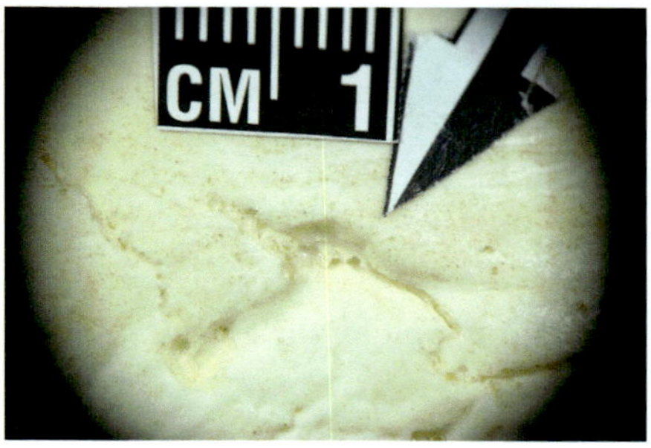

Figure 3.11 This photograph was taken with a lens of 18–200 mm with a focal length of 150 mm using the macro lens.

Source: Photograph by the author.

Lighting

4

The Built-in Flash

This flash is useful and generally used either to fill in shadows on a subject and thus improve its exposure or to illuminate a subject in low light.

However, it is essential to keep in mind that its use carries risks, such as reflections, shadows, underexposure, and overexposure if not properly controlled.

Figures 4.1 and 4.2 present two examples of problems caused by improper flash use. Figure 4.3 illustrates a photograph taken with appropriate flash settings, while Figure 4.4 demonstrates that satisfactory image quality can be achieved without flash through the use of an appropriate ISO setting.

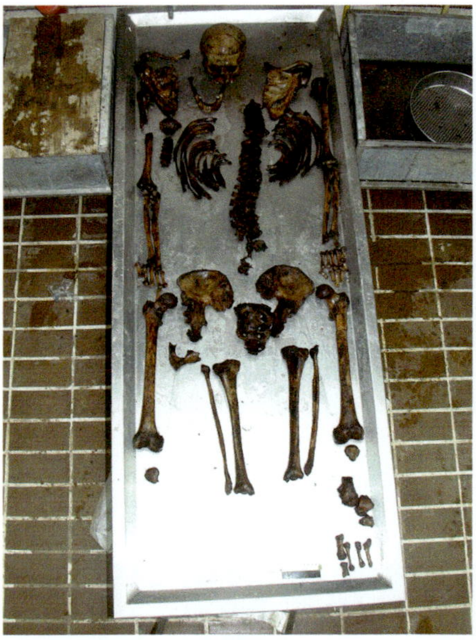

Figure 4.1 Due to the reflection of additional flash, the ruler and the case number are not visible in this photo.

Source: Photograph by the author.

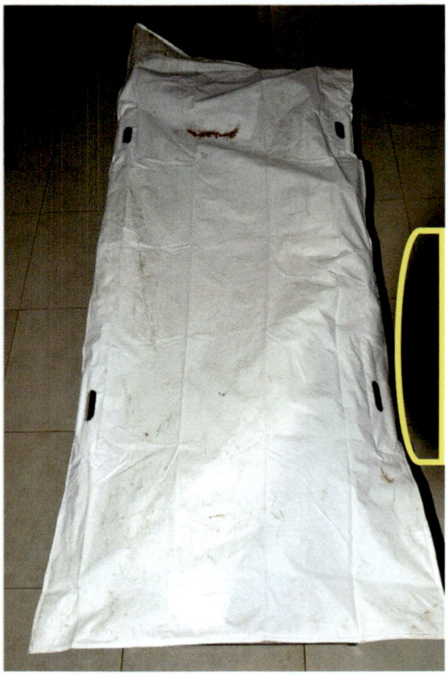

Figure 4.2 The photo, which was taken with the built-in flash and lens hood, shows a region of darkness. This is because the camera was held in the vertical position when the picture was taken.

Source: Photograph by the author.

DOI: 10.4324/9781003768838-7

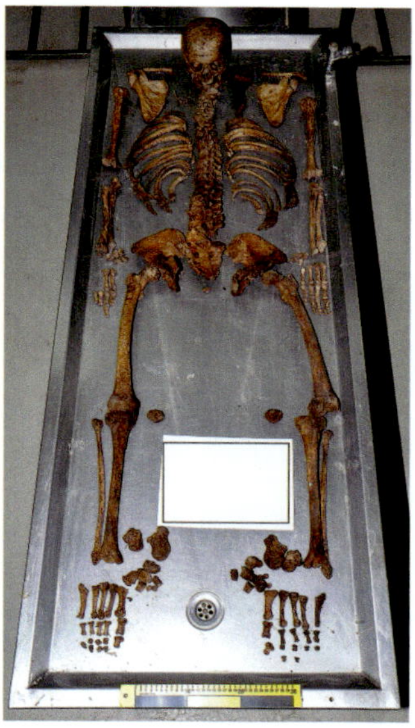

Figure 4.3 Shows a photo taken with a good flash setting.

Source: Photograph by the author.

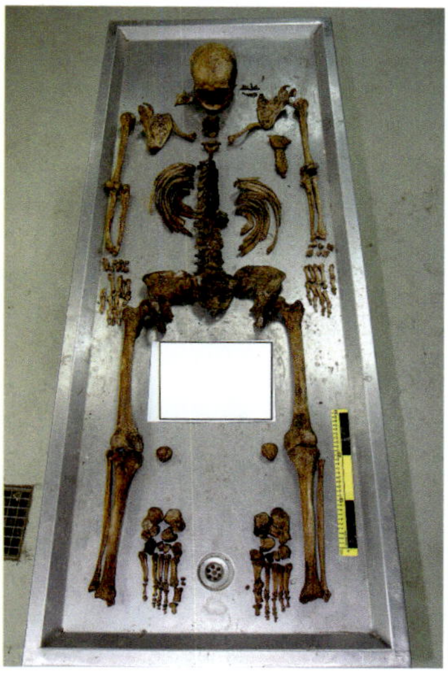

Figure 4.4 Shows a photo taken without flash, with an ISO of 800.

Source: Photograph by the author.

Additional Flash

Compared with a built-in flash, an external flash offers greater light output, increased working distance, and enhanced control over the direction of illumination. It can also be used with a variety of accessories that enable the production of soft or diffused lighting, depending on the application. Figure 4.5 presents an example of an external flash.

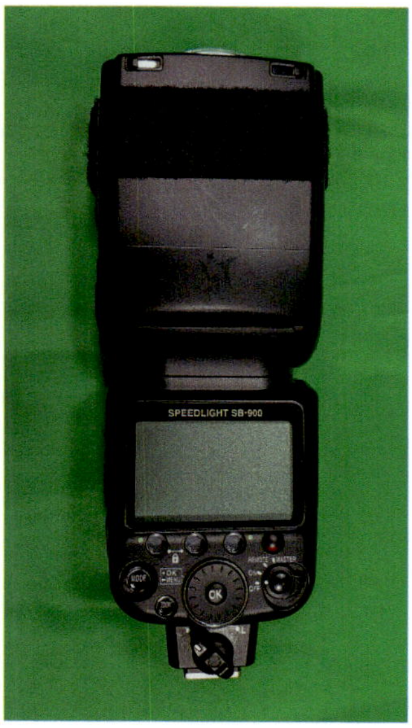

Figure 4.5 Example with an additional flash.

Source: Photograph by the author.

Ring Light Flash

Figure 4.6 illustrates another type of external flash that is mounted around the lens. It consists of two semicircular flash units that can be operated either together or independently, depending on the required level and distribution of illumination.

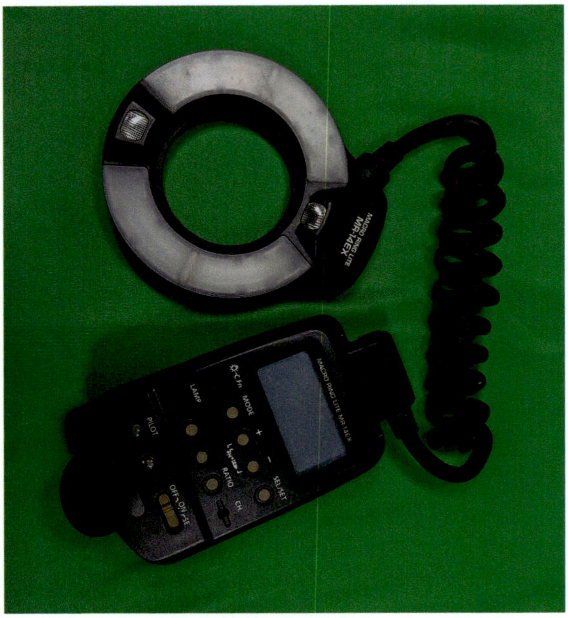

Figure 4.6 Ring light flash.

Source: Photograph by the author.

Additional Lamps

I use two distinct types of lighting. The first is a softbox lighting kit, and the second is a desk lamp with an articulated arm that provides continuous light. In photography, these lamps are very useful to me, especially when photographing details. Both options allow me to take photos without a flash, compensate for insufficient lighting, and direct the light precisely.

To avoid color temperature variations, it is recommended to use a daylight bulb, from 15 to 23 W, which offers faithful colors in photography.

Figures 4.7 and 4.8 present two examples of alternative lighting: desk lamps and softbox lighting. Despite the difference in their cost, both options offer comparable lighting conditions and excellent photo quality.

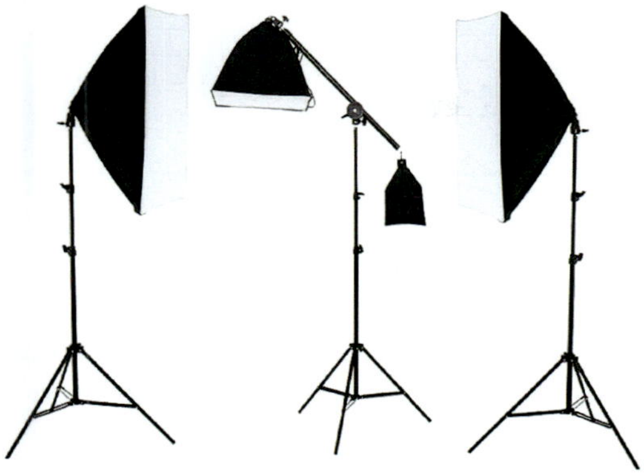

Figure 4.7 Example of a softbox lighting kit.

Source: Photograph by the author.

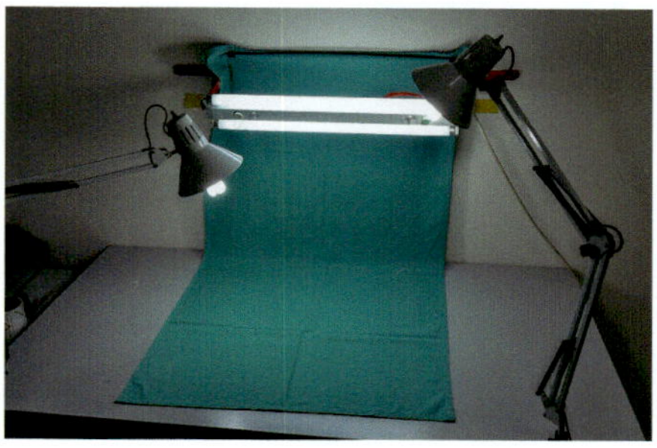

Figure 4.8 Example of a desk lamp with an articulated arm.

Source: Photograph by the author.

Accessories

5

In certain circumstances, accessories will be able to assist you in shooting images, or they will allow you to improve your photography skills. There are two accessories that are required to be present on every photograph that is taken for forensic photography: a scale and a case number. To identify each piece of evidence, an additional number will be utilized.

Tripod

During the shooting process, a tripod will typically assist in stabilizing a camera, which is helpful for low-speed photography, macro photography, and other types of photography.

Figure 5.1 illustrates the various ways a center-column tripod can be used. In addition to supporting a camera, a tripod can also be used to hold a flash, a video camera, or other accessories. Figure 5.2 shows a different tripod configured in a single position.

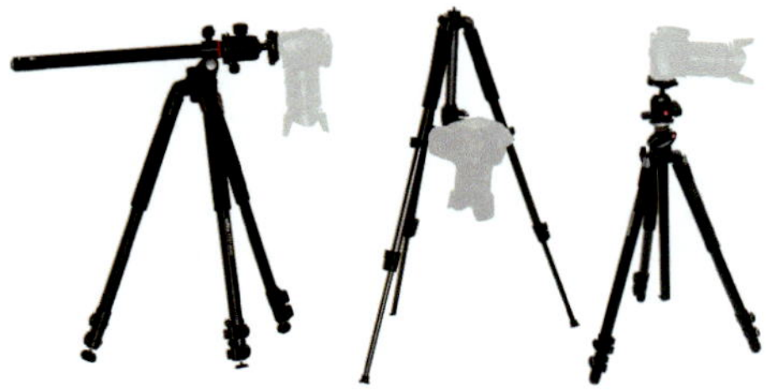

Figure 5.1 A tripod that has a center column that can pivot horizontally is an example of a tripod that offers greater flexibility.

Source: Photograph by the author.

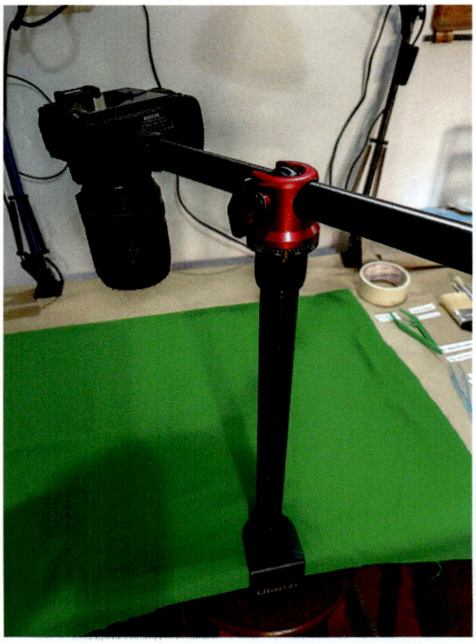

Figure 5.2 Another example, the MT-88 camera mount can be modified in length and can rotate horizontally through 360 degrees, making it an ideal choice for photographing details, evidence, documents, and infrared photography.

Source: Photograph by the author.

DOI: 10.4324/9781003768838-8

Ruler

To provide a metric reference for the subject, it is necessary to have a selection of rulers of different lengths, widths, and colours, depending on the type of photograph being taken, as shown in Figure 5.3.

You can make your own rulers by using Word, and then you can print them out in a variety of sizes using adhesive paper so that they can be adhered to the bones.

When printing, use matte adhesive paper to minimize reflection issues.

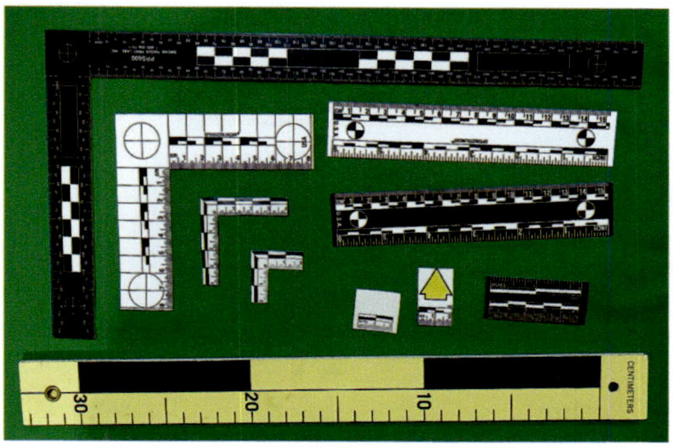

Figure 5.3 An assortment of scales that might be utilized, depending on the subject that is going to be shot.

Source: Photograph by the author.

Arrow

To indicate details such as bullet wounds, fractures, or other injuries in a photograph, arrows of different sizes are used, as illustrated in Figures 5.4 to 5.6.

You can make your own arrows by using Word, and then you can print them out in a variety of sizes using adhesive paper so that they can be adhered to the bones.

When printing, use matte adhesive paper to minimize reflection issues.

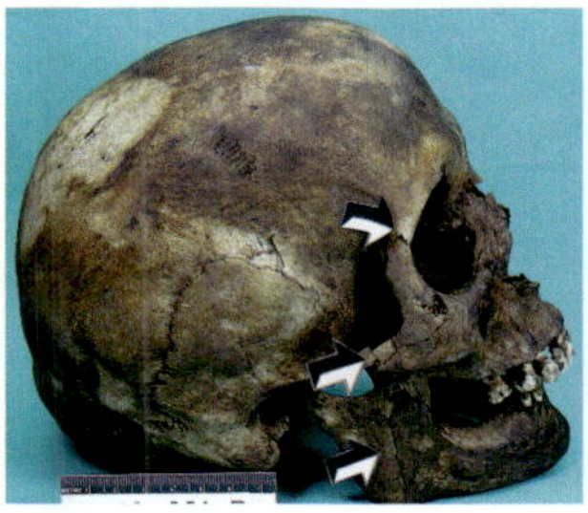

Figure 5.4 Example of three injuries to the skull.

Source: Photograph by the author.

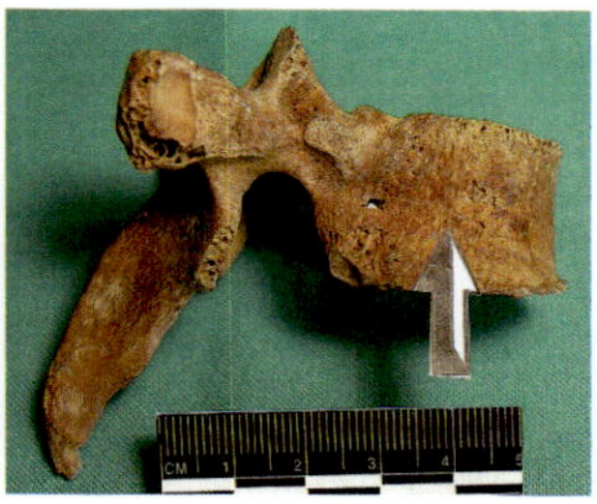

Figure 5.5 Example of a vertebra injury.

Source: Photograph by the author.

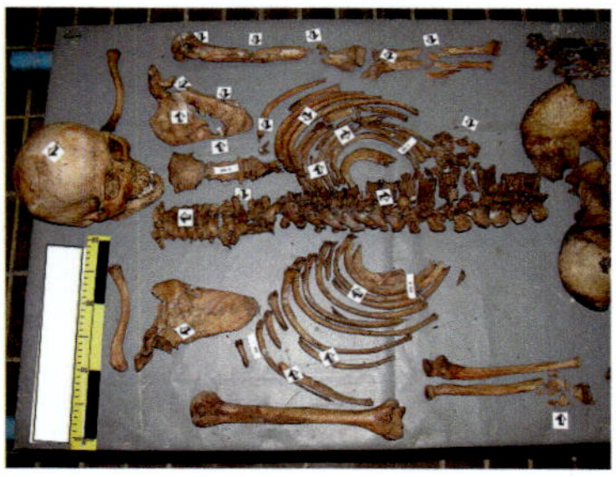

Figure 5.6 Example of upper-body injuries.

Source: Photograph by the author.

Support

The support shown in Figure 5.7 is a device designed to hold an object and facilitate macro or close-up photography, enabling the capture of high-quality images, as illustrated in Figures 5.8 and 5.9.

Depending on the type of support used, it is essential to protect the claws to avoid leaving marks on the bones.

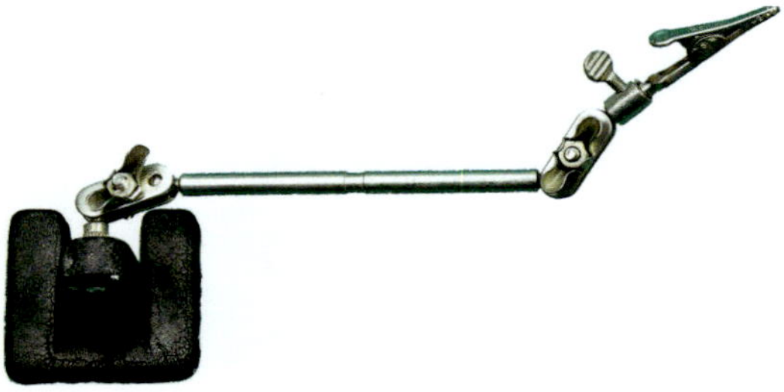

Figure 5.7 Example of the support that may be utilized.

Source: Photograph by the author.

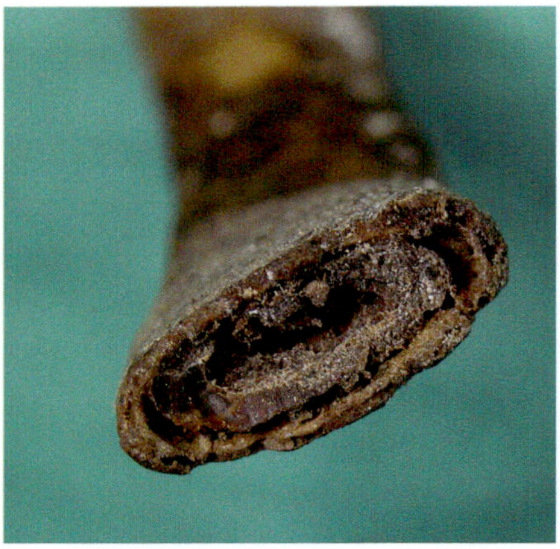

Figure 5.8 Example with a rib sternal end.

Source: Photograph by the author.

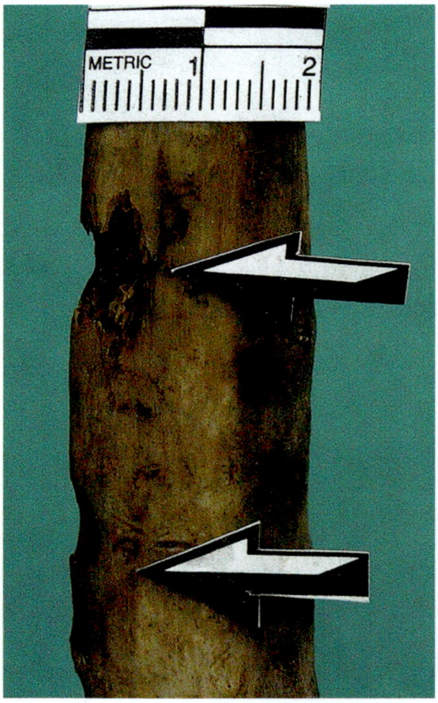

Figure 5.9 Example with a rib.

Source: Photograph by the author.

Dymo

Figure 5.10 shows an example of a Dymo label maker, which is a compact and portable label printer that allows you to print letters and numbers in a variety of font sizes. It can also be used to generate the case code, evidence number, or other relevant numbers in forensic photography.

Using Dymo, you will be able to create self-adhesive labels of a size that is tailored to your photographs without the risk of numbers or letters being misread. As shown in Figure 5.11

Figure 5.12 illustrates a reflection problem caused by laminated labels.

Use a paper refill to avoid any risk of reflection.

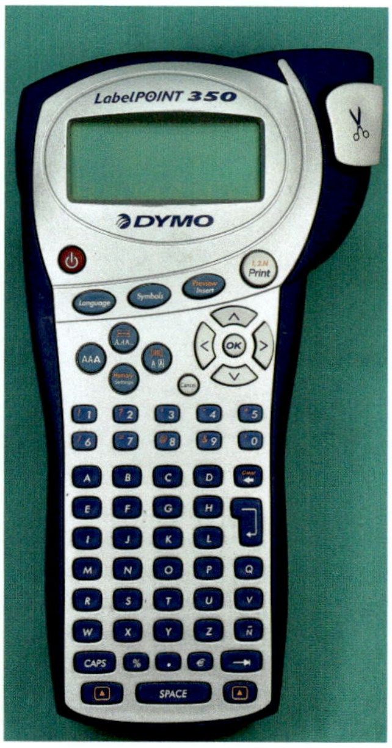

Figure 5.10 Example of Dymo.

Source: Photograph by the author.

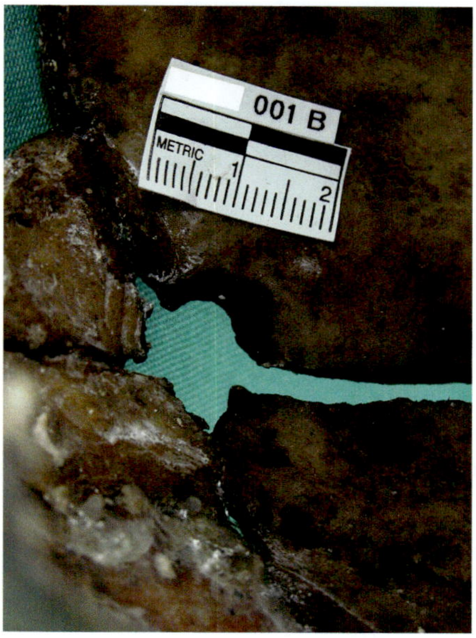

Figure 5.11 Example of its application on a skull—internal view.

Source: Photograph by the author.

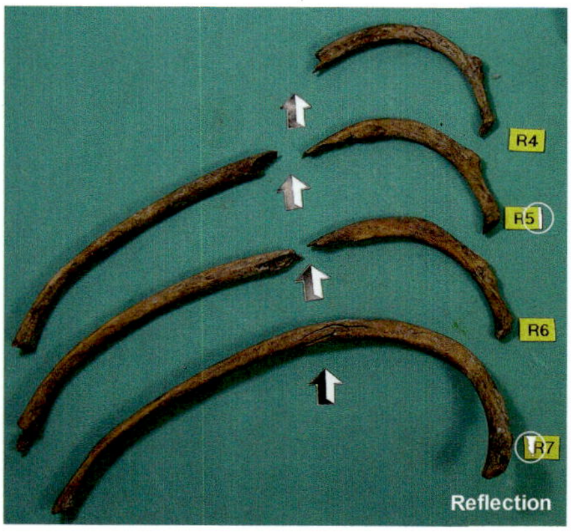

Figure 5.12 Here is an example of a photograph that was taken with a plastic refill; the reflections are visible.

Source: Photograph by the author.

Number

During an autopsy, we are required to assign a number to each piece of evidence found, such as bullets. We can also use numbers to determine where the bullet entered and exited the body, as well as to identify fractures or any other injury. As shown in Figures 5.13 and 5.14.

You can make your own numbers by using Word, and then you can print them out in a variety of sizes using adhesive paper so that they can be adhered to the bones.

When printing, use matte adhesive paper to minimize reflection issues.

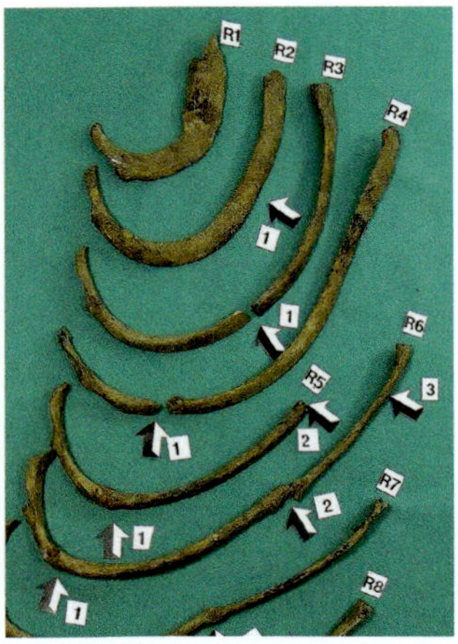

Figure 5.13 An example of how to number ribs.

Source: Photograph by the author.

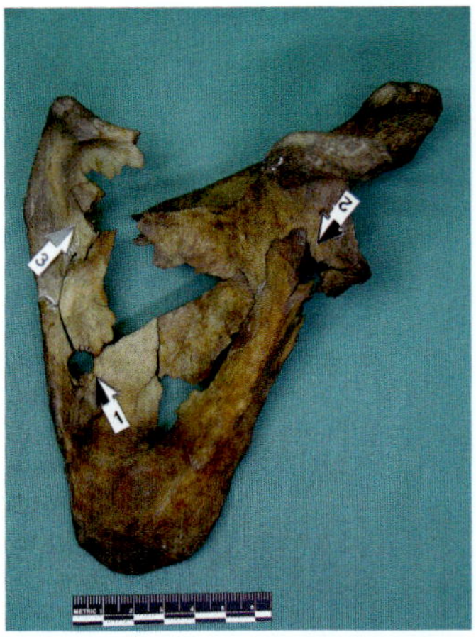

Figure 5.14 As an illustration of how to number lesions.

Source: Photograph by the author.

Forensic Rods

Forensic rods , as shown in Figure 5.15, are a tool used to determine the trajectory of a projectile, from entry to exit. Generally, trajectories of different colors are used to identify each trajectory.

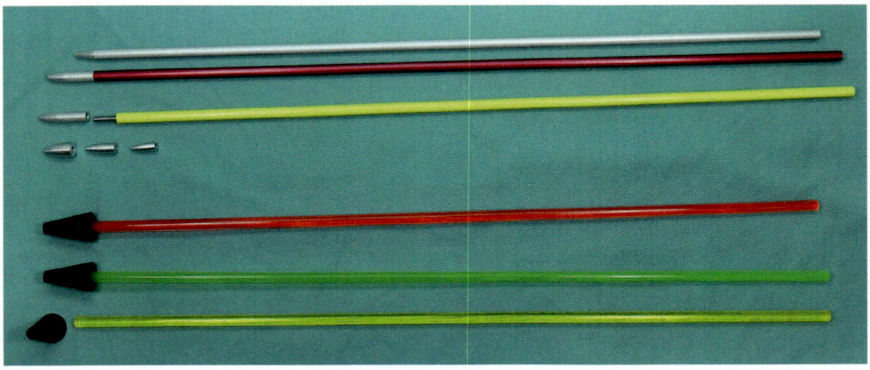

Figure 5.15 Example of different rods.

Source: Photograph by the author.

Making your own forensic rods is simple to do; the materials that you will require are a wooden stick, colored tape, and an arrow.as shown in Figure 5.16 and Figure 5.17 illustrates a completed example. Figure 5.18 illustrates an example of the use of forensic rods.

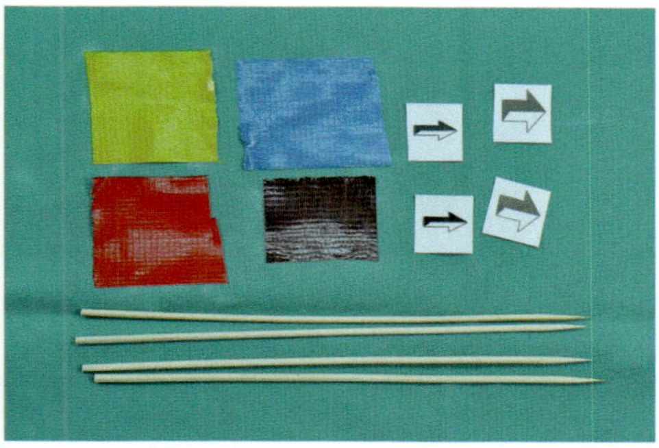

Figure 5.16 Example of required components.

Source: Photograph by the author.

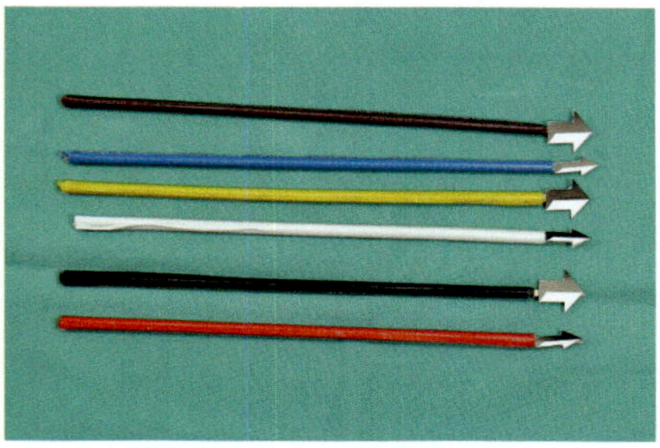

Figure 5.17 Example of rods that have been finished.

Source: Photograph by the author.

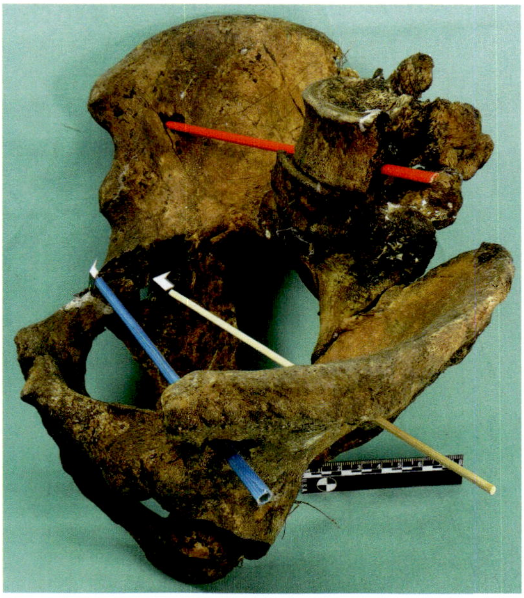

Figure 5.18 An example of the usage of rods of differing colors for the purpose of interpreting the trajectory of three different gunshots.

Source: Photograph by the author.

Background

It is essential to have an adequate background to achieve satisfactory results in photography; often, we focus on the subject to be photographed and completely forget about the background.

When choosing the background for the photograph, it is important to consider the contrast between the subject matter and the background.

This is demonstrated by the three Figures 5.19 to 5.21, which show that the outcome will vary depending on the background that is utilized.

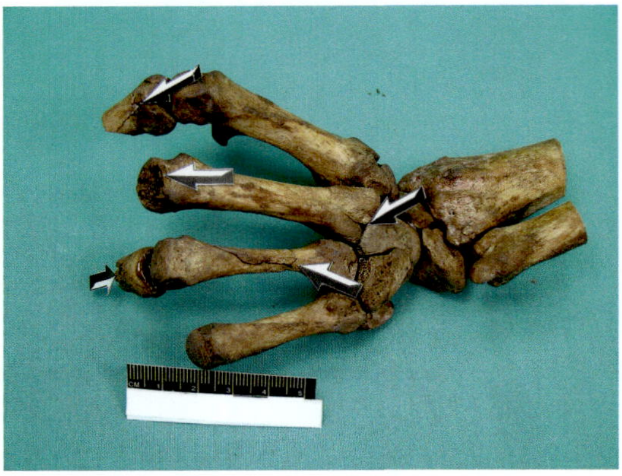

Figure 5.19 The background is green, which creates a sufficient contrast between the subject and the background.

Source: Photograph by the author.

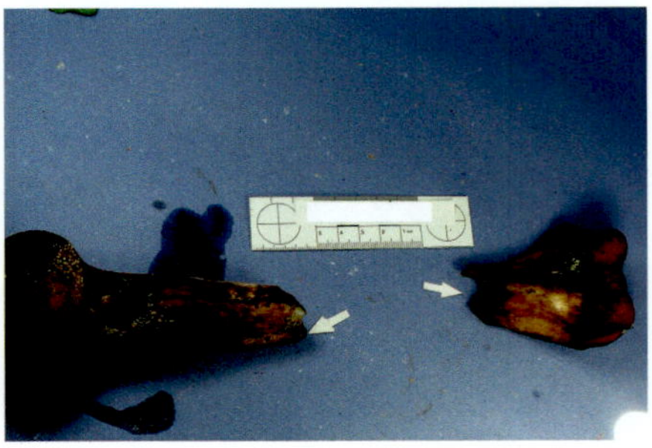

Figure 5.20 Consists of a blue paper background, which results in a lack of contrast between the subject and the background.

Source: Photograph by the author.

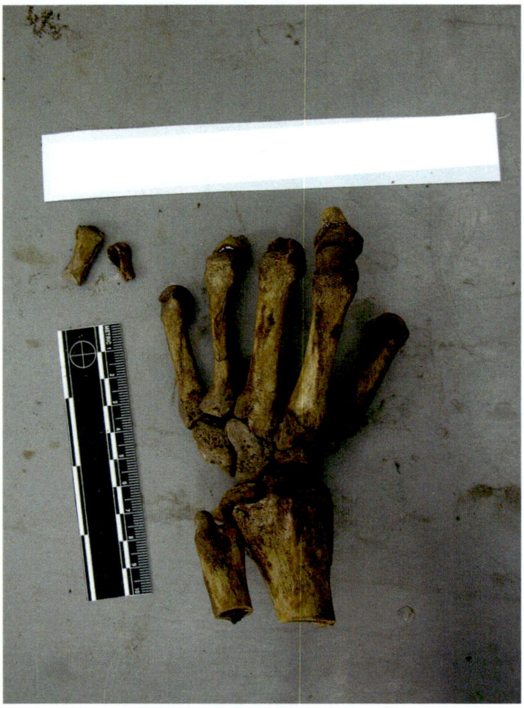

Figure 5.21 The bone is photographed on a table that does not have a background; thus, there is not a lot of contrast between the subject and the background.

Source: Photograph by the author.

Photo Log

When taking photographs, it is essential to keep a record of each one, including a description of the subject of the shot and/or any other pertinent information. To prevent having a variety of cases and images contained within the same photo log, it is recommended to utilize a separate photo log for each individual case. Figure 5.22 shows an example which can be used to document photographs.

Photo Log

Date: **Photographer:**
Case N°:

Photo N°	Body N°	Art. N°	Descriptions

Note:

Signature:

Figure 5.22 This is an example of a basic photo log that can be utilized.

Source: Photograph by the author.

Photographic ID Cards

Photographic identity cards, which are typically included in the original photograph, allow for the identification of the photographer as well as the information regarding the case. The following details are included in this information: the date, the agency, the case number, and the place.

Before Photographing

6

Before you start shooting, take some time to think about how you want to take the photo and what type of equipment you will need.

Preparation

The photographs that are presented below demonstrate the distinction between a photograph that has not been prepared and one that has been properly prepared.

As illustrated in Figures 6.1 and 6.2, these photographs contain certain elements that prevent us from seeing or understanding what the photographer is trying to demonstrate.

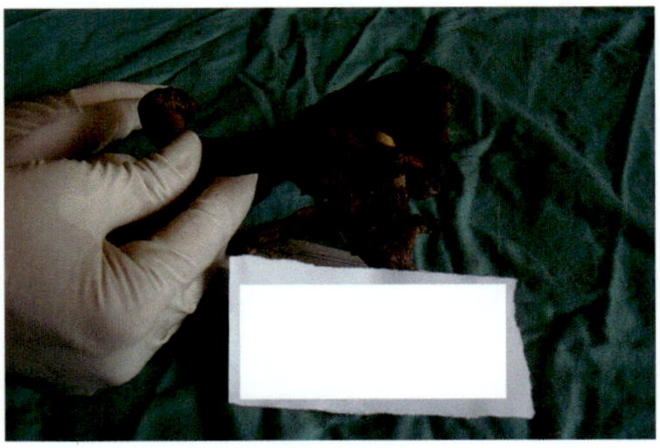

Figure 6.1 It is intended that this photograph depicts a gunshot wound to the scapula and clavicle; nevertheless, the hands and the label divert attention away from the subject of the photograph.

Source: Photograph by the author.

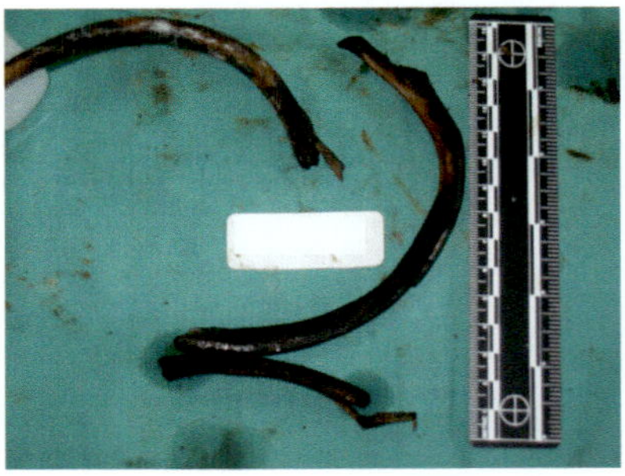

Figure 6.2 The purpose of this photograph is to illustrate fractured ribs; however, which rib is present and which fracture is being depicted?

Source: Photograph by the author.

 DOI: 10.4324/9781003768838-9

In contrast to images that have been prepared to have a clear and concise explanation as shown in Figures 6.3 to 6.5.

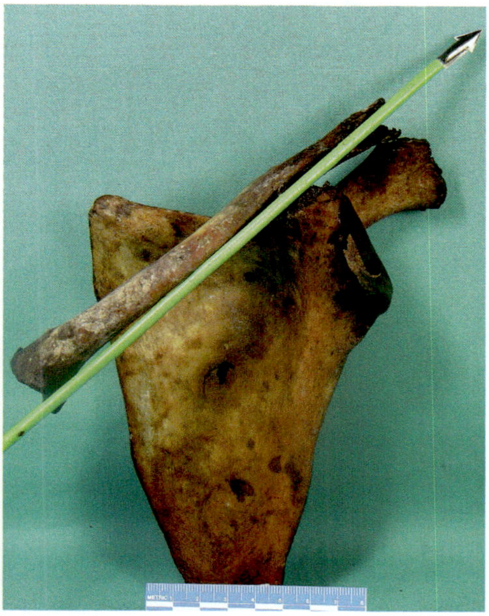

Figure 6.3 The scapula and clavicle are visible in this photograph, which depicts a bullet trajectory.

Source: Photograph by the author.

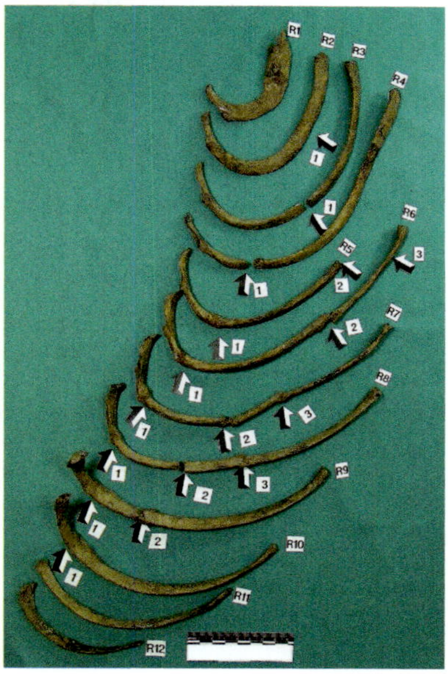

Figure 6.4 In this photograph, it is possible to identify each rib and the fracture that it has.

Source: Photograph by the author.

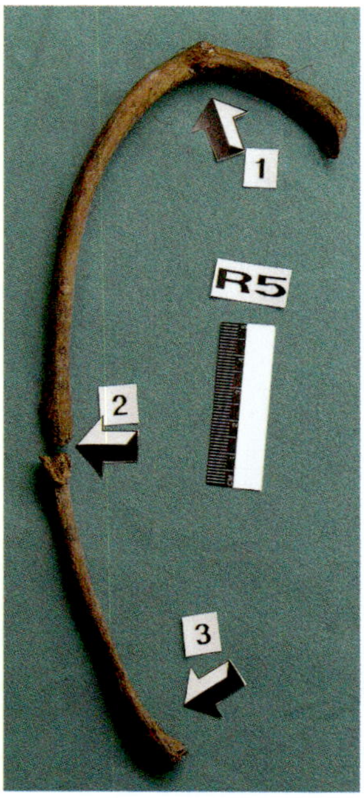

Figure 6.5 In this photograph, you can see that the procedure is the same for a single rib.

Source: Photograph by the author.

Before taking a photo, the photographer should carefully assess what elements will enhance the final image and, if needed, clean the subject (such as a bone). This preparation helps ensure the photograph clearly conveys the intended focus or message.

The number, letter, and ruler all need to be adjusted according to the size of the subject. Figure 6.6 shows improper use of a ruler. For example, if the subject is relatively small, the number and ruler should be adjusted aesthetically to match the size of the subject. As shown in Figures 6.7.

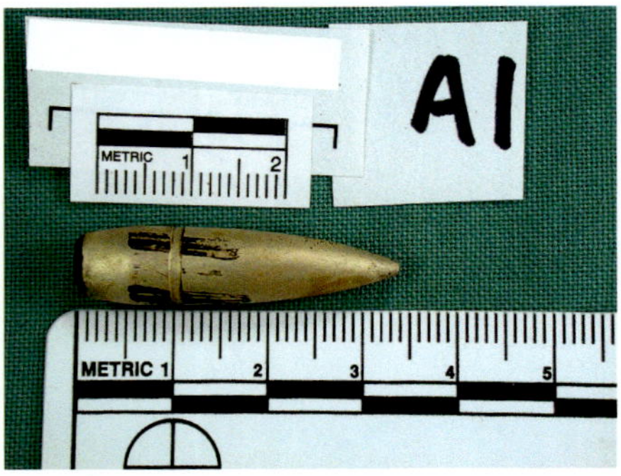

Figure 6.6 Inadequate photo. One of the rulers is excessively huge, the other is superfluous, and the item number is big, which results in the primary topic appearing to be of a smaller size.

Source: Photograph by the author.

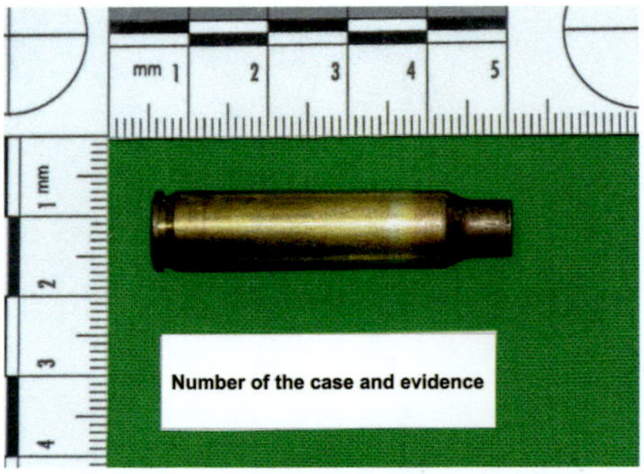

Figure 6.7 Adequate photo. This photograph, on the other hand, features a scale and a label that have been adapted for this photograph, which gives the impression that the primary subject is normal.

Source: Photograph by the author.

Orientations (Vertical or Horizontal)

The orientation of the subject will determine how to frame the photograph. By framing the shot according to the orientation of the subject, you will be able to eliminate any extra space, obtain a closer image, and prevent the inclusion of unnecessary objects in the frame.

Figures 6.8 through 6.12 illustrate the distinction between framing that is unsuccessful and framing that frames the subject in an appropriate manner.

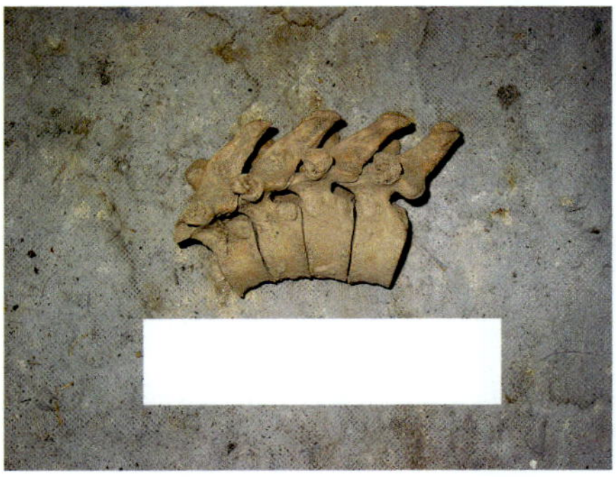

Figure 6.8 This photograph shows vertebrae that were taken using a horizontal frame, which wastes space and gives the impression that the subject is smaller than it is.

Source: Photograph by the author.

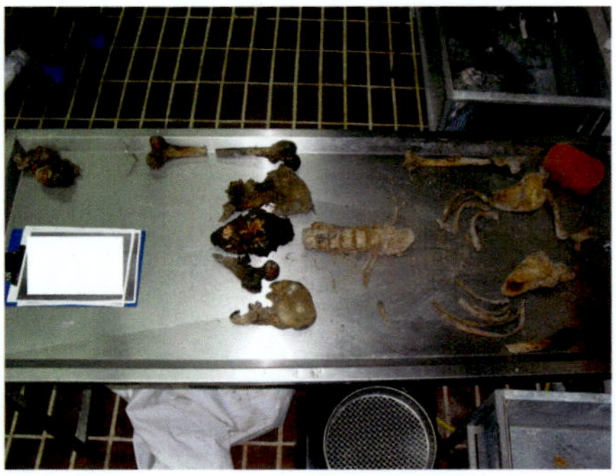

Figure 6.9 Here is another example of a photo taken with a horizontal frame, which includes objects that should not be present in the photo.

Source: Photograph by the author.

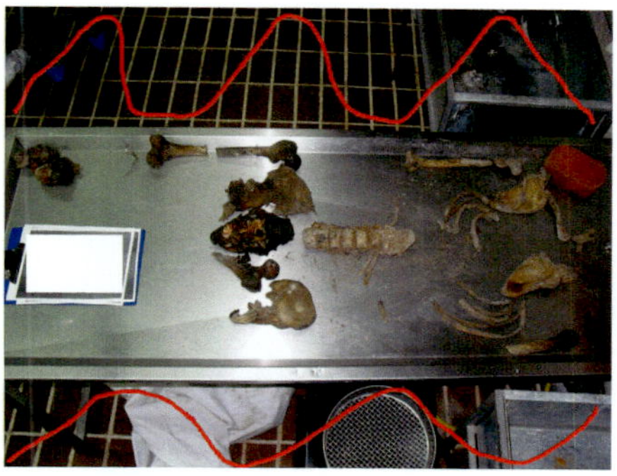

Figure 6.10 This photograph illustrates the space that may be removed in red by employing effective framing and bringing the subject closer.

Source: Photograph by the author.

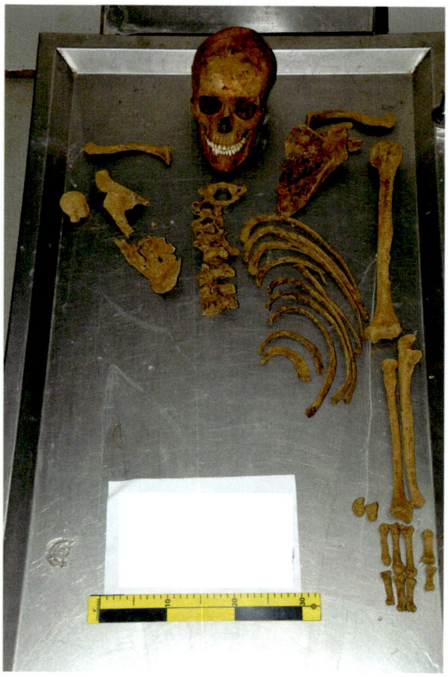

Figure 6.11 Photo taken with vertical framing, which allows the subject to be brought closer and eliminates unnecessary space.

Source: Photograph by the author.

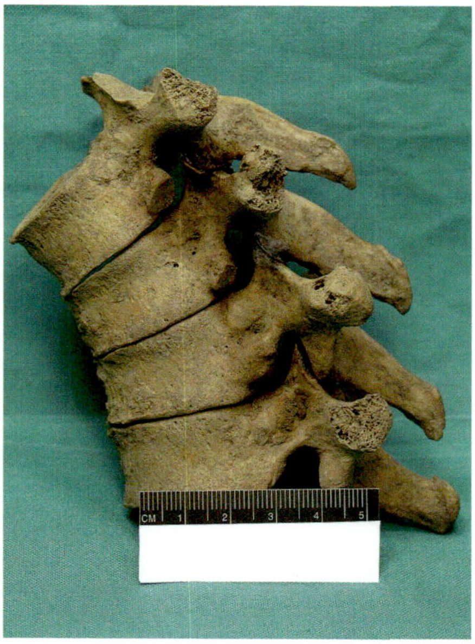

Figure 6.12 When compared to Figure 6.8, a photograph that was taken utilizing a vertical frame allows the subject to be brought closer.

Source: Photograph by the author.

Figures 6.13 and 6.14 demonstrate the suitable framing that corresponds with the issue. To have an image that is good quality, it is vital to keep in mind that this is one of the components that will help you achieve that goal.

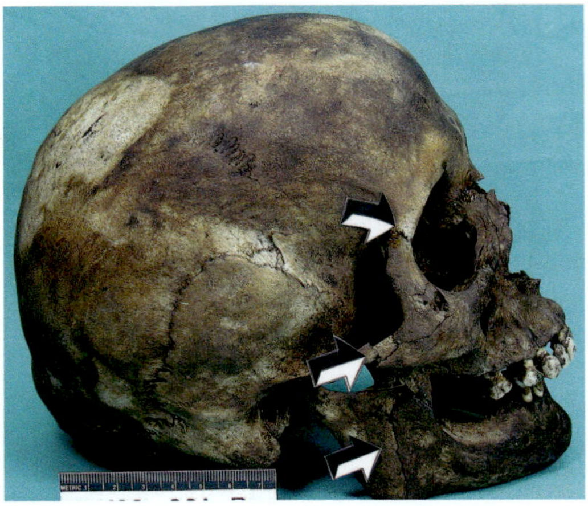

Figure 6.13 Photo taken with horizontal framing corresponding to the subject.

Source: Photograph by the author.

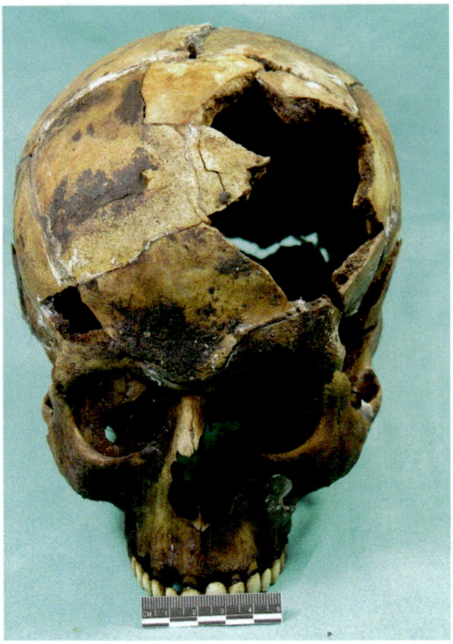

Figure 6.14 Photo taken with vertical framing corresponding to the subject.

Source: Photograph by the author.

Position

When working on details, a tripod is beneficial while working at a slow speed. If you do not have a tripod or if you do not prefer to use one, you should make sure that you adopt a correct and stable posture to avoid up-and-down body movements during shooting. As shown Figure 6.15, additionally, you should make sure that your shutter speed is quick enough to prevent blurring. The distance that separates the subject and the photographer will be determined by the lens used.

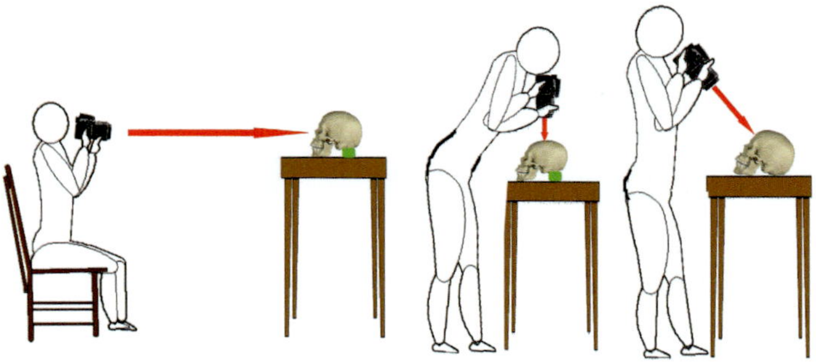

Figure 6.15 This illustration shows possible positions during a photography session without using a tripod.

Source: Photograph by the author.

To capture the most amount of information in the photograph, it is vital to select a viewpoint that is suitable for the subject that you wish to emphasize when you are taking the photograph.

Figures 6.16 and 6.18 show an image that was taken without choosing a good viewpoint and that lacks information.

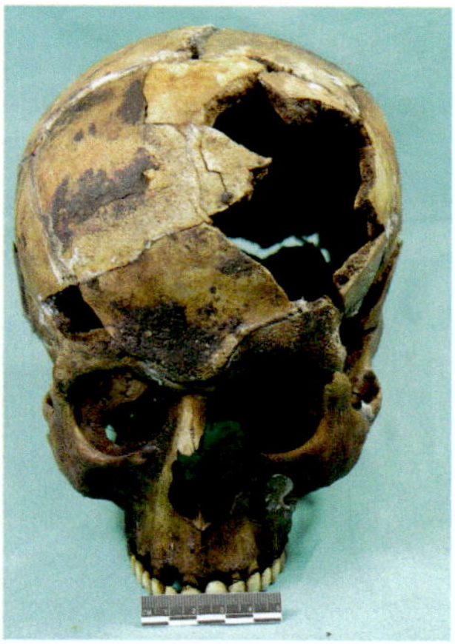

Figure 6.16 Shows an image from an inadequate viewpoint; the photograph does not show the point where the bullet entered.

Source: Photograph by the author.

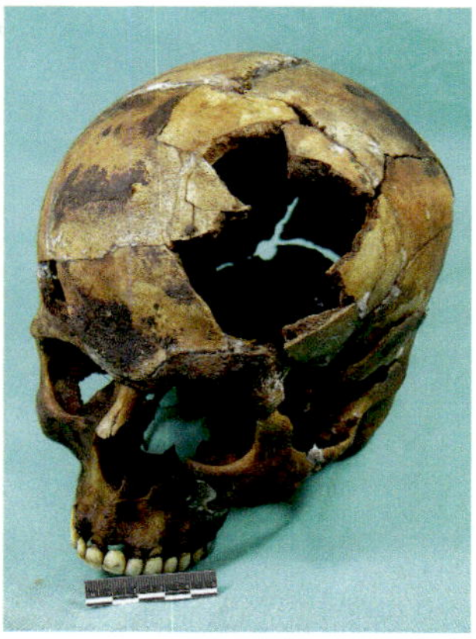

Figure 6.17 A photograph taken from an advantageous viewpoint, allowing you to see the bullet exit as well as its entry point.

Source: Photograph by the author.

Figures 6.17 and 6.19 show an image with an appropriate viewpoint and more information on the photograph.

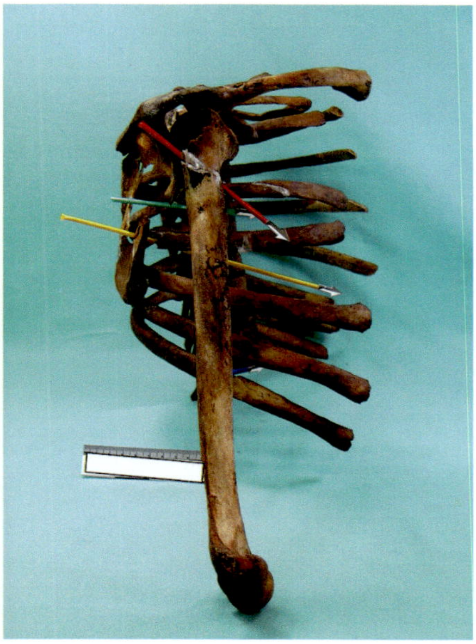

Figure 6.18 Another example with a negative perspective, the trajectory of the bullet, which is depicted in blue, is not apparent in this picture.

Source: Photograph by the author.

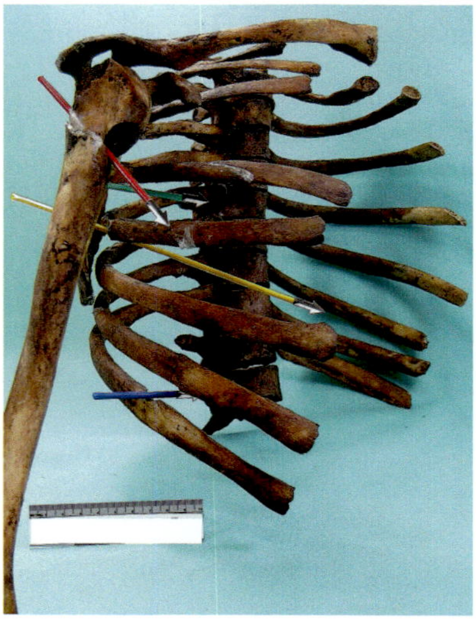

Figure 6.19 In comparison, this photograph demonstrates clearly the blue bullet trajectory.

Source: Photograph by the author.

Shooting

In addition to a sluggish shutter speed or an inaccurate focus setting, pushing the shutter button can also result in blurry images. It could appear to be a straightforward process to take a picture by pushing the shutter button, but unfortunately, certain precautions must be taken.

When you wish to take a picture, you should avoid pressing the button firmly and all the way down because doing so will cause the camera to move, which will result in a blurry picture.

Press the shutter button halfway to activate autofocus, and the camera will display the focusing position being used. As illustrated in Figures 6.20 and 6.21, depending on the subject being photographed, the autofocus point will be different.

The next step is to take the photo by pressing the button all the way down in a gentle manner.

It is important to keep in mind that when taking a picture, it is necessary to push the shutter button softly to prevent the possibility of the camera shaking.

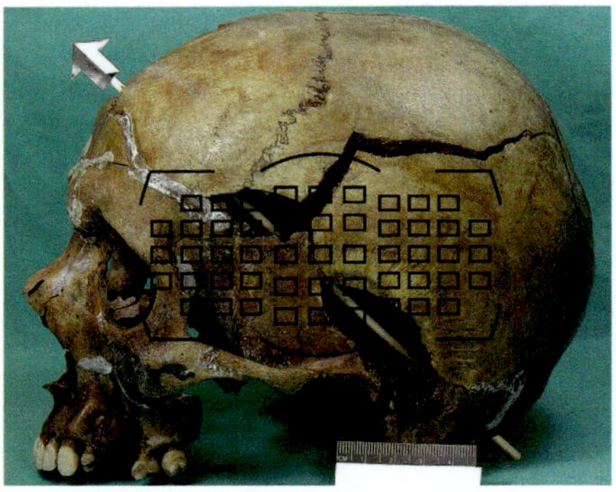

Figure 6.20 Example with multiple autofocus points.

Source: Photograph by the author.

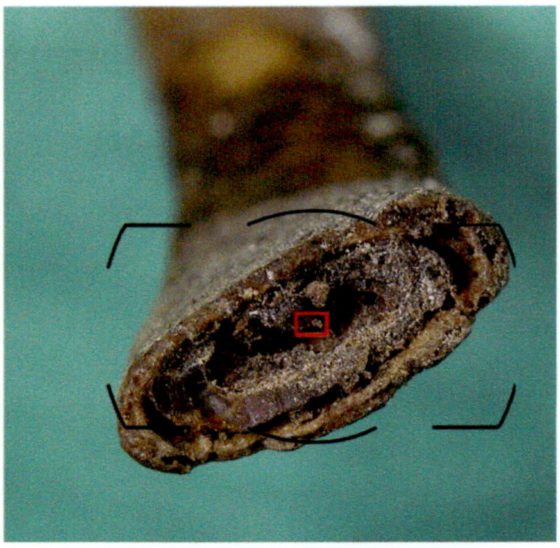

Figure 6.21 Example with a single autofocus point.

Source: Photograph by the author.

Skeleton

7

When working with human bones, it is necessary for a forensic photographer to have minimal knowledge of anatomy and to know that the adult human skeleton is composed of 206 bones. When taking photographs, the photographer needs to be aware of both the subject being photographed and its anatomical position to avoid any misunderstanding.

Figures 7.1 and 7.2 show respectively the anterior and posterior views of human skeletons, along with some names of the bones that are depicted in each image. Figure 7.3 illustrates two examples of incorrect anatomical positioning during photographic documentation.

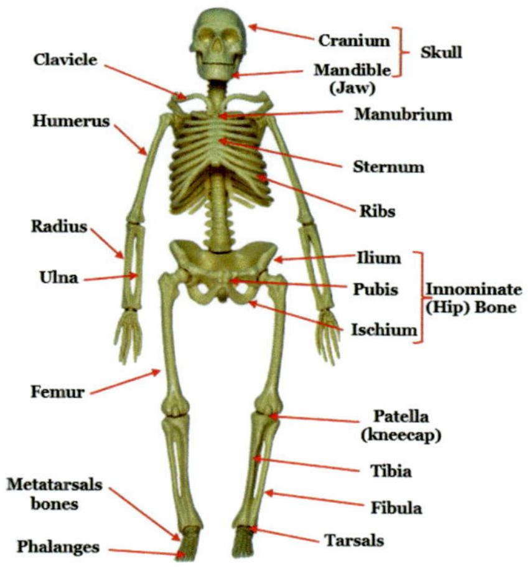

Figure 7.1 Anterior view of skeleton.

Source: Photograph by the author.

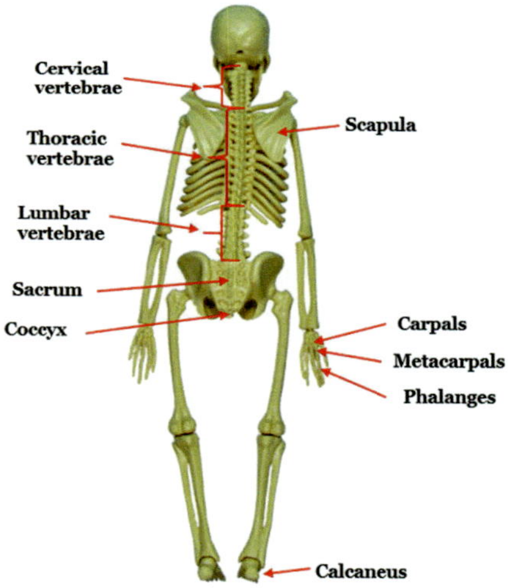

Figure 7.2 Posterior view of skeleton.

Source: Photograph by the author.

DOI: 10.4324/9781003768838-10

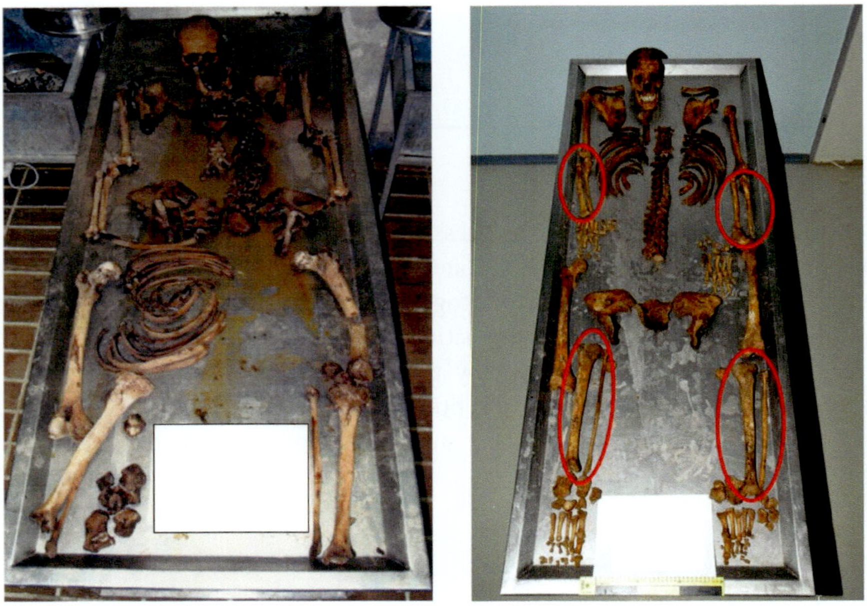

Figure 7.3 Two skeletons that are positioned in an anatomically wrong manner. The bones are mixed up on the left side, while an anatomical mistake is indicated by the red circles on the right side of the image.

Source: Photograph by the author.

Reconstruction 8

In addition to taking detailed photographs of aspects such as a bullet entry or exit point, a cut, an old fracture, or another detail that the anthropologist may request, depending on what has been diagnosed, the photographer will sometimes be asked to interpret these observations in a didactic manner. As shown in Figure 8.1, a photographer may encounter difficulties when attempting to correctly interpret an injury, so you will therefore sometimes have to collaborate with a forensic anthropologist to obtain a reconstruction corresponding to the requirements.

It is essential to collaborate with a forensic anthropologist when dealing with complex cases, and reconstruction will often make an essential contribution to a deeper understanding of the current situation.

After a case has been reconstructed, it is a great deal less difficult to arrive at a more correct interpretation and to take photographs that are richer in detail.

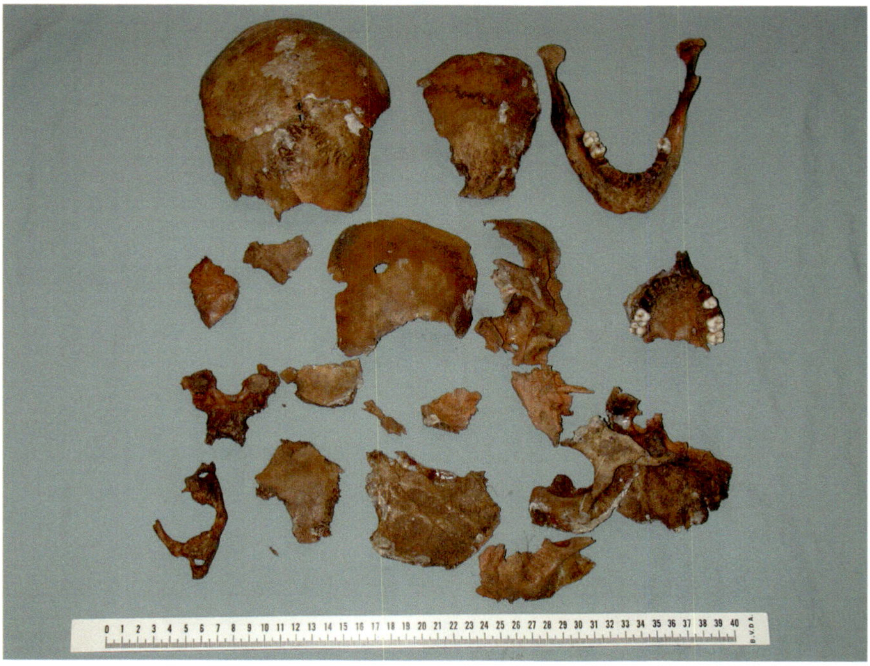

Figure 8.1 Fragments of a skull prior to its reconstruction.

Source: Photograph by the author.

DOI: 10.4324/9781003768838-11

Figures 8.2 to 8.5: Using glue and a catalyst as tools, Professor Edixon Quiñones is currently engaged in the process of reconstructing the skull into its original form.

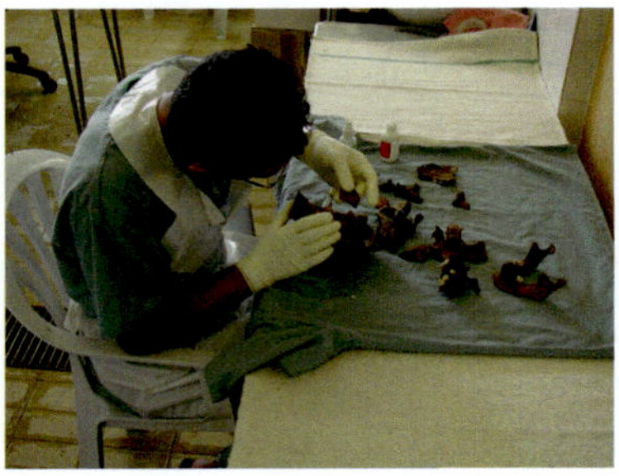

Figure 8.2 Before reconstruction.

Source: Photograph by the author.

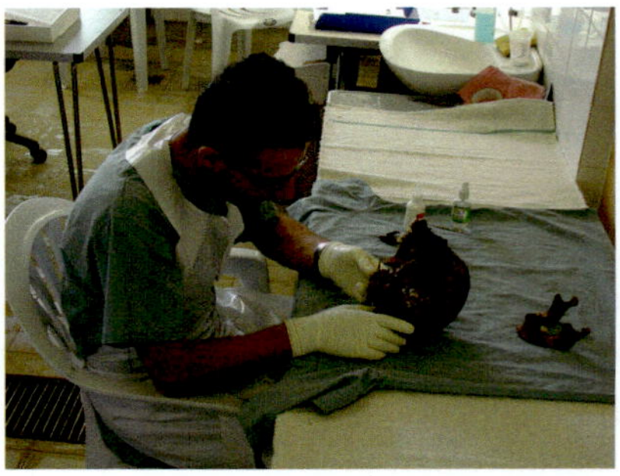

Figure 8.3 During the process of reconstruction.

Source: Photograph by the author.

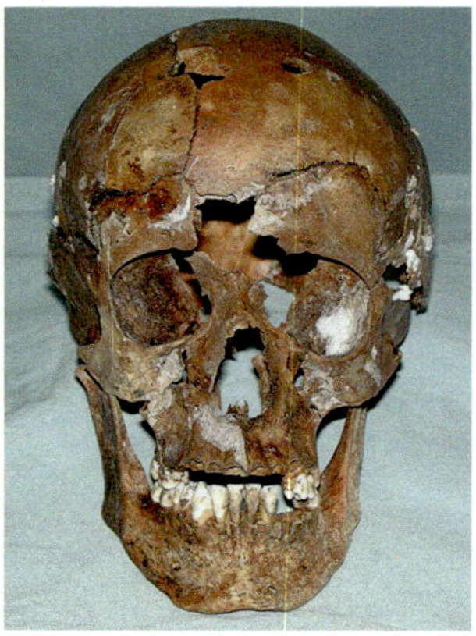

Figure 8.4 Illustration of the skull after it has been reconstructed.

Source: Photograph by the author.

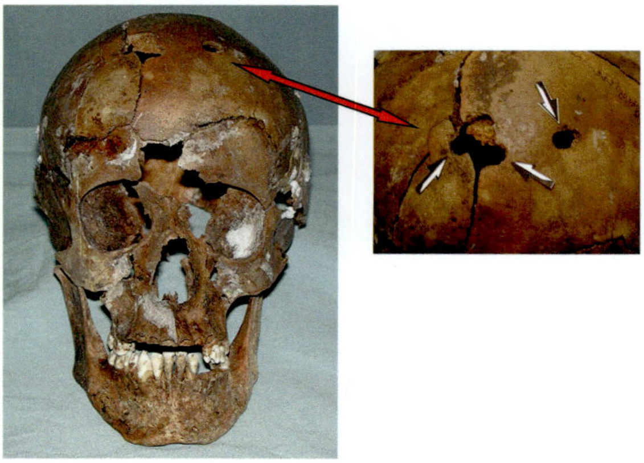

Figure 8.5 After the reconstruction, three bullet entrances can be seen on the parietal bone. Without a reconstruction, it would not have been possible to see those three bullet entrances.

Source: Photograph by the author.

Figures 8.6 to 8.13 illustrate several examples of reconstructions that assist in understanding and interpreting the events that took place, or that may be used for possible identification.

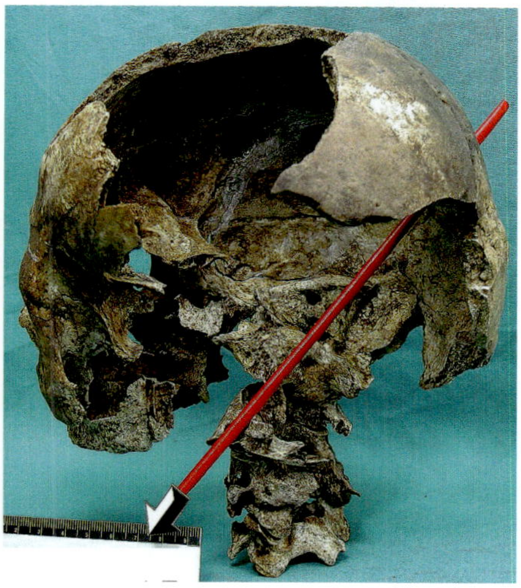

Figure 8.6 The trajectory of a bullet from the parietal to the cervical vertebrae is depicted by the red rod.

Source: Photograph by the author.

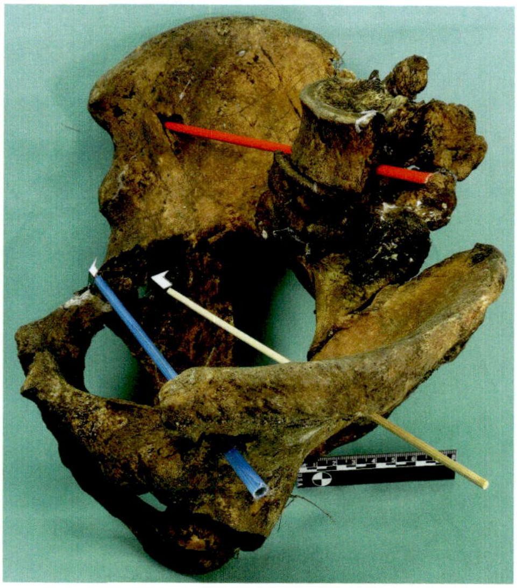

Figure 8.7 Shows three bullet trajectories, each represented by a red, yellow, and blue rod.

Source: Photograph by the author.

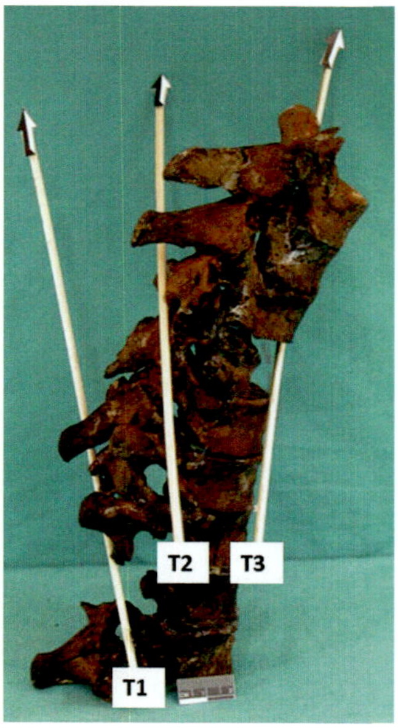

Figure 8.8 Shows three bullets' trajectories in the thoracic vertebrae labeled T1, T2, and T3. As seen in this picture, you can use labels to distinguish each trajectory if you do not have colored rods.

Source: Photograph by the author.

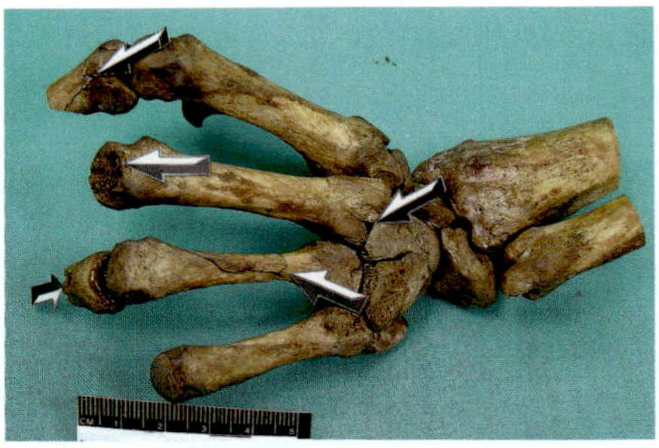

Figure 8.9 After reconstruction of the right hand, the fractures indicated by an arrow can be seen.

Source: Photograph by the author.

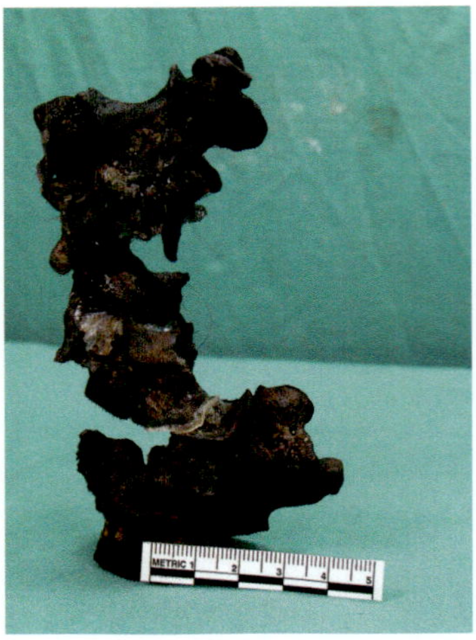

Figure 8.10 After reconstruction, the gunshot wounds in the thoracic vertebrae can be seen.

Source: Photograph by the author.

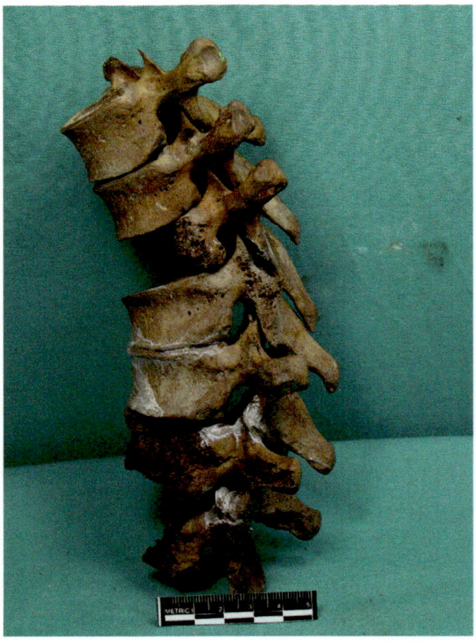

Figure 8.11 Other examples of reconstruction, the gunshot wounds in the vertebrae can be seen.

Source: Photograph by the author.

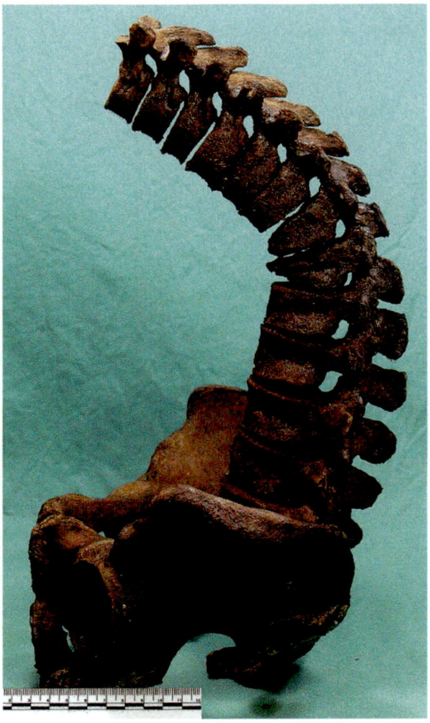

Figure 8.12 After spinal reconstruction, we observe a kyphosis and compression of thoracic vertebrae 11th and 12th, which can be useful for identification.

Source: Photograph by the author.

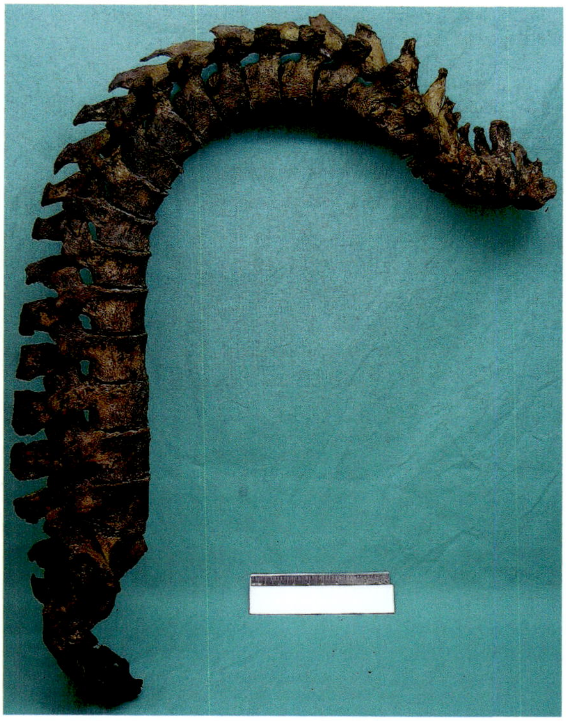

Figure 8.13 Another example of spinal reconstruction, which can be useful for identification.

Source: Photograph by the author.

9 Basic Recommendations

Listed below are some suggestions that you should consider before beginning to photograph your subject:

- Take a picture of the closed body bag as well as the open body bag in its entirety.
- When you find evidence in the body bag, take a general and a detailed photo, and make sure to include the evidence number in the photo.
- Take a general photo in the anatomical position first, then move on to photograph the lesion in greater detail (anterior and posterior views depending on the possibility or condition of the bones).
- Make sure you choose a background that is suitable for bones and evidence.
- Capture photographic detail in order, beginning with the head and working all the way down to the feet.
- Include at least six different general views of the skull, including the front, right, back, left, top, and base views, as well as any necessary details.
- Take at least four photographs of the teeth (both the maxilla and the mandible, when possible, with the front, right, left, and top views included).
- Photograph all available evidence, such as fractures (antemortem or postmortem) or any other findings.
- Take a general picture of the clothes, including details.

Where Applicable, Make Sure You Don't Neglect These

- Examine the light that is used, paying attention to its intensity, quantity, direction, and shading.
- ISO, shutter speed, aperture, and white balance should be adjusted according to the circumstances.
- Discard any items that you do not need to capture in the photo.
- Ensure you have a strong point (what we want to show).
- Each photograph must include, where possible, the case number, a graduated ruler that corresponds to the subject's size, and, if required, an evidence number.
- If possible, position the ruler so that the image is correctly oriented.
- Study carefully the components that will make up the final image before you shoot.
- Take time to consider how you want to shoot the picture and the equipment you will need to do so properly.
- Move around and select the best possible position in relation to the subject.
- Frame the photograph based on the orientation of the subject to create a closer image and eliminate any unnecessary space.

DOI: 10.4324/9781003768838-12

- Keep a steady position to prevent a blurry image.
- Choose the correct autofocus point and press the button halfway; once focused, gently press the button all the way down to prevent the camera from moving while shooting.

Method of Work 10

1. X-ray
2. General photography
3. Detail

X-Ray

Before the autopsy begins, make sure that the body has been inspected using X-rays or a fluoroscope to check for any contents in the body bag, such as sharp or pointed objects, bullets, or other important discoveries.

Whenever feasible, a photograph should be taken to guarantee the preservation of the radiograph, depending on the type of X-ray machine used.

Photographs from an X-ray are shown in Figures 10.1 and 10.2.

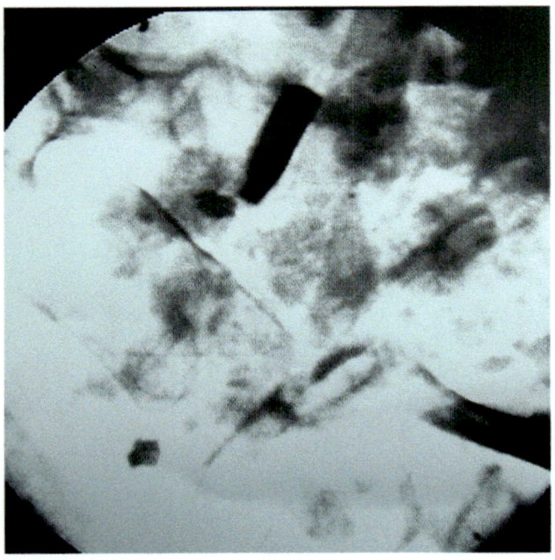

Figure 10.1 Shell case in a body bag.

Source: Photograph by the author.

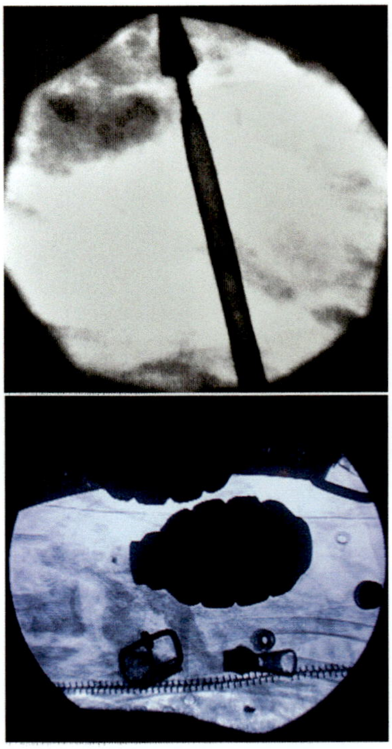

Figure 10.2 Show a sharp and two hand grenades in a body bag.

Source: Photograph by the author.

DOI: 10.4324/9781003768838-13

General Photography

Before, during, and after the autopsy, photos will be taken. There will be more or fewer pictures to capture based on the specifics of each situation. The first pictures will either show the body bag, box, or other container open or closed, depending on the conditions.

The use of a ladder will enable you to get a better view of the overall body bag, as displayed below in Figures 10.3 to 10.6.

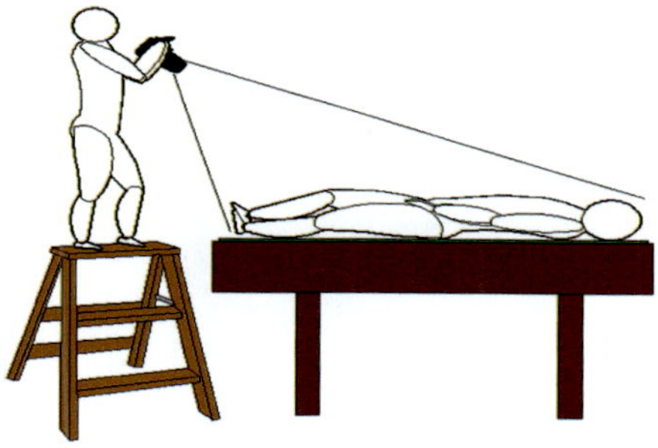

Figure 10.3 This illustration shows an example of the use of a stepladder. The photographer will decide where the stepladder should be placed.

Source: Photograph by the author.

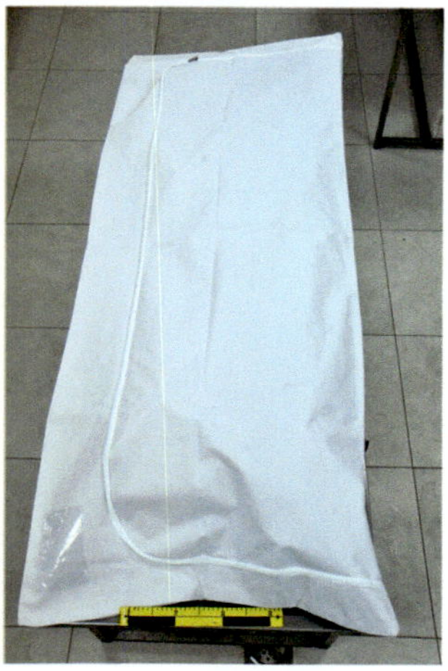

Figure 10.4 Example of how the photo will look.

Source: Photograph by the author.

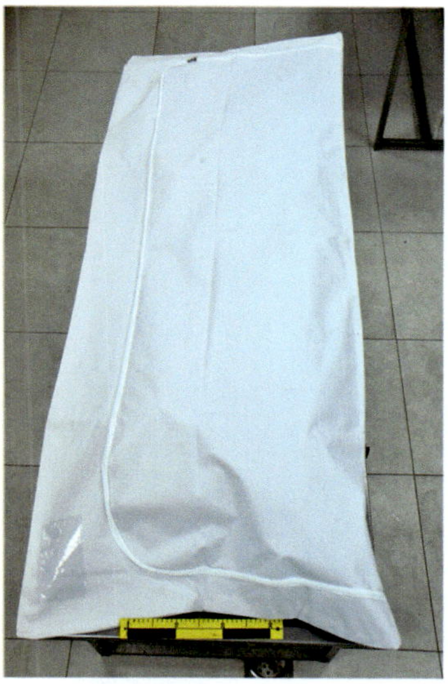

Figure 10.5 Body bag close.

Source: Photograph by the author.

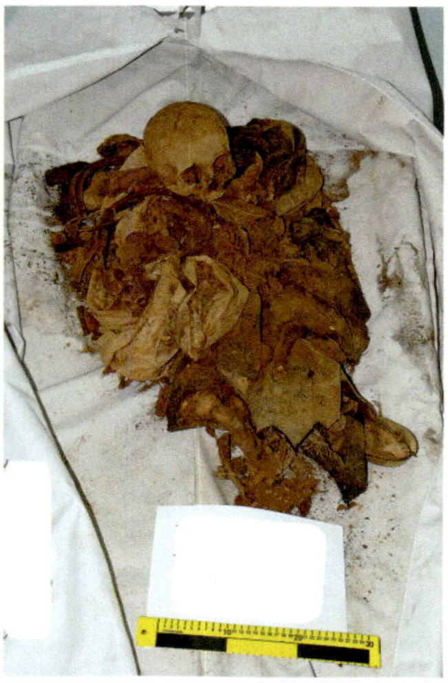

Figure 10.6 Body bag open

Source: Photograph by the author.

If there are artifacts in the body bag (like ligatures or a bullet, for instance), a general and detailed photograph with an evidence number must be taken before they are removed.

A mid-range photograph illustrating the region where the artifact is located will be the first image, as seen in Figure 10.7, and a detailed image will be the second, as seen in Figure 10.8.

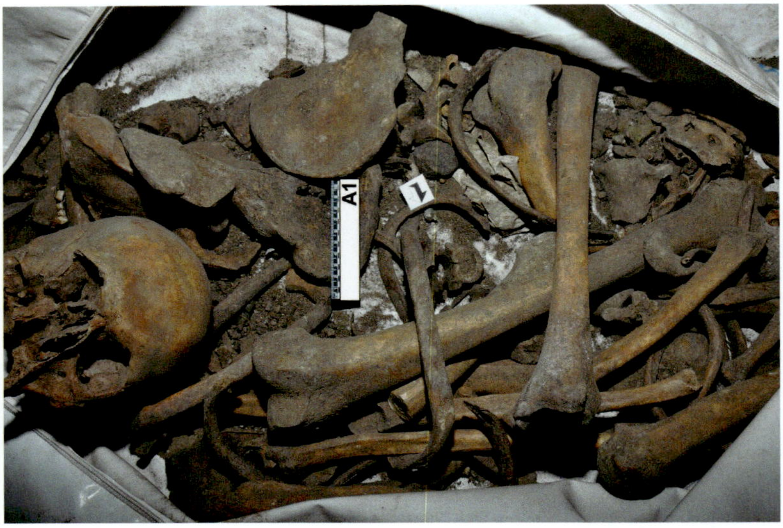

Figure 10.7 Image displaying the artifact location indicated by the arrow along with its evidence number.

Source: Photograph by the author.

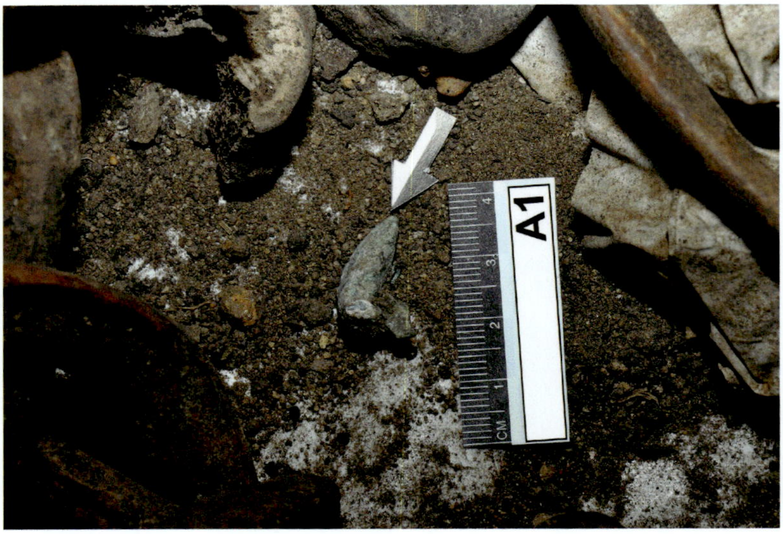

Figure 10.8 Image showing the bullet's details indicated by an arrow with its evidence number.

Source: Photograph by the author.

After being cleaned, the bones will be arranged on a table in the proper anatomical position so that a general view of the skeleton may be taken, as seen in Figure 10.9, followed, if appropriate, by a photo displaying the body's fractures, as seen in Figure 10.10. Figure 10.11 shows an example with a newborn.

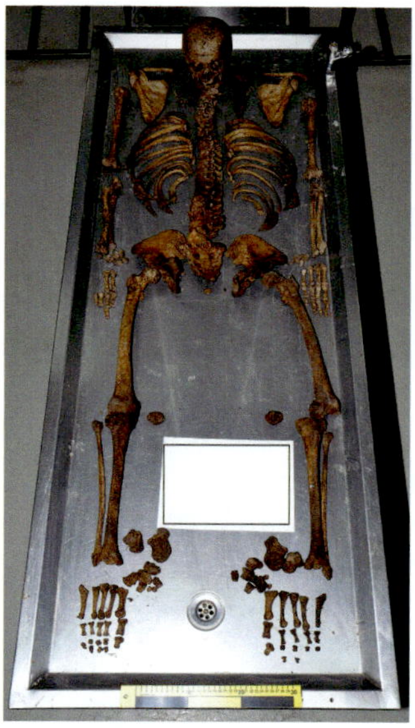

Figure 10.9 Anatomical position.

Source: Photograph by the author.

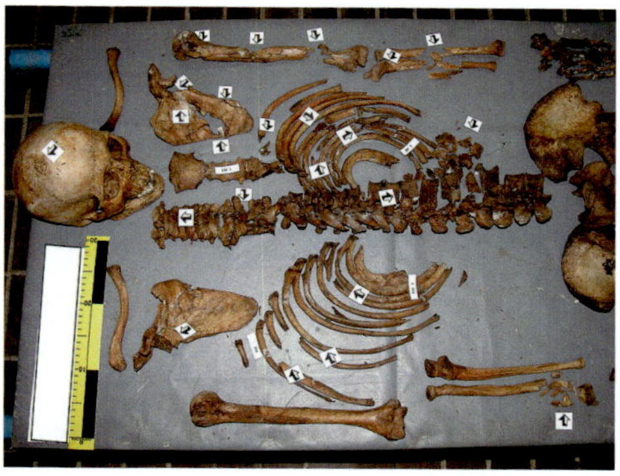

Figure 10.10 The body fractures are shown by the arrows.

Source: Photograph by the author.

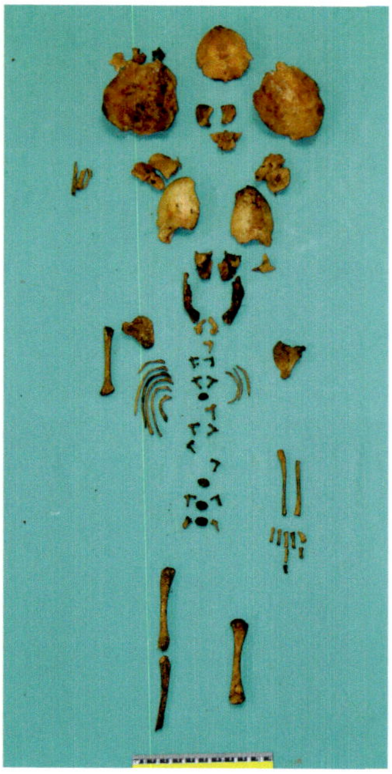

Figure 10.11 As seen in this picture, it is advised to place the newborn on an appropriate background when photographing it to achieve better contrast.

Source: Photograph by the author.

Detail

The specifics of any fractures or other findings seen during the skeletal examination must be photographed once the anatomical position has been captured.

The details must be presented to support and validate the anthropologist's and/or pathologist's findings and conclusions. These could include a cut, an injury, a bullet entry and exit, and so on.

A general overview of the bone should always be the first image taken, followed by a second, more in-depth image that highlights the crucial detail (or details), then, if possible, an inside shot.

Beginning with the most anatomically correct order, starting with the head and working our way down to the toes.

It is advised to set up a "mini studio" specifically for taking quality photos. This could take place in the autopsy room or another room, depending on the situation and the amount of space available.

There are several methods to have a "mini studio." You can buy a Mini Photo Studio Box, but it is only good for small bones, with limitations; you can buy studio lights, like in Figure 10.12, which are very helpful but somewhat bulky; or you can just make one yourself using simple materials, like the one in Figure 10.13, which will let you get great details of all kinds of bones, long or small, and even reconstructions.

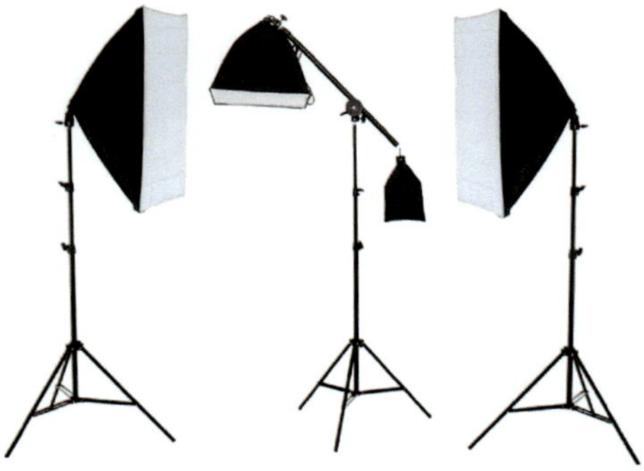

Figure 10.12 Example of studio lighting.

Source: Photograph by the author.

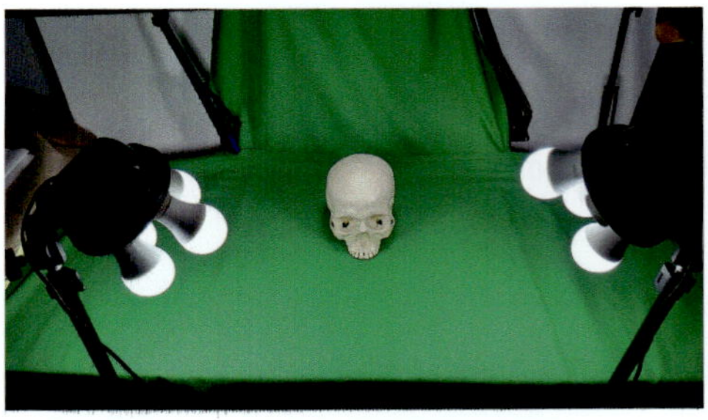

Figure 10.13 Example of use without softbox.

Source: Photograph by the author.

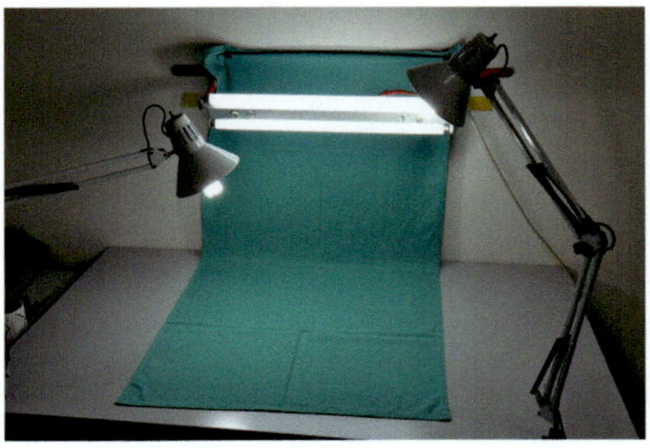

Figure 10.14 An illustration of a basic studio constructed using simple tools.

Source: Photograph by the author.

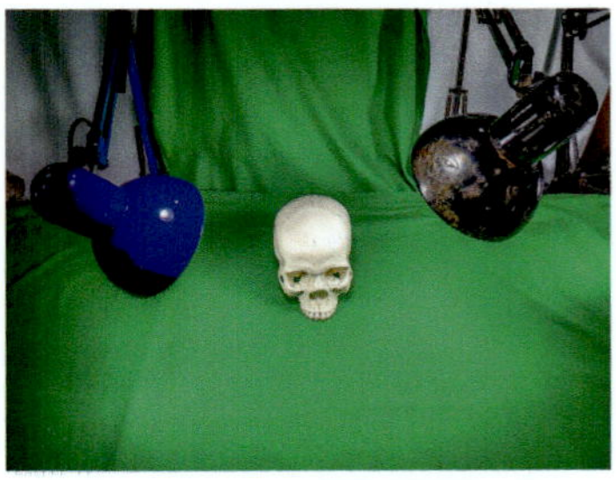

Figure 10.15 Another example of a basic studio.

Source: Photograph by the author.

With Studio Lighting

If there is adequate room surrounding the shooting table, this style of studio lighting is appropriate for illuminating the subject from above and the sides. It can be used with or without softbox, as demonstrated in the Figure 10.13

With Basic Materials

Building a mini studio is a relatively simple process; you only need a table, two or four adjustable desk lamps with 20 W so-called daylight bulbs, and a matte cotton backdrop with the right amount of contrast, as shown in Figure 10.14, and followed by an example using articulated desk lamps, as shown in Figures 10.15 and 10.16.

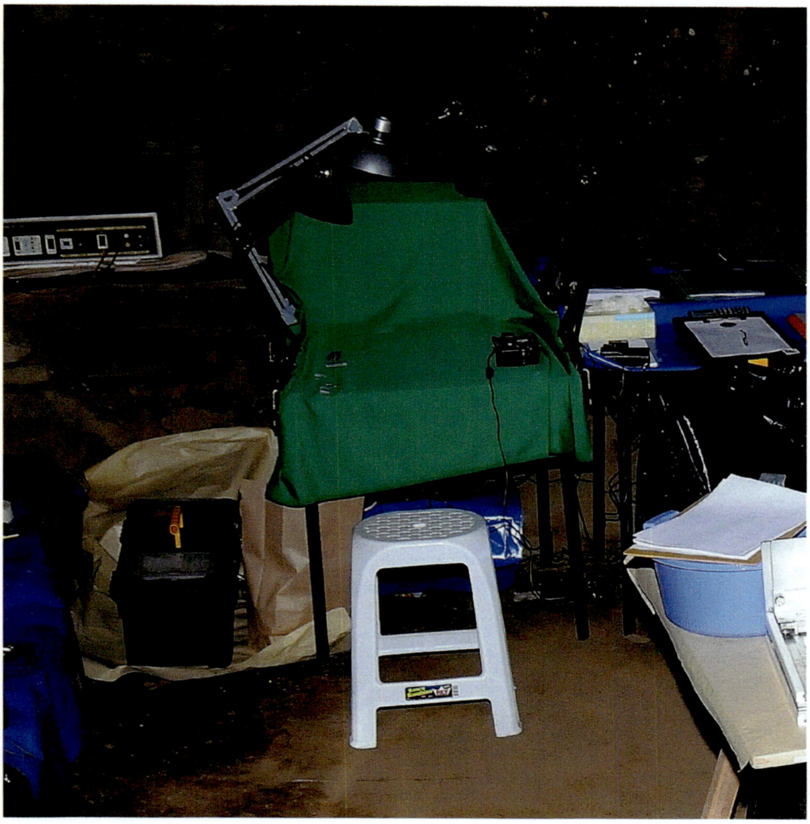

Figure 10.16 Another illustration of a basic studio that was constructed on-site at a height of 3,200 m and ran on a car battery.

Source: Photograph by the author.

In our case, we could assume that an excellent mini photography studio requires high-quality equipment, but this is not always the case. All the images used to illustrate this manual were taken in a mini studio, like the Figure 10.14, which allowed me to get great detail photographs without the need for a flash, tripod, or software editing.

Photographs of Bones Taken in Various Contexts

11

To prevent the disclosure of sensitive information, several photographs have been retouched.

To avoid potential issues arising from differences in photographic equipment and shooting conditions, the ISO setting, shutter speed, and aperture used for each photograph in this manual are not provided. These parameters vary according to the camera model, lens, and lighting conditions. Consequently, the settings used to produce the images in this manual may not be suitable for other equipment and attempting to replicate these settings could result in photographs of unsatisfactory quality.

Figures 11.1 to 11.149 demonstrate a proper preparation of photographic images for various subjects, using appropriate indicators (e.g., arrows, rulers, and forensic rod) to identify and emphasize points of interest. This approach ensures that the viewer's attention is focused on the relevant features of the image.

Bone Fractures, Diseases, and Other

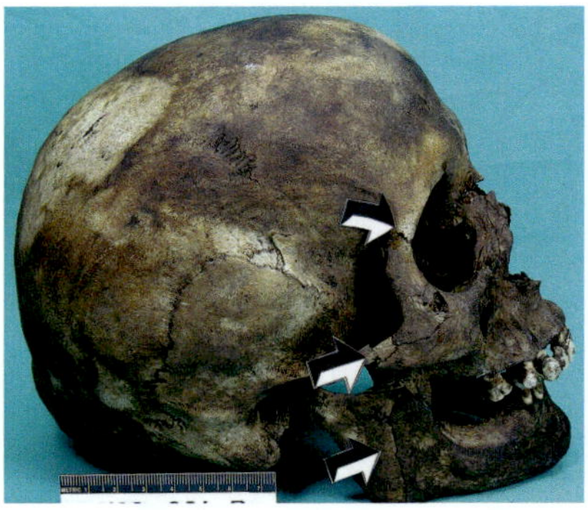

Figure 11.1 Three injuries on the skull indicated by arrows; two on the zygomatic bones and one on the mandibular ramus.

Source: Photograph by the author.

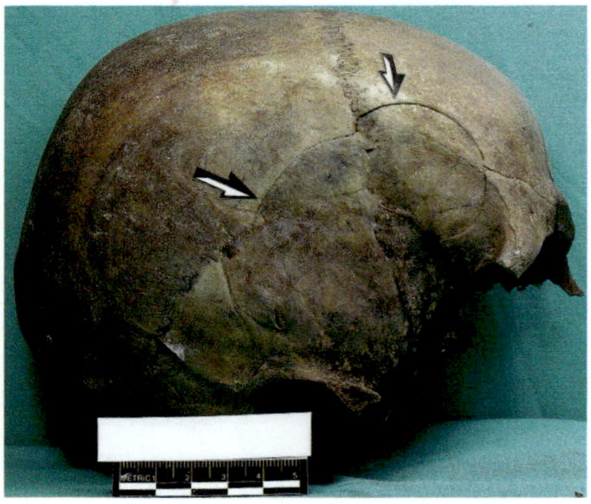

Figure 11.2 Arrows on the frontal and parietal bones indicating a skull fracture.

Source: Photograph by the author.

DOI: 10.4324/9781003768838-14

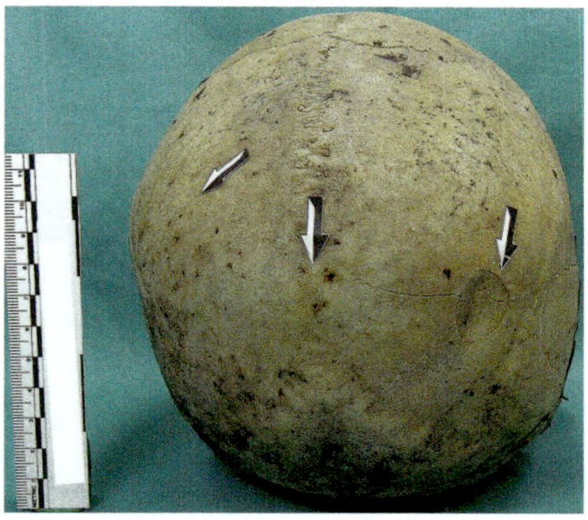

Figure 11.3 Arrows show a fracture and focal injury on the parietal.

Source: Photograph by the author.

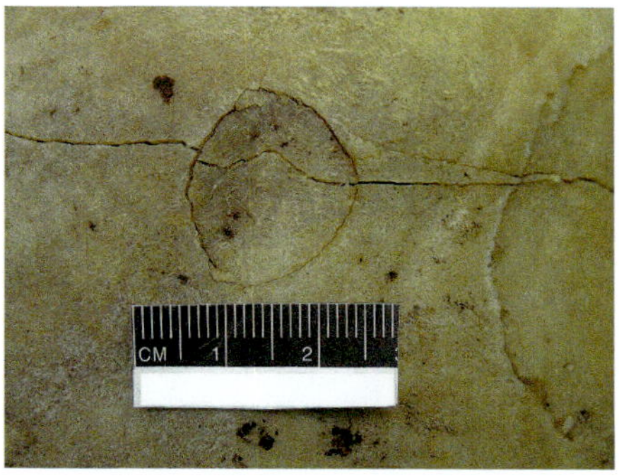

Figure 11.4 Close-up of the injury.

Source: Photograph by the author.

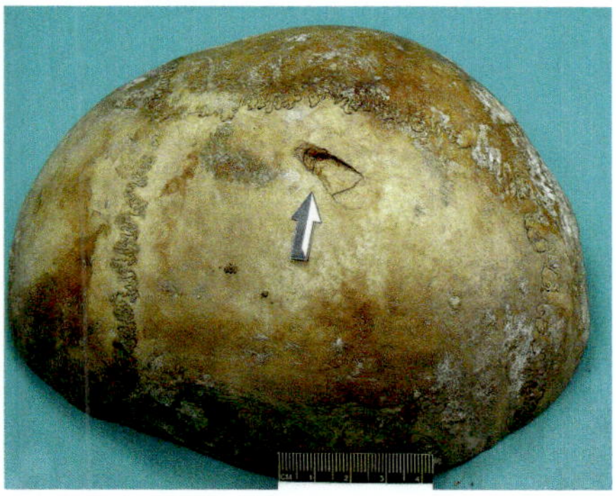

Figure 11.5 Arrows show a depressed fracture on the left parietal.

Source: Photograph by the author.

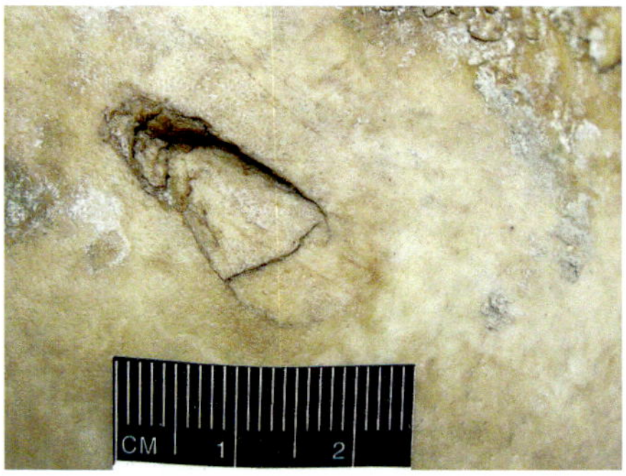

Figure 11.6 Close-up of the injury.

Source: Photograph by the author.

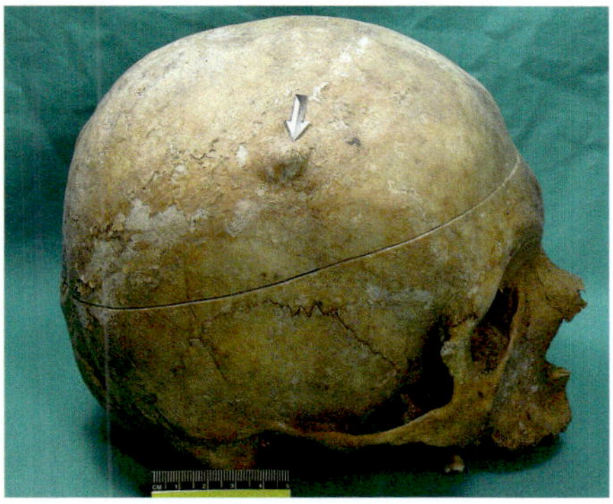

Figure 11.7 Arrow shows an Osteoid Osteoma on the right parietal.

Source: Photograph by the author.

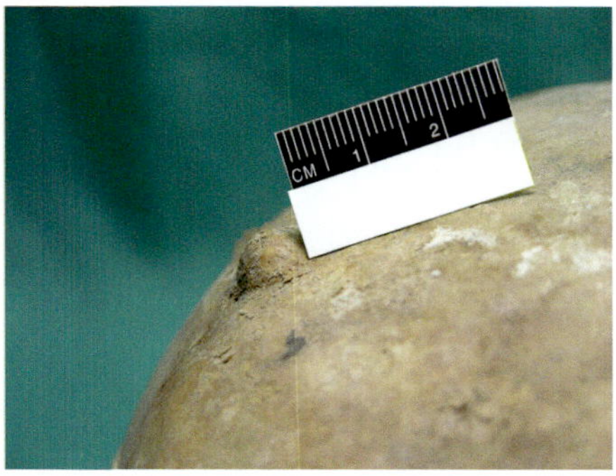

Figure 11.8 Detail of the Osteoid Osteoma.

Source: Photograph by the author.

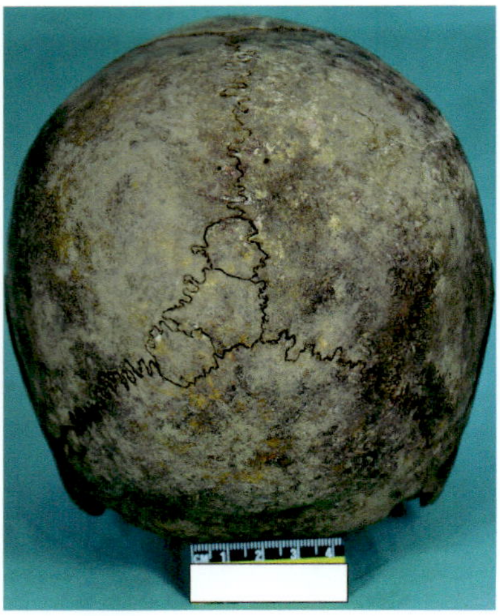

Figure 11.9 Wormian bones and parietal foramina.

Source: Photograph by the author.

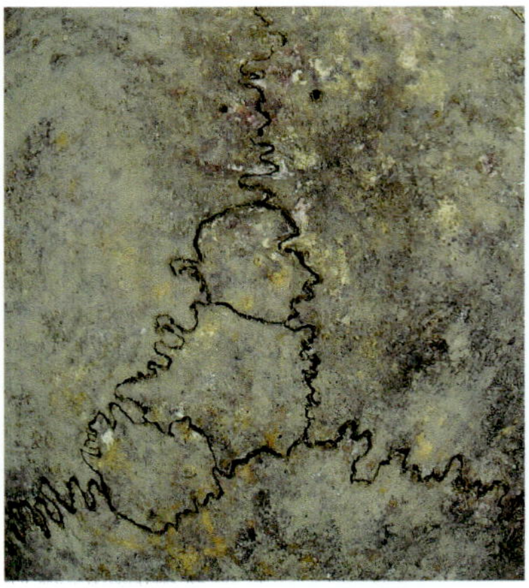

Figure 11.10 Close-up of the Wormian bones and parietal foramina

Source: Photograph by the author.

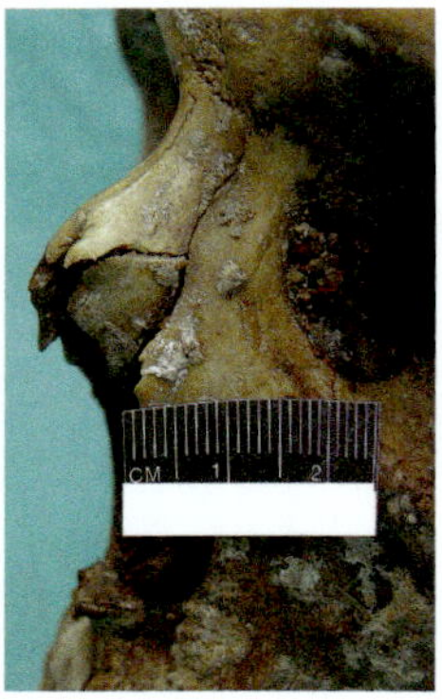

Figure 11.11 Nasal bone fracture.

Source: Photograph by the author.

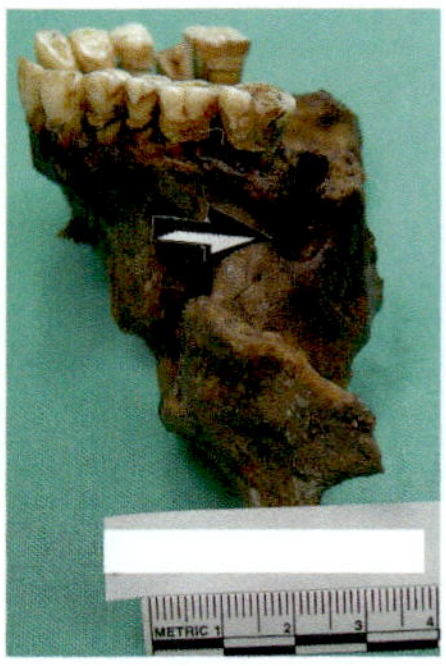

Figure 11.12 Abscess on the upper jaw indicated by the arrow.

Source: Photograph by the author.

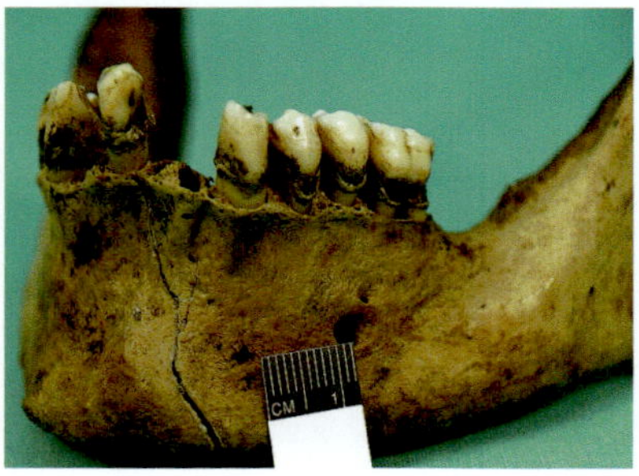

Figure 11.13 Symphyseal fracture

Source: Photograph by the author.

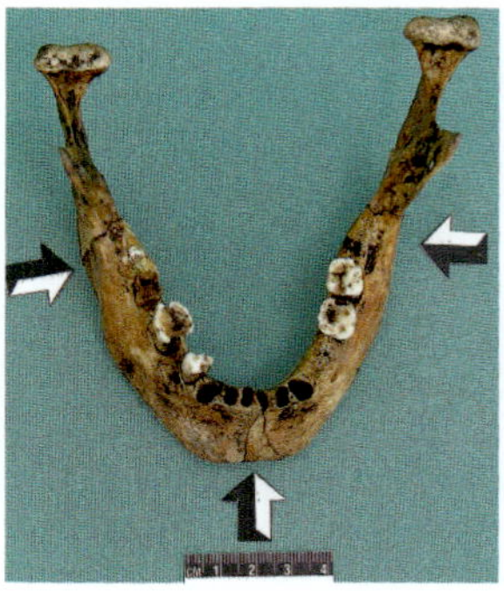

Figure 11.14 Arrows showing three mandibular fractures.

Source: Photograph by the author.

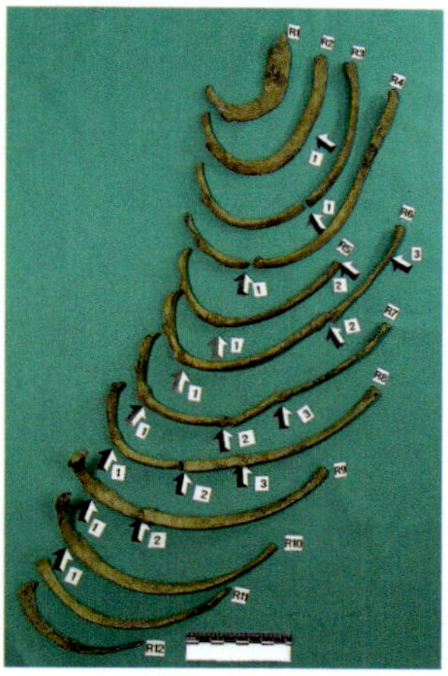

Figure 11.15 Right ribs, second to tenth (labeled); fractures indicated by arrows.

Source: Photograph by the author.

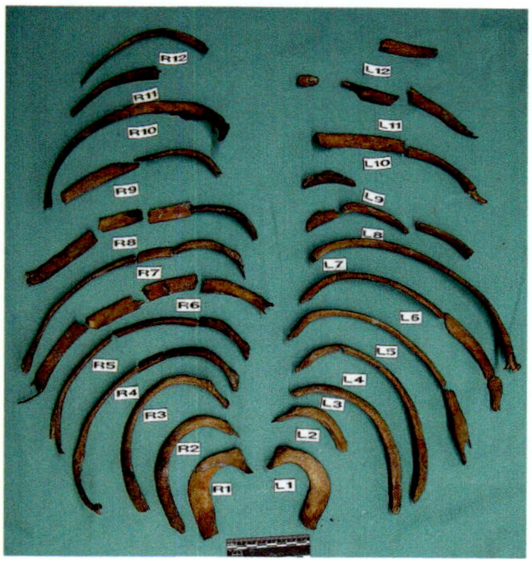

Figure 11.16 Fractures to the rib cage. Each label contains the rib number and side.

Source: Photograph by the author.

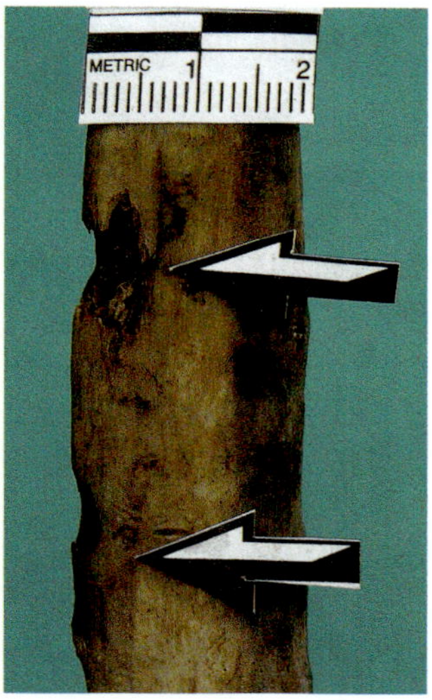

Figure 11.17 Left rib 9th, internal side showing pellet injuries indicated by arrows.

Source: Photograph by the author.

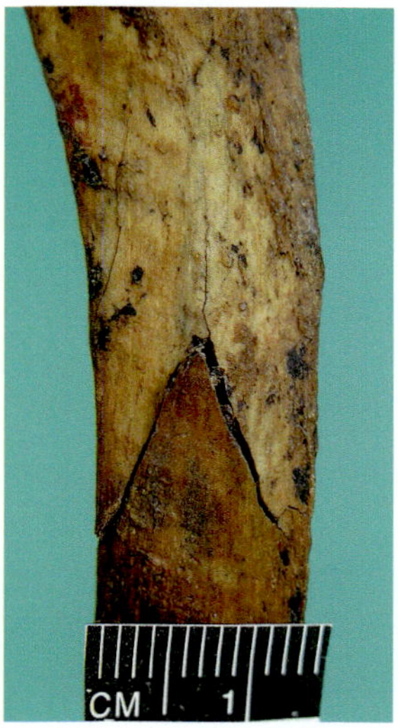

Figure 11.18 Fracture of 8th right rib.

Source: Photograph by the author.

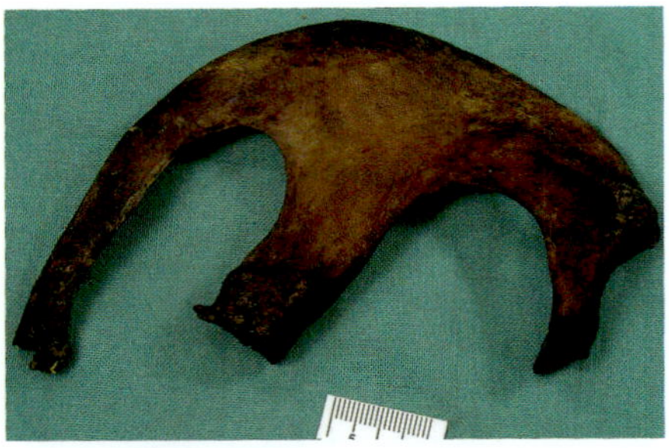

Figure 11.19 Show that the first and second ribs are fused.

Source: Photograph by the author.

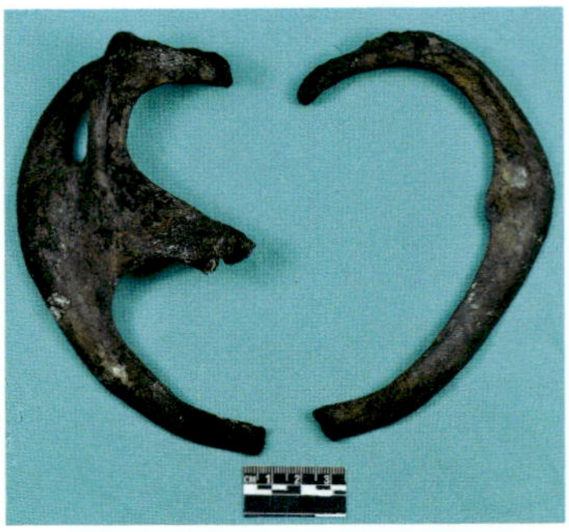

Figure 11.20 Show the first and second left ribs are fused with an old fracture on the second right rib.

Source: Photograph by the author.

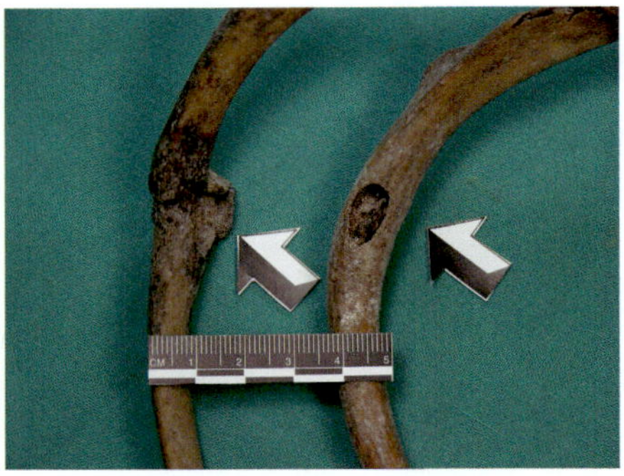

Figure 11.21 Arrow indicates callus formation on the 7th right rib and osteomyeloma of the 10th right rib.

Source: Photograph by the author.

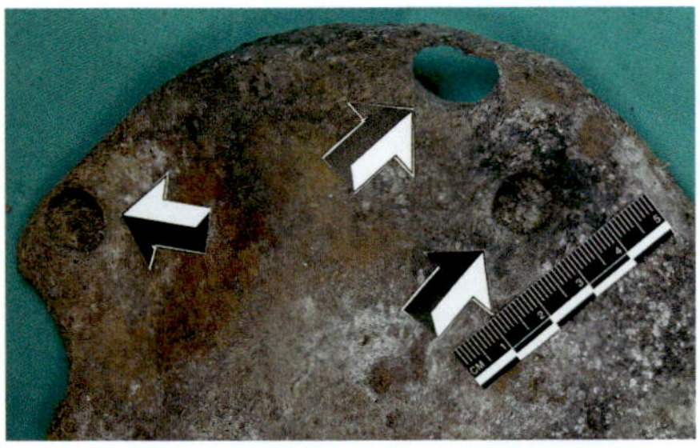

Figure 11.22 Arrows show multiple myeloma on the left ilium.

Source: Photograph by the author.

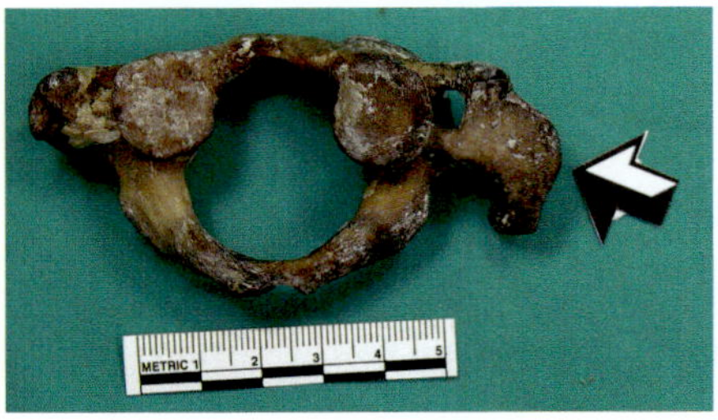

Figure 11.23 Arrow points at a congenital malformation of the transverse foramen of the atlas.

Source: Photograph by the author.

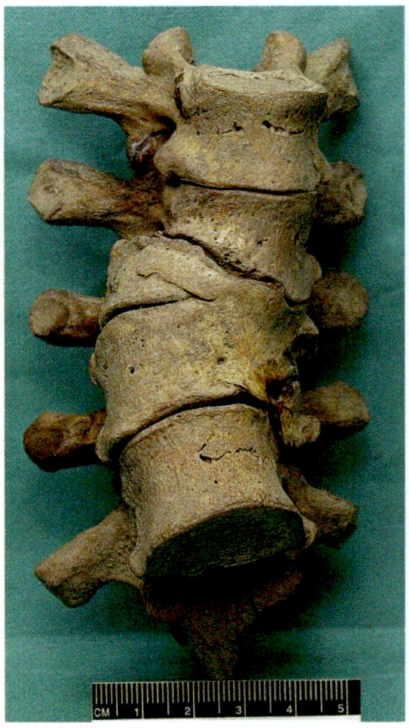

Figure 11.24 Thoracic spine T5-T9 with compression fracture of T6 and T7.

Source: Photograph by the author.

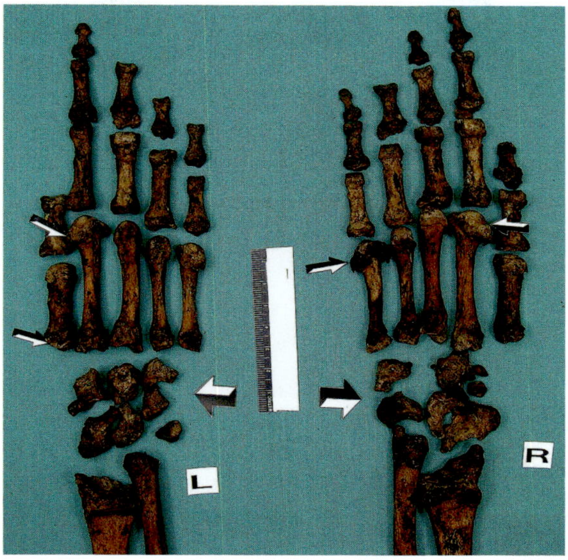

Figure 11.25 Arrow points to healed fracture on different bones of both hands.

Source: Photograph by the author.

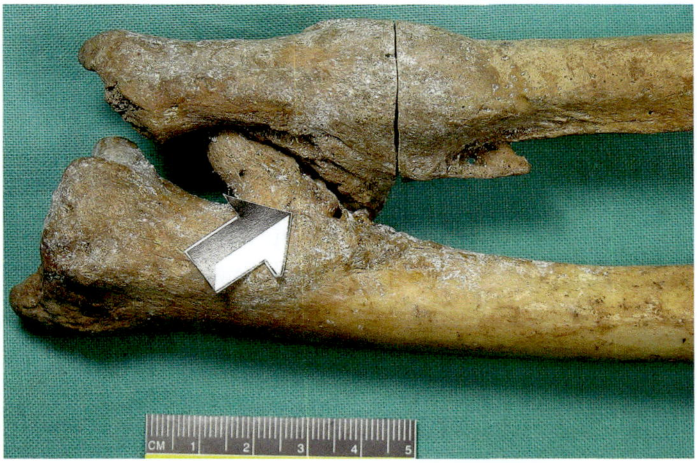

Figure 11.26 Arrow shows pseudoarthrosis of the ulna and radius.

Source: Photograph by the author.

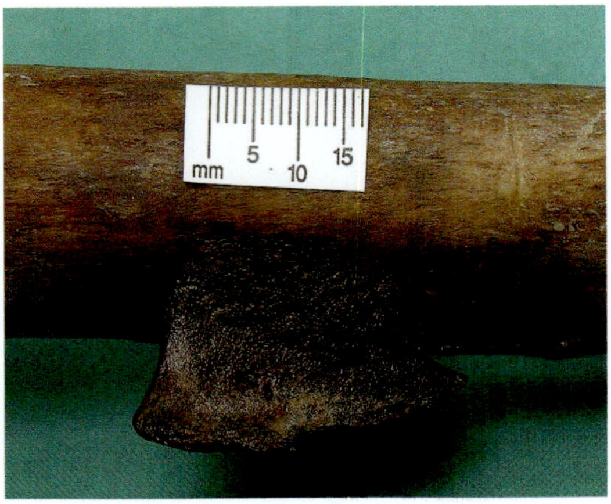

Figure 11.27 Femoral enthesopathy.

Source: Photograph by the author.

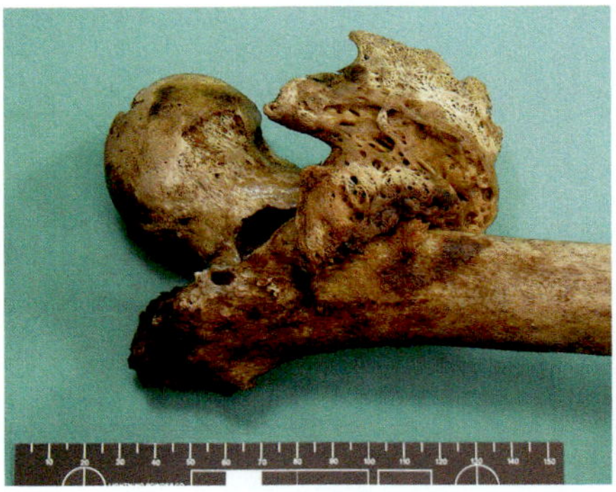

Figure 11.28 Show a femur with a callus formation (old fracture).

Source: Photograph by the author.

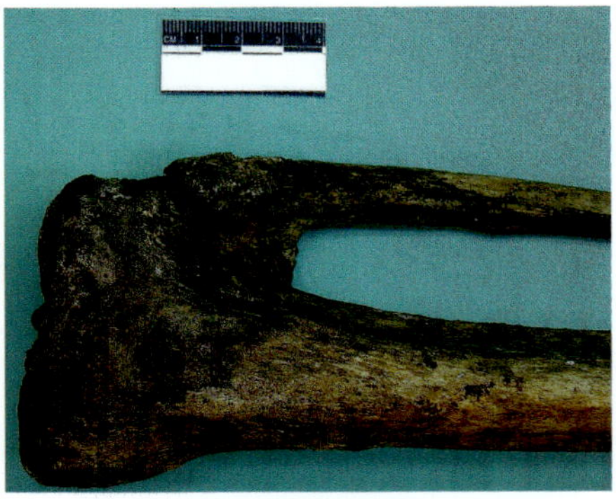

Figure 11.29 Proximal fusion of the fibula and tibia.

Source: Photograph by the author.

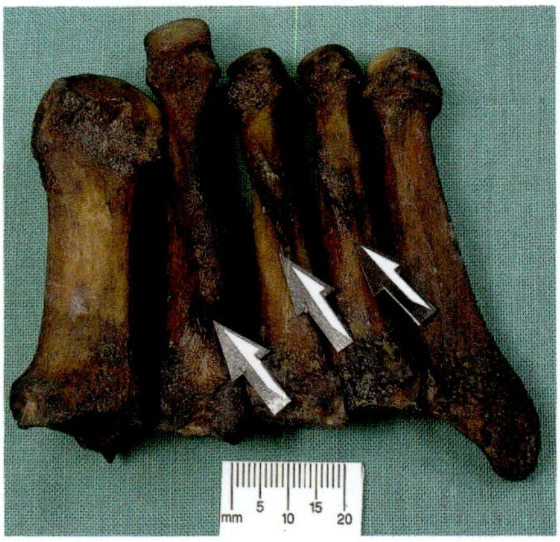

Figure 11.30 Three healed fractures on the right metatarsals indicated by arrows.

Source: Photograph by the author.

Surgical

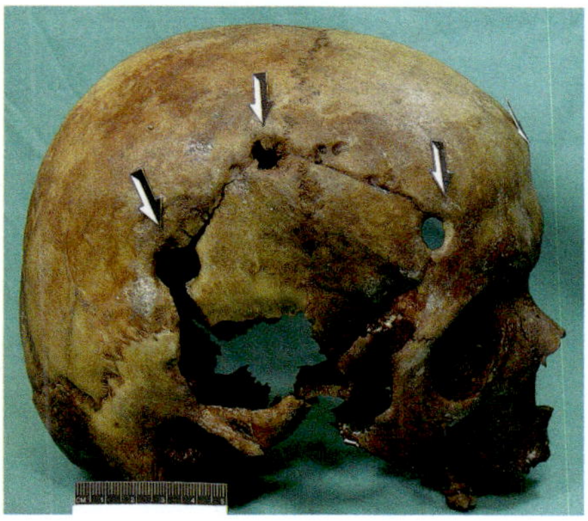

Figure 11.31 Craniotomy on the right side of the skull indicated by arrows

Source: Photograph by the author.

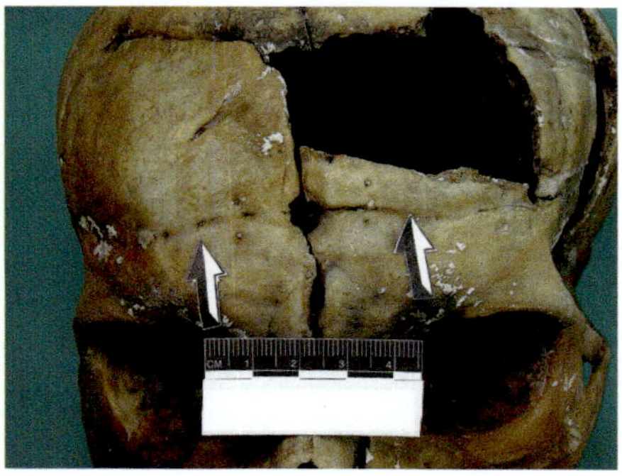

Figure 11.32 Craniotomy on the frontal bone indicated by arrows.

Source: Photograph by the author.

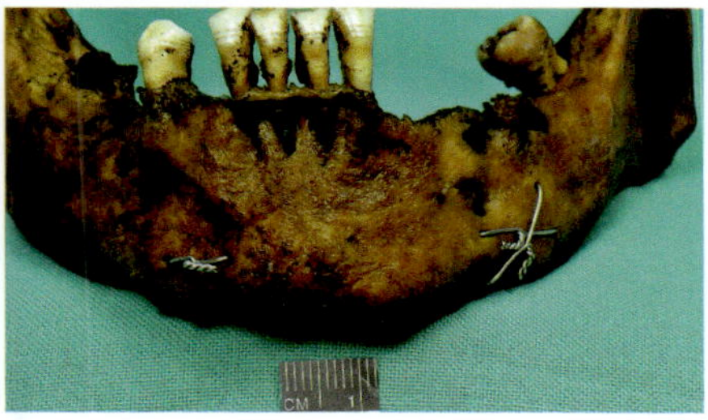

Figure 11.33 Surgical K-wire on the symphysis and body.

Source: Photograph by the author.

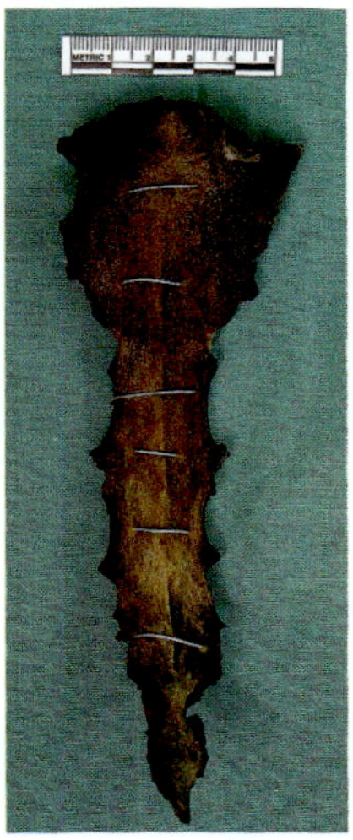

Figure 11.34 Sternotomy posterior view.

Source: Photograph by the author.

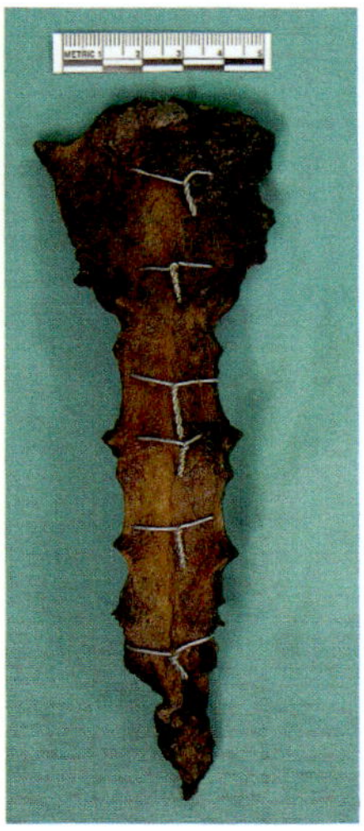

Figure 11.35 Sternotomy anterior view.

Source: Photograph by the author.

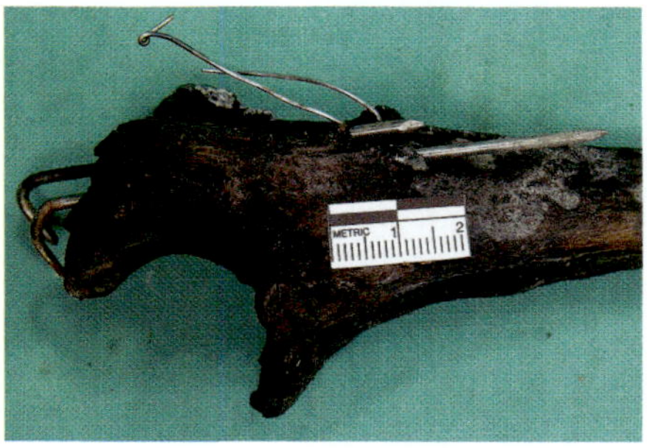

Figure 11.36 K-Wire through the proximal aspect of the ulna.

Source: Photograph by the author.

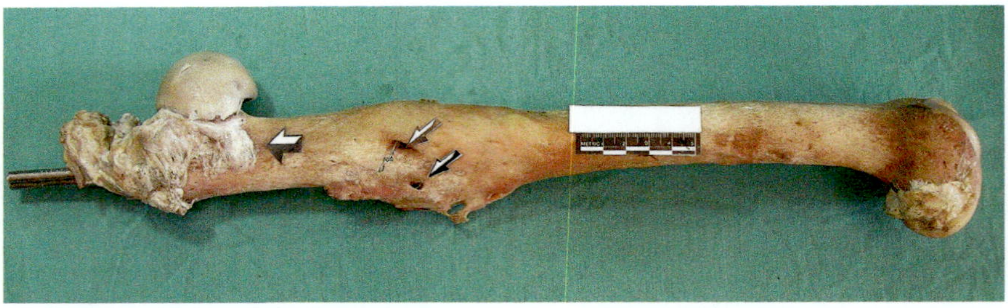

Figure 11.37 General view of the femur with an intramedullary rod with K-wire indicated by arrows.

Source: Photograph by the author.

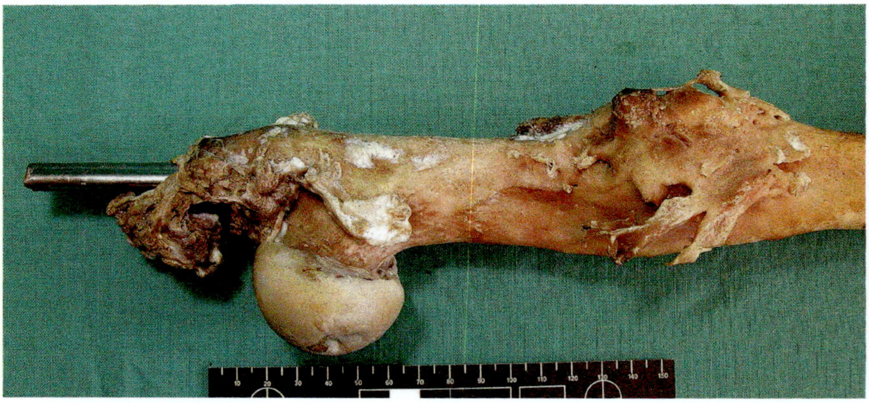

Figure 11.38 Head of femur with Intramedullary rod.

Source: Photograph by the author.

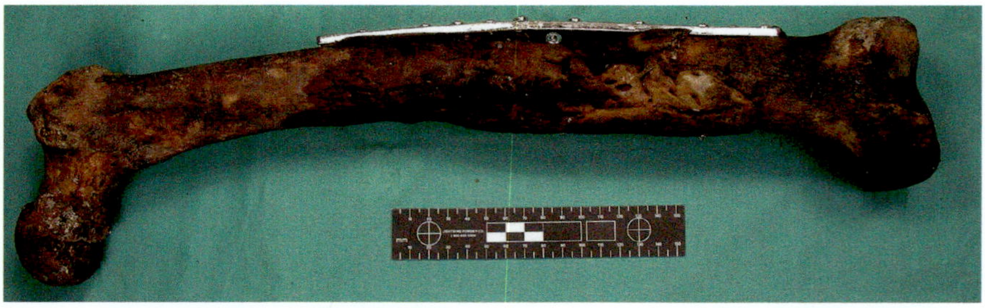

Figure 11.39 Left femur with a compression plate.

Source: Photograph by the author.

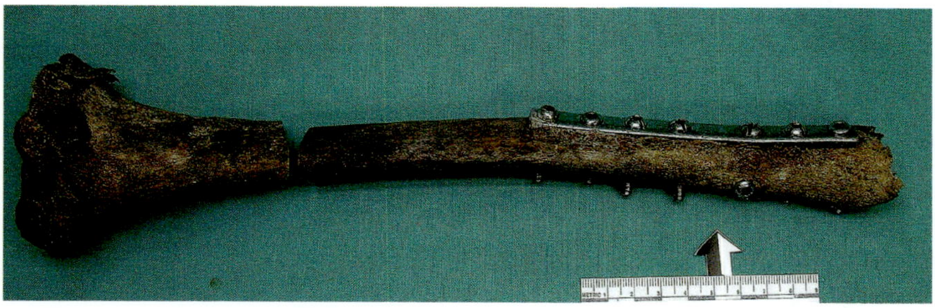

Figure 11.40 Tibia with a compression plate and surgical screw indicated by arrows.

Source: Photograph by the author.

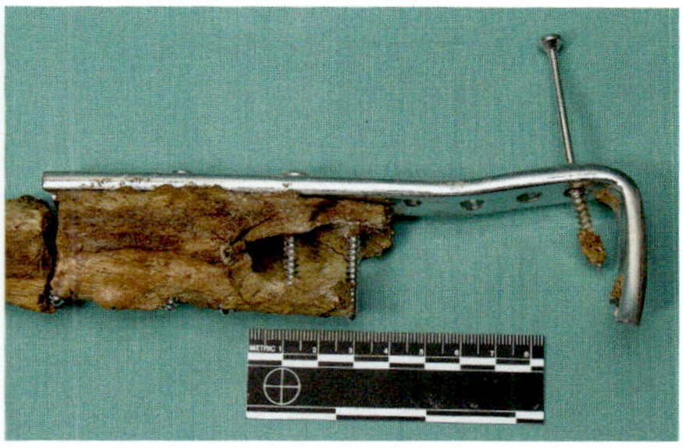

Figure 11.41 Bridge plate and screws.

Source: Photograph by the author.

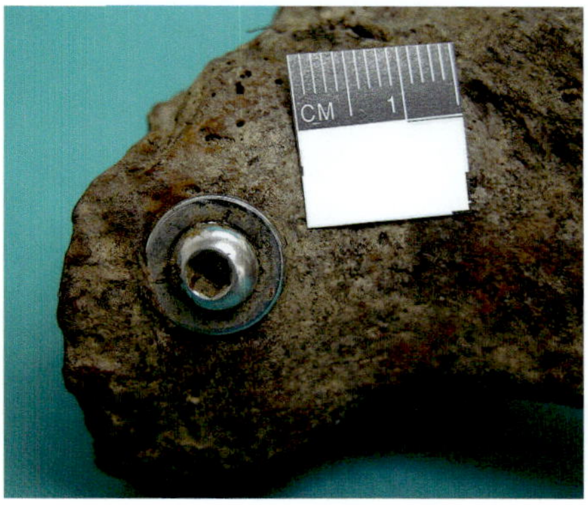

Figure 11.42 Surgical screw through the tibia.

Source: Photograph by the author.

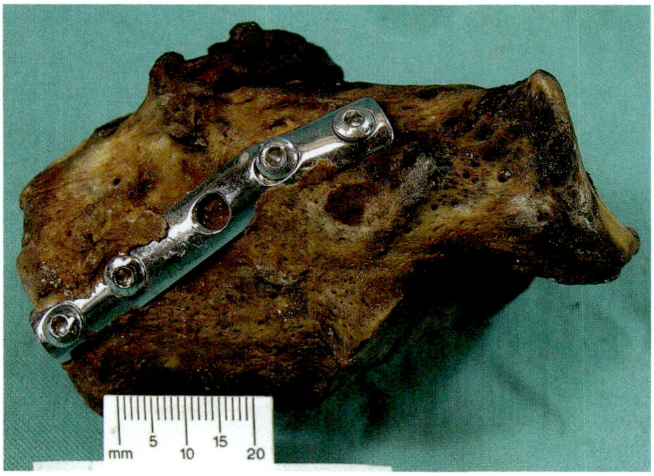

Figure 11.43 Left calcaneus with a compression plate.

Source: Photograph by the author.

Injuries Related to GSW

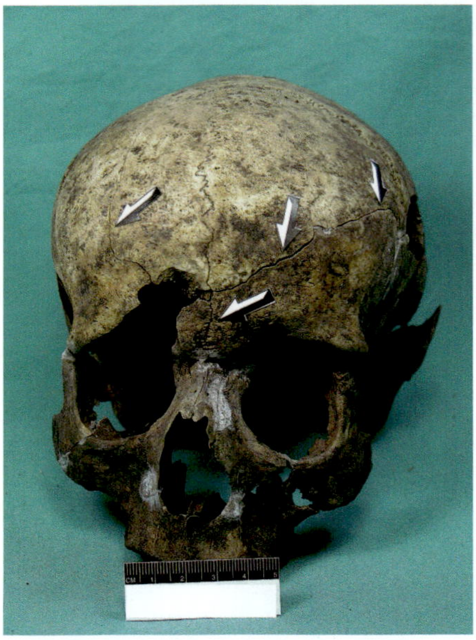

Figure 11.44 Skull front view. Note: Arrows point to fractures related to the entrance (Keyhole).

Source: Photograph by the author.

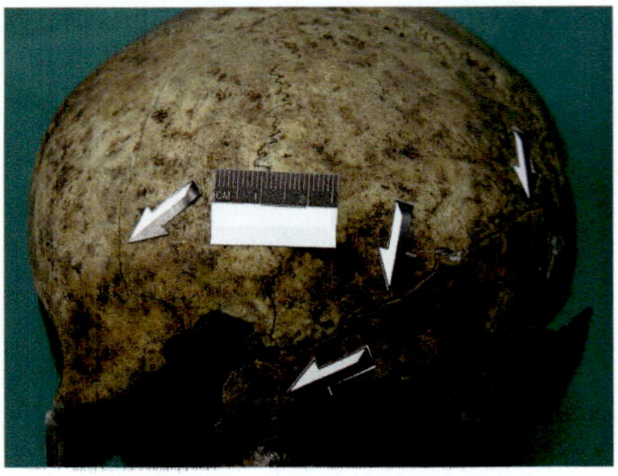

Figure 11.45 Close up of the fractures.

Source: Photograph by the author.

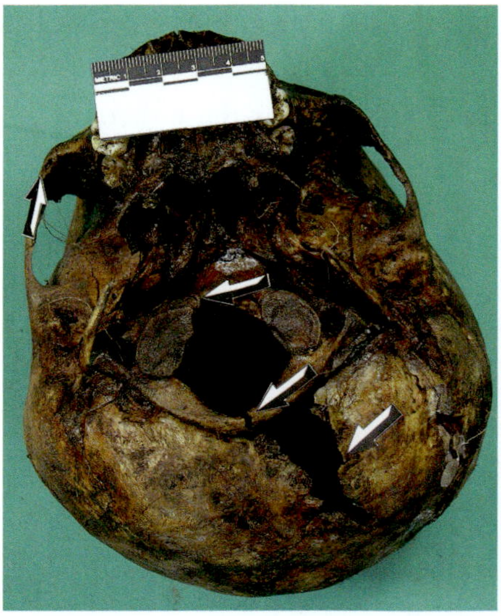

Figure 11.46 Arrows show the gunshot trajectory through the zygomatic, C1, and occipital bone.

Source: Photograph by the author.

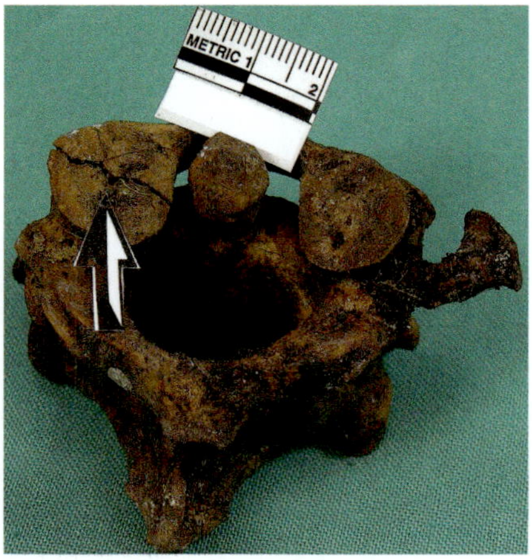

Figure 11.47 Fracture on the superior articular facet of C1 related to GSW, indicated by the arrow.

Source: Photograph by the author.

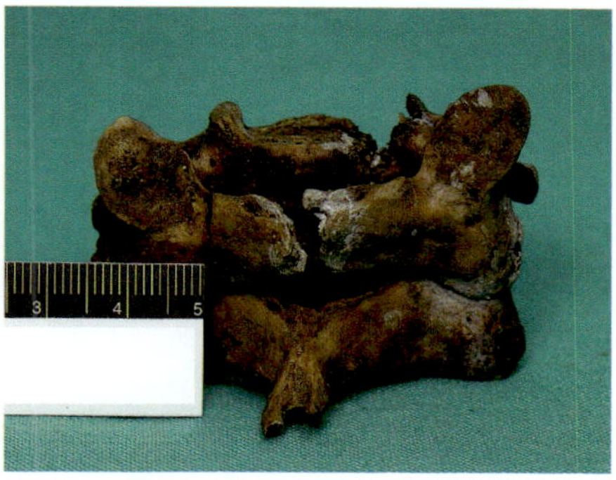

Figure 11.48 Fracture of the spinous process related to GSW.

Source: Photograph by the author.

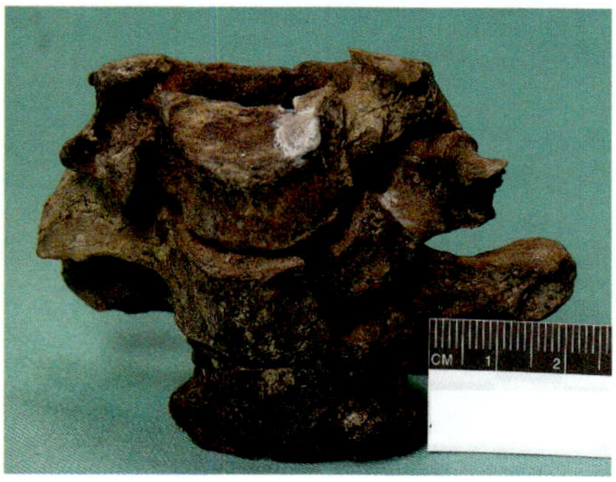

Figure 11.49 Fracture on body of the vertebra related to GSW.

Source: Photograph by the author.

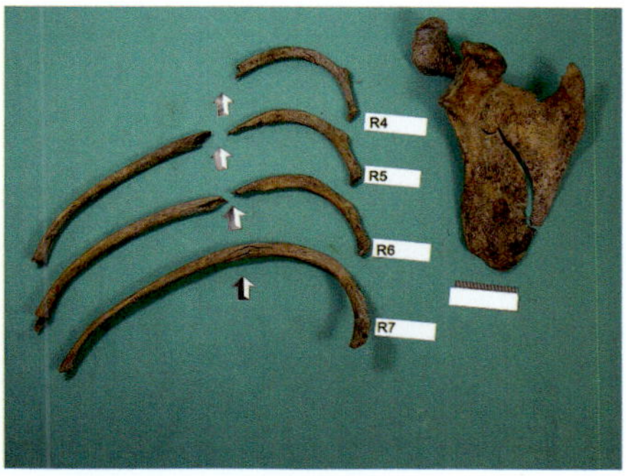

Figure 11.50 Fractures to the 4th to 7th right ribs indicated by arrows and scapula related to GSW.

Source: Photograph by the author.

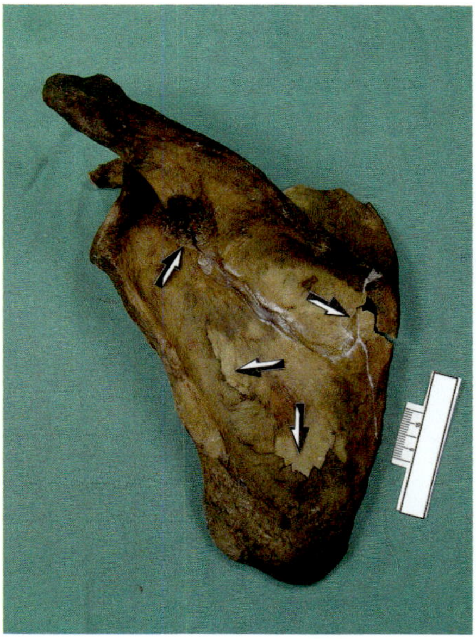

Figure 11.51 Fractures to the left scapula related to GSW indicated by arrows.

Source: Photograph by the author.

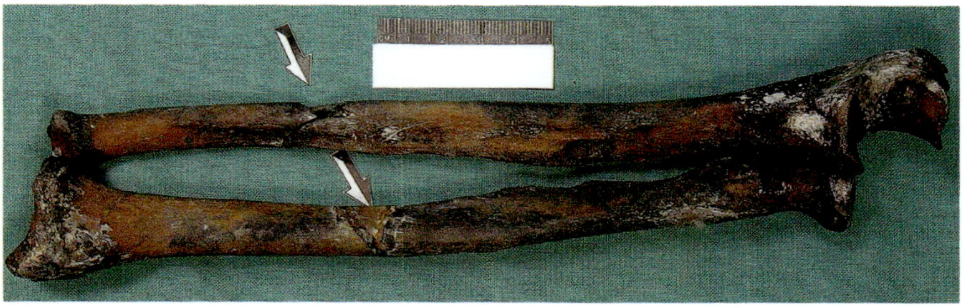

Figure 11.52 Fractures of the radius and ulna as a result of GSW, indicated by arrow.

Source: Photograph by the author.

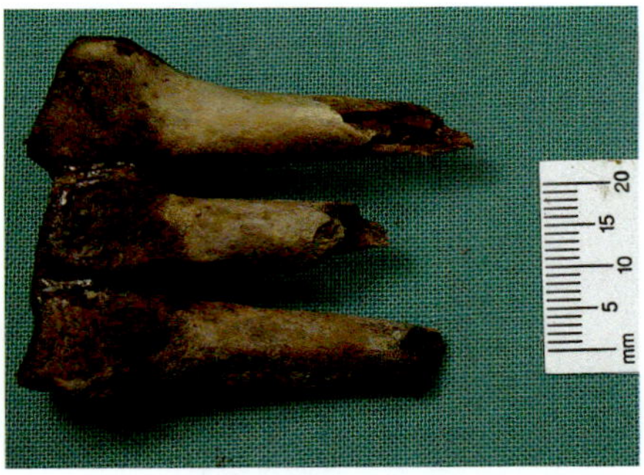

Figure 11.53 Three right metatarsals with fractures that occurred by GSW.

Source: Photograph by the author.

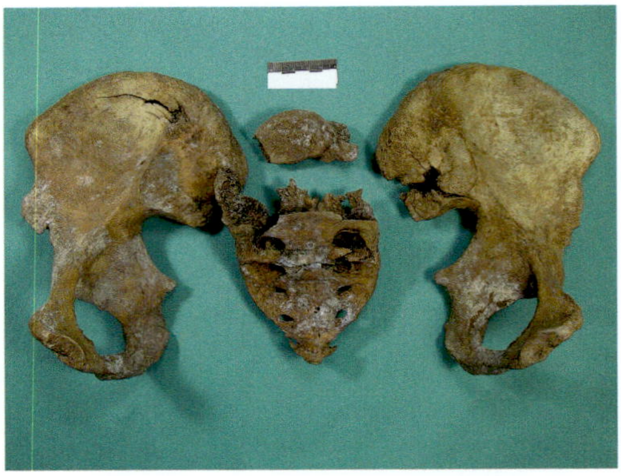

Figure 11.54 Pelvis anterior view fractures that occurred by GSW.

Source: Photograph by the author.

Bullet Entrance

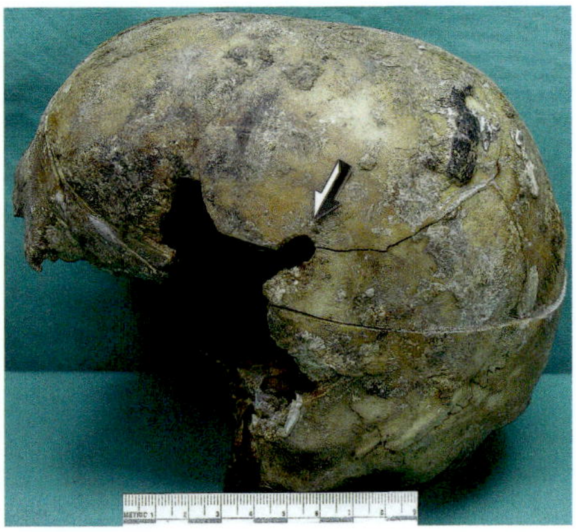

Figure 11.55 Arrow points to the bullet entrance (possible keyhole) through the left parietal bonnet.

Source: Photograph by the author.

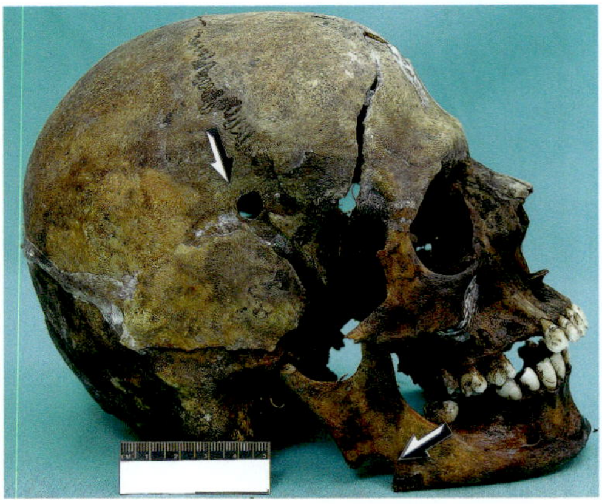

Figure 11.56 Arrows indicate two bullet entrances on the right side of the skull.

Source: Photograph by the author.

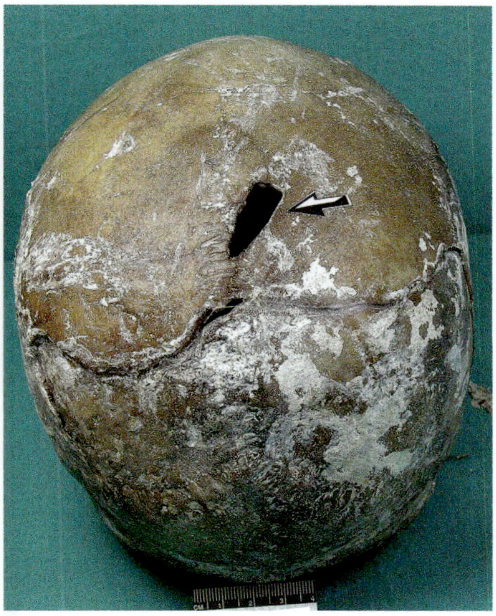

Figure 11.57 Arrows point to the bullet entrance (sideways impact).

Source: Photograph by the author.

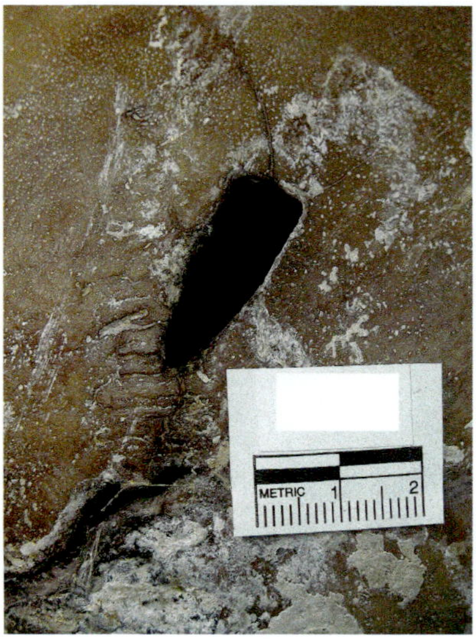

Figure 11.58 Close-up of the bullet entrance (sideways impact).

Source: Photograph by the author.

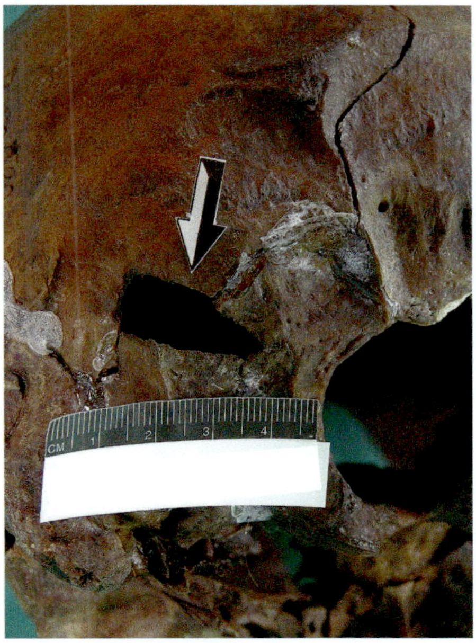

Figure 11.59 Arrow point to the bullet entrance (sideways) through the occipital region.

Source: Photograph by the author.

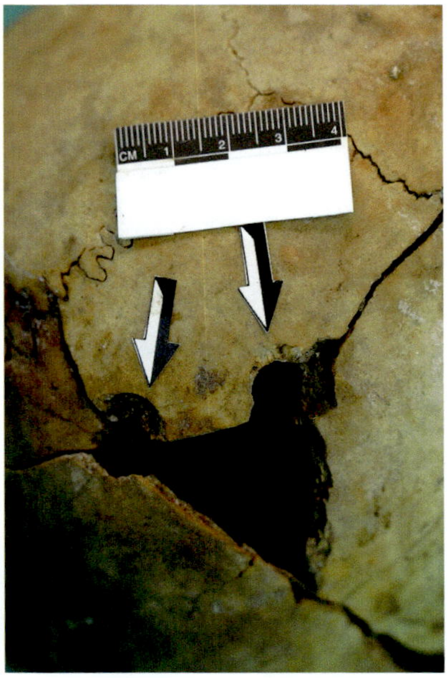

Figure 11.60 Skull keyhole and entrance.

Source: Photograph by the author.

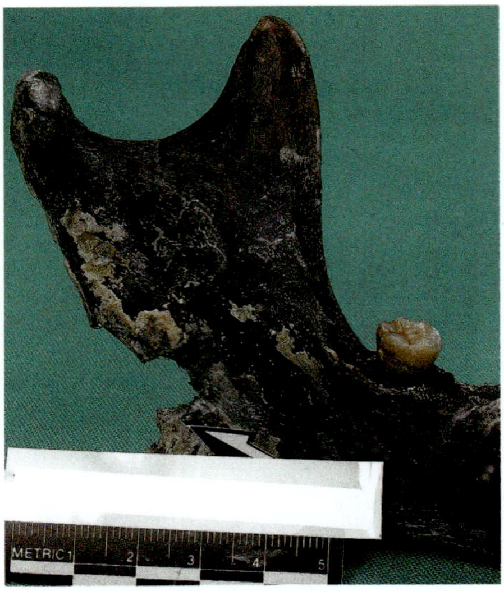

Figure 11.61 Bullet entrance in the mandible indicated by an arrow.

Source: Photograph by the author.

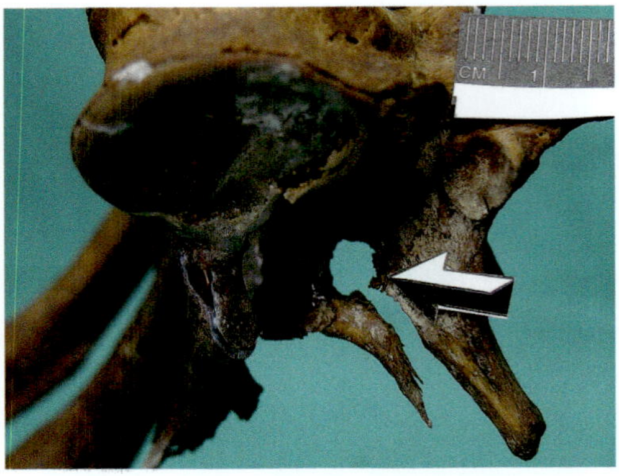

Figure 11.62 Thoracic vertebra, GSW through the posterior lamina indicated by an arrow.

Source: Photograph by the author.

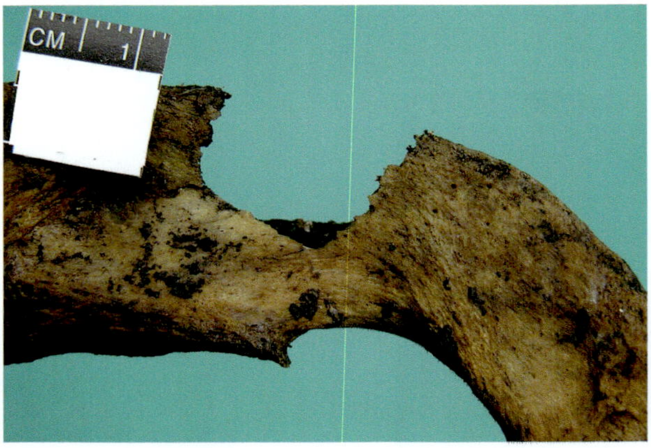

Figure 11.63 Detail of the GSW through a rib.

Source: Photograph by the author.

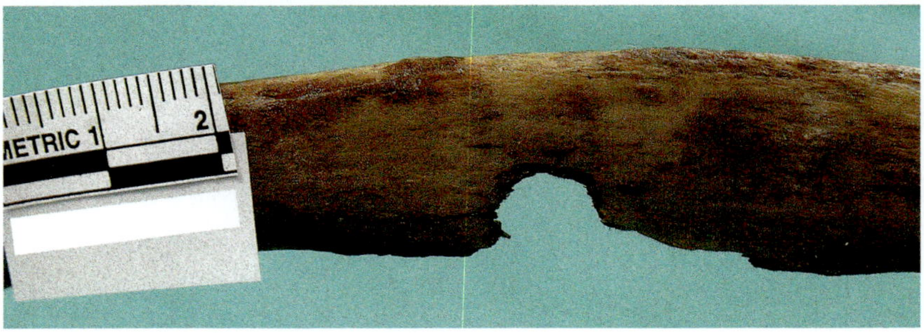

Figure 11.64 Detail of exit GSW through a rib.

Source: Photograph by the author.

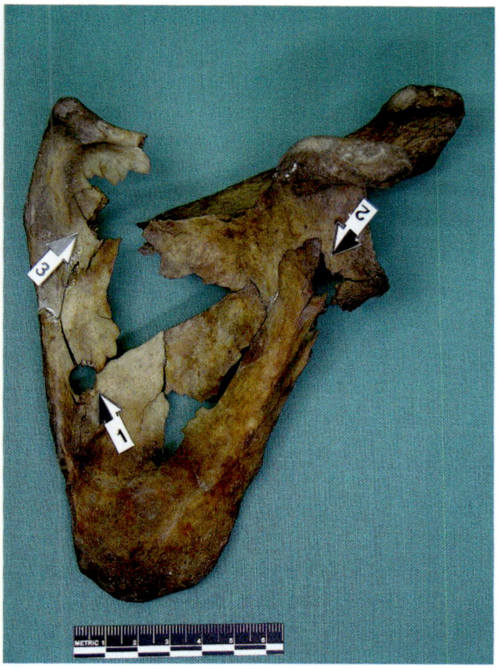

Figure 11.65 Arrows point to three GSWs through the right scapula. Each injury is numbered.

Source: Photograph by the author.

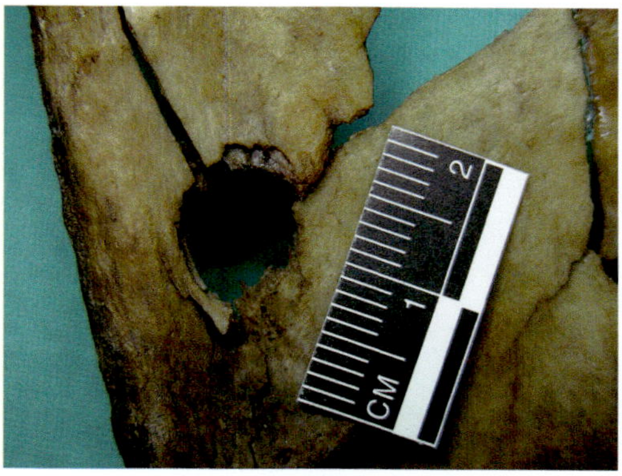

Figure 11.66 Right scapula. Note: Detail of GSW exit (number 1 in previous photograph).

Source: Photograph by the author.

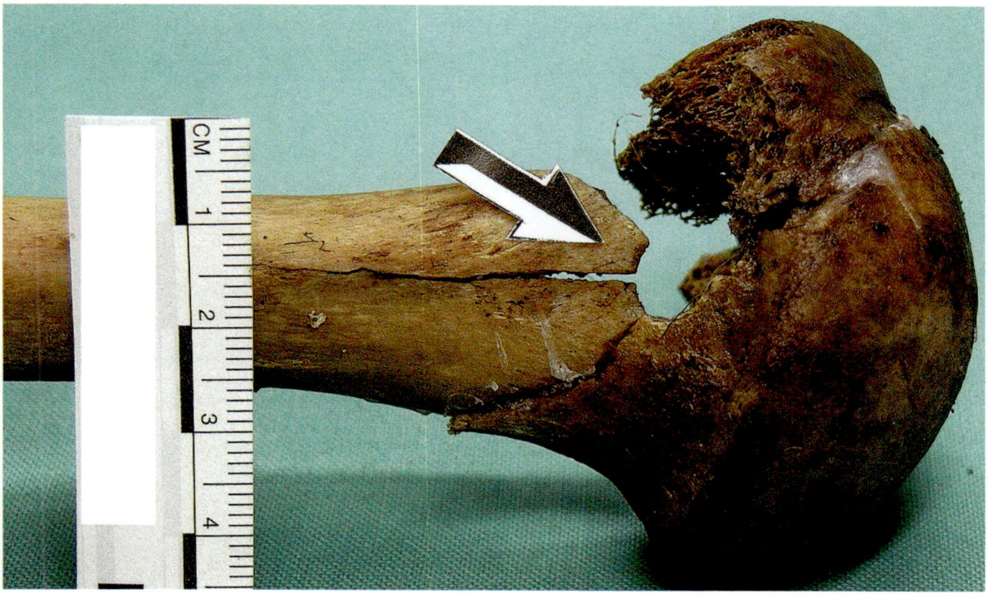

Figure 11.67 Arrow points to GSW entrance through humeral head.

Source: Photograph by the author.

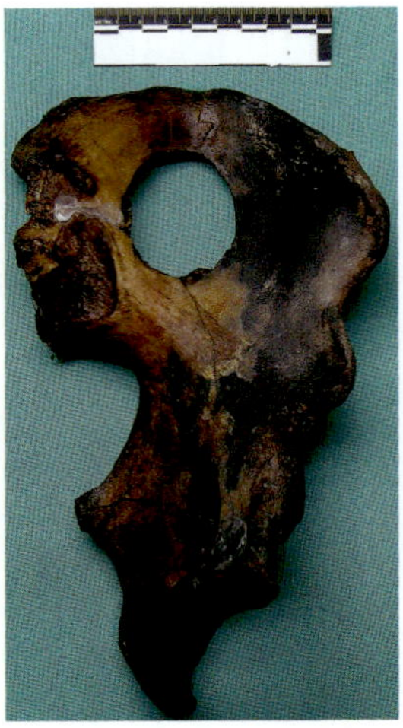

Figure 11.68 Shrapnel injury through the left ilium.

Source: Photograph by the author.

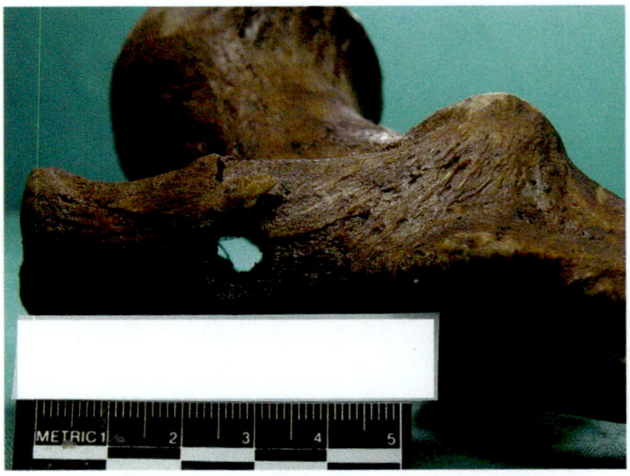

Figure 11.69 GSW through the greater trochanter of the femur.

Source: Photograph by the author.

External and Internal View of Bullet Entrance

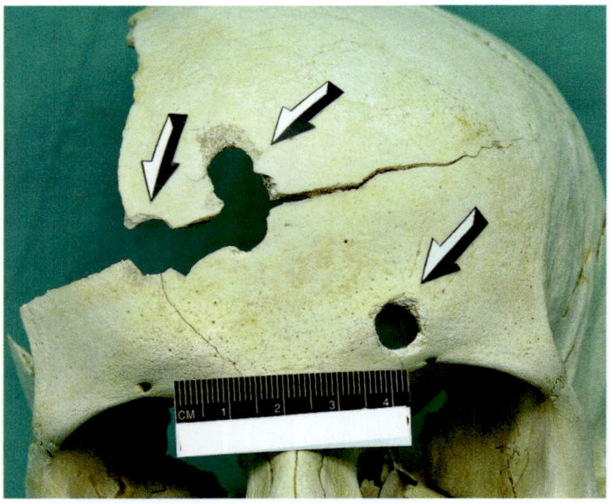

Figure 11.70 External view of the frontal bone with three gunshot entrance wounds, pointed out by arrows.

Source: Photograph by the author.

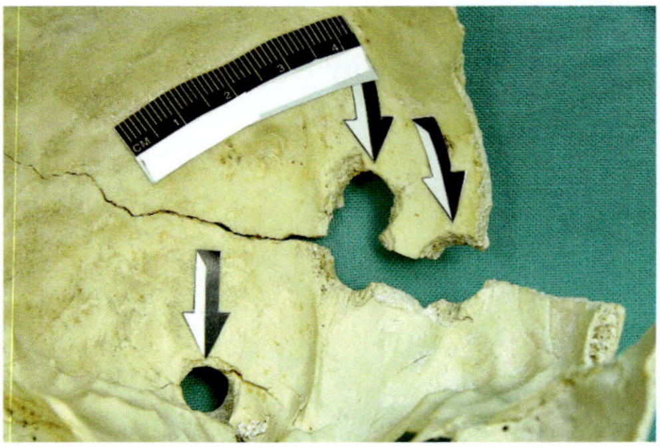

Figure 11.71 Internal view of the frontal bone shows three gunshot entrance wounds pointed out by arrows.

Source: Photograph by the author.

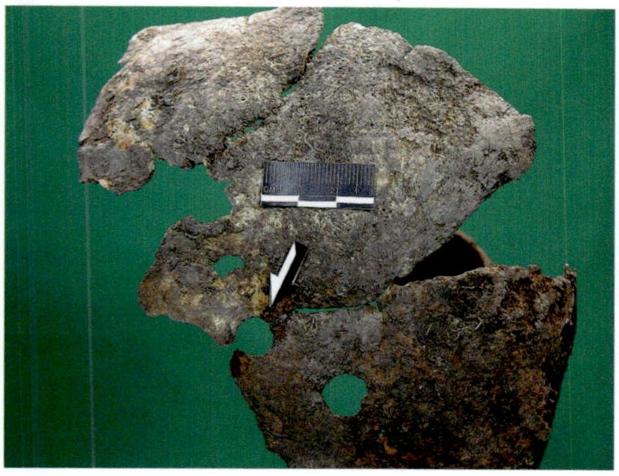

Figure 11.72 External view of a piece of the skull with a gunshot entrance pointed by an arrow.

Source: Photograph by the author.

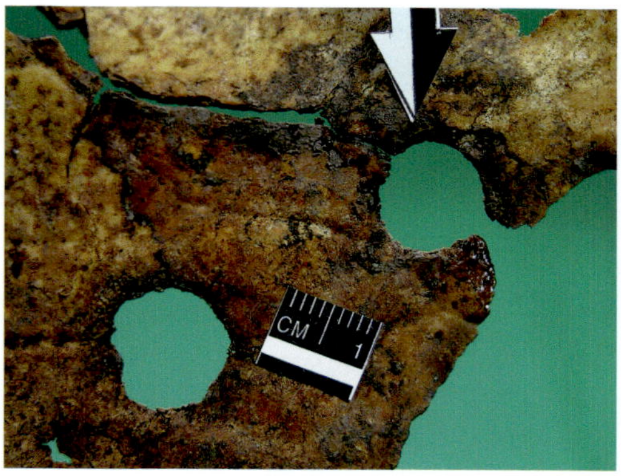

Figure 11.73 Internal view of a piece of the skull with a gunshot entrance pointed by an arrow.

Source: Photograph by the author.

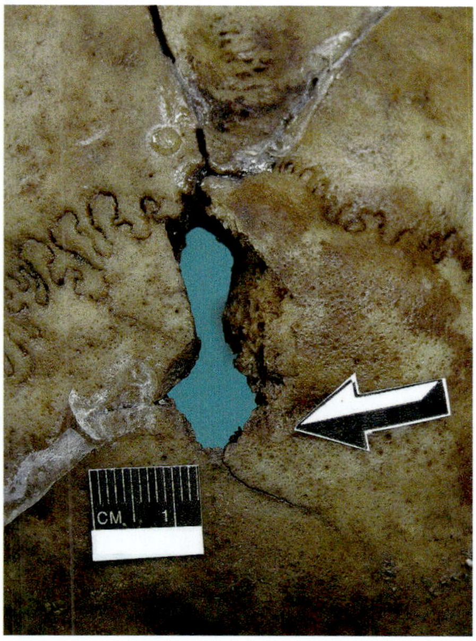

Figure 11.74 External view of the skull with a keyhole marked by an arrow.

Source: Photograph by the author.

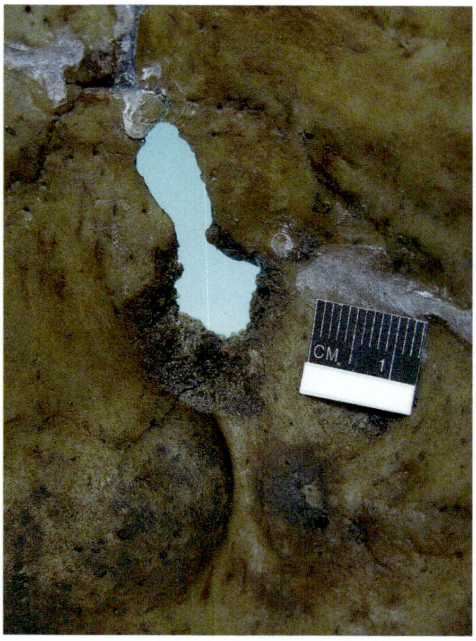

Figure 11.75 Internal view of the keyhole showing beveling.

Source: Photograph by the author.

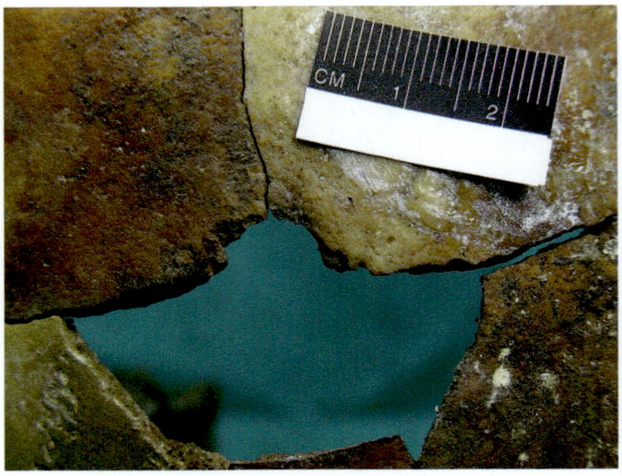

Figure 11.76 External view of the occipital with a gunshot entrance.

Source: Photograph by the author.

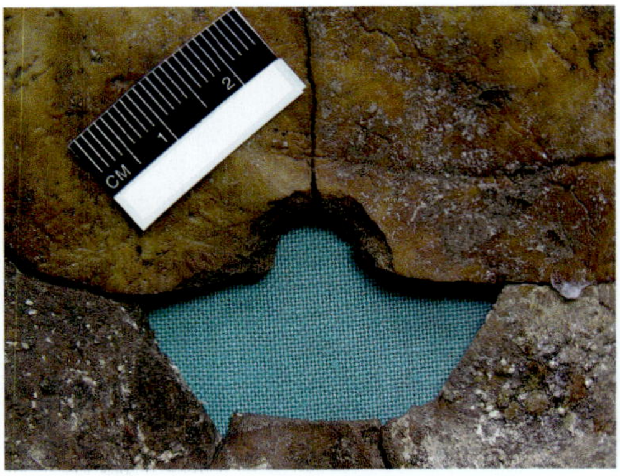

Figure 11.77 Internal view of the entrance showing beveling.

Source: Photograph by the author.

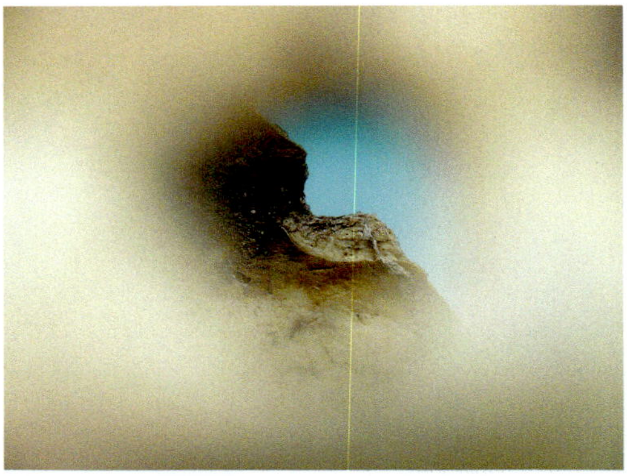

Figure 11.78 Internal view of the entrance wound as seen through the exit and following the trajectory of the bullet.

Source: Photograph by the author.

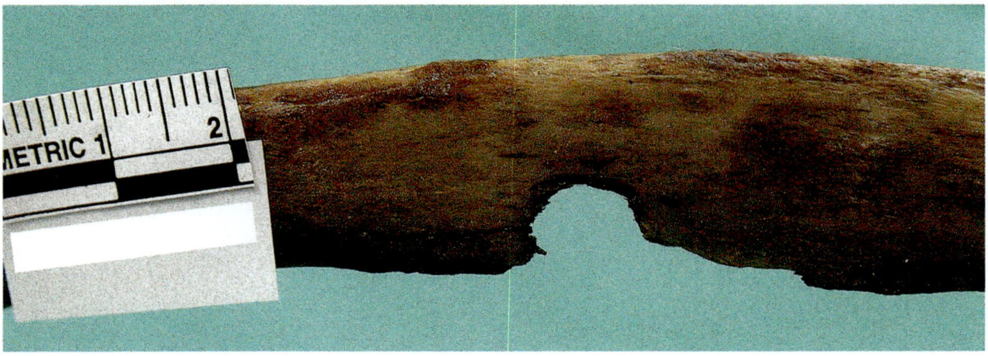

Figure 11.79 Anterior view of the right rib 11th with gunshot entrance.

Source: Photograph by the author.

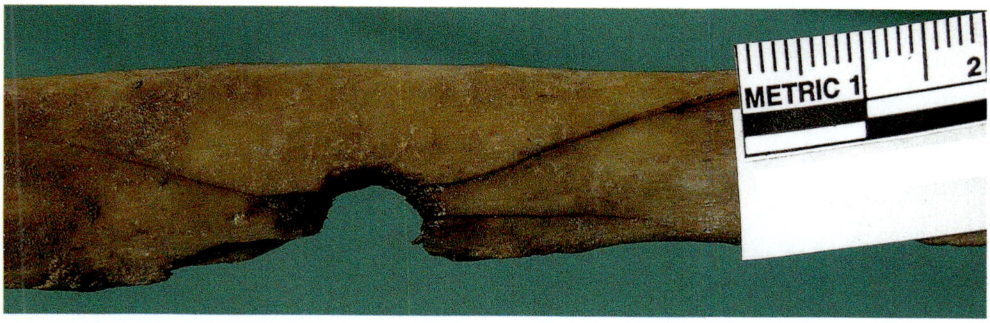

Figure 11.80 Internal view of the right rib 11th with gunshot entrance.

Source: Photograph by the author.

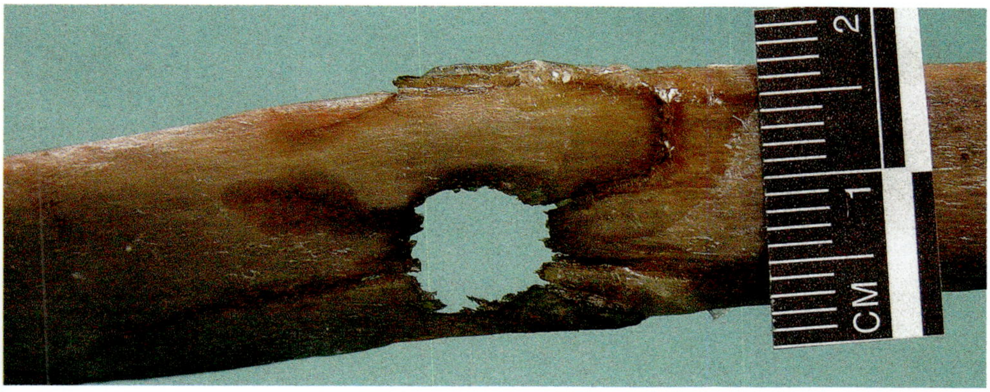

Figure 11.81 Anterior view of a rib with a gunshot entrance.

Source: Photograph by the author.

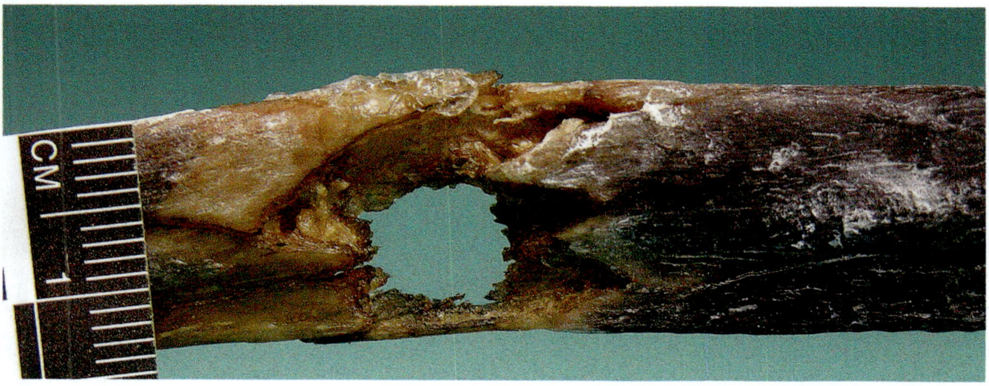

Figure 11.82 Internal view of a rib with gunshot entrance.

Source: Photograph by the author.

Bullet Exits

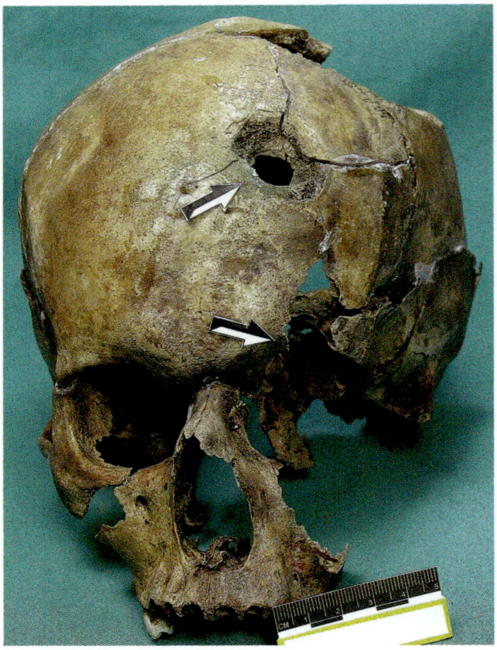

Figure 11.83 Two gunshot exits on the frontal points by arrows.

Source: Photograph by the author.

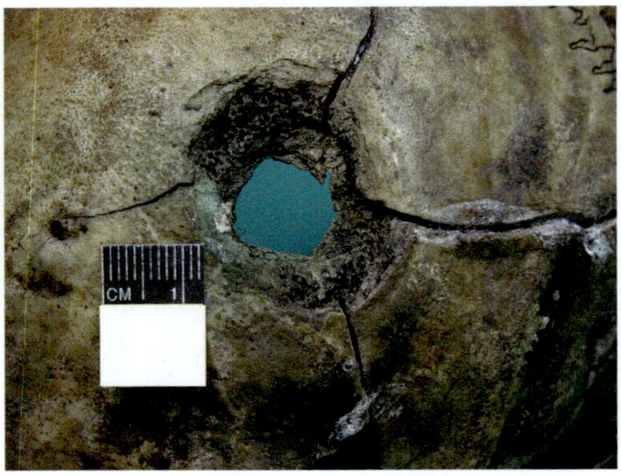

Figure 11.84 Detail of the exit and beveling.

Source: Photograph by the author.

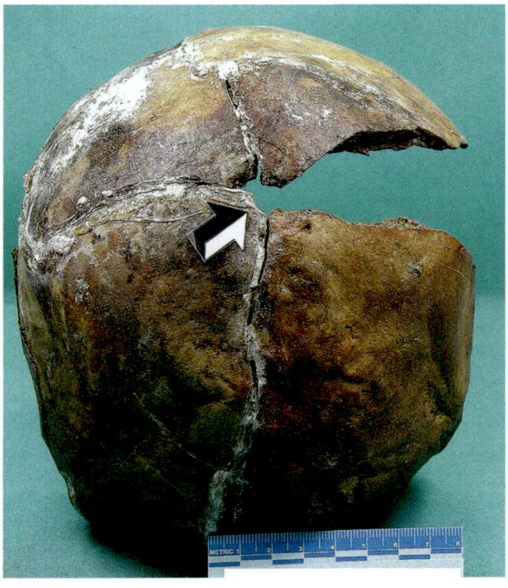

Figure 11.85 Gunshot exit through sagittal suture.

Source: Photograph by the author.

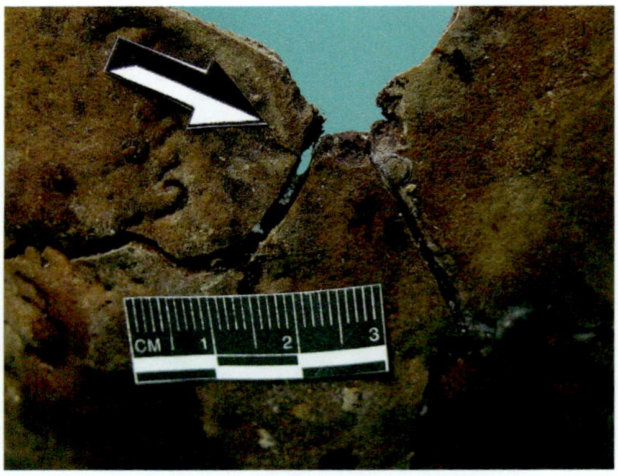

Figure 11.86 Gunshot exit with external beveling through the skull, indicated by arrows.

Source: Photograph by the author.

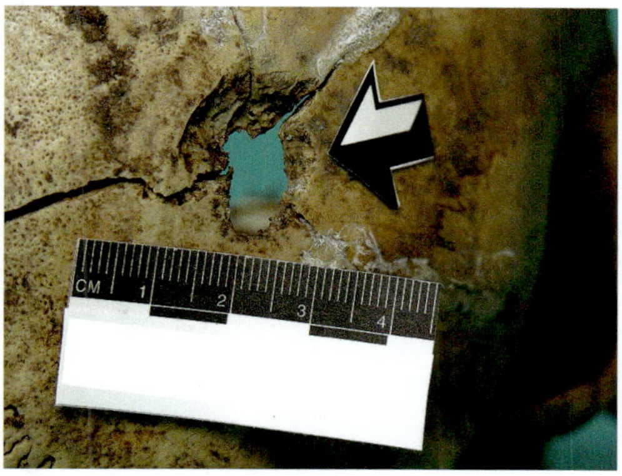

Figure 11.87 Gunshot exit through the skull with external beveling indicated by arrows.

Source: Photograph by the author.

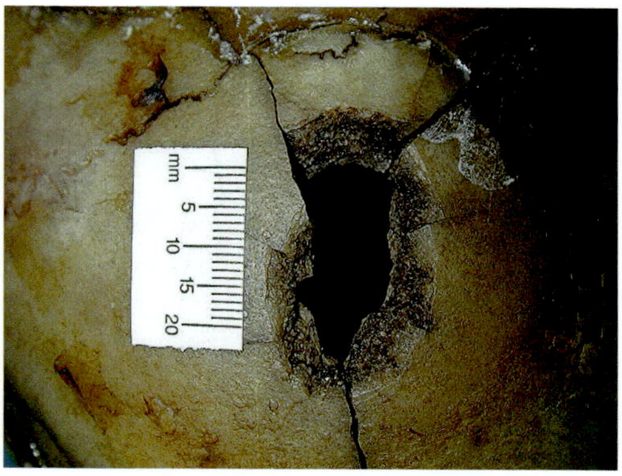

Figure 11.88 Gunshot exit through the skull with the outline of the bullet (sideways).

Source: Photograph by the author.

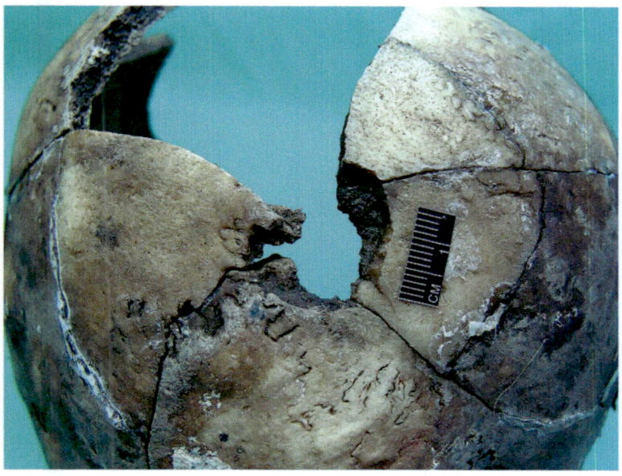

Figure 11.89 Gunshot exit through the skull with external beveling.

Source: Photograph by the author.

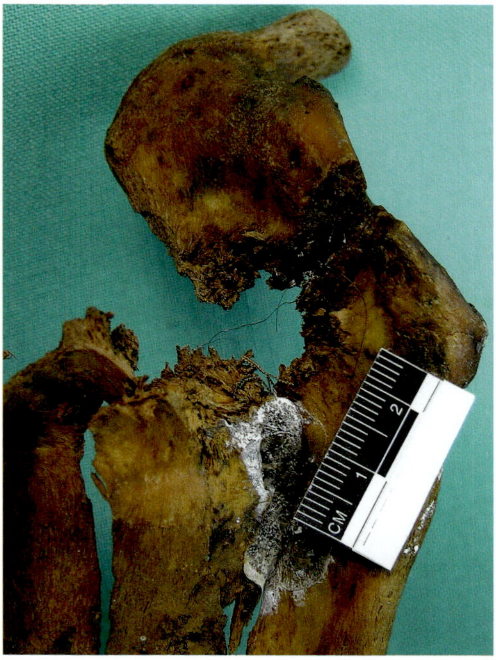

Figure 11.90 Gunshot exit through the scapula with beveling.

Source: Photograph by the author.

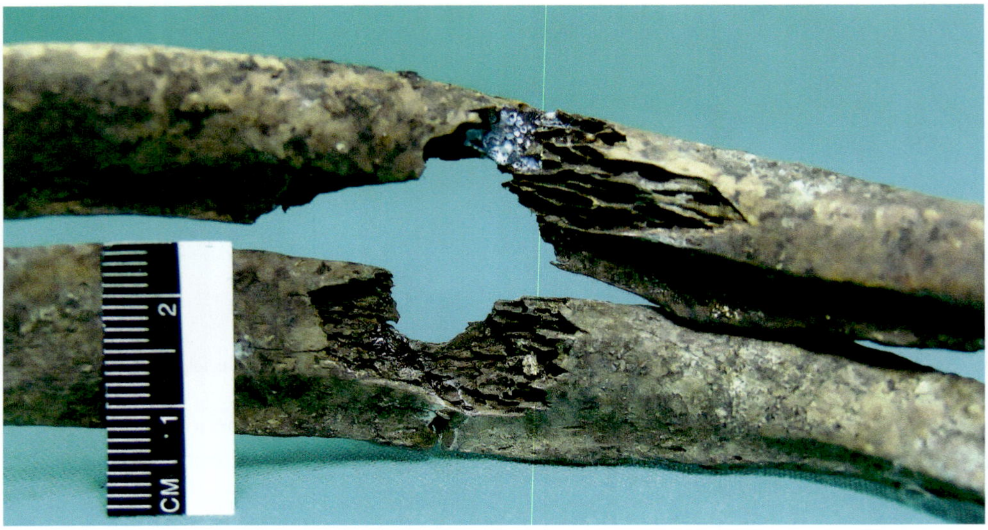

Figure 11.91 Posterior view of two ribs revealing gunshot exit with the external beveling.

Source: Photograph by the author.

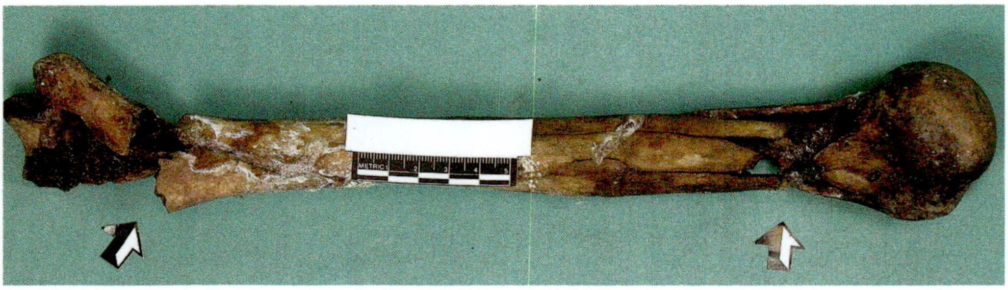

Figure 11.92 Two gunshot exits through the humerus indicated by arrows.

Source: Photograph by the author.

Bullet Exits with Entrance

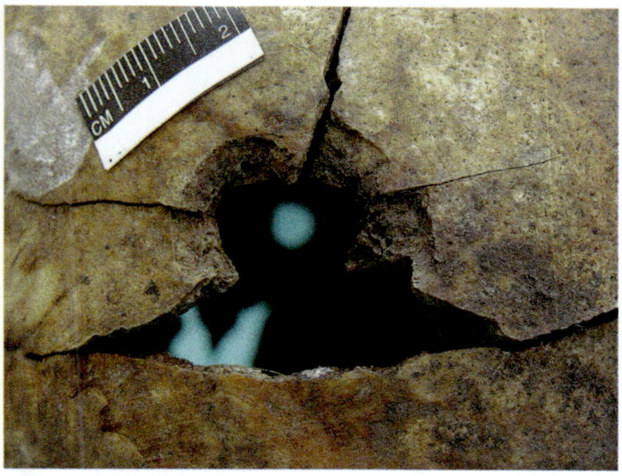

Figure 11.93 Gunshot exit with a beveling through the skull, entrance visible in the background.

Source: Photograph by the author.

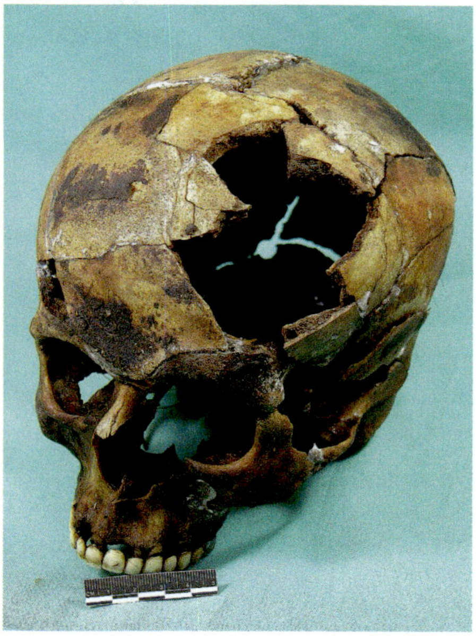

Figure 11.94 Gunshot exit through the frontal, in the background, entrance through the parietal.

Source: Photograph by the author.

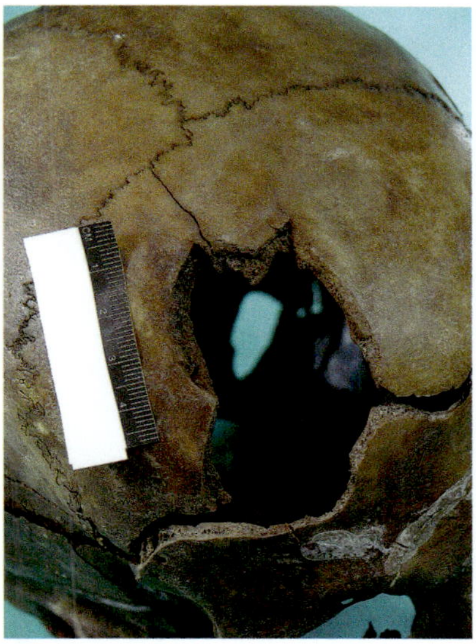

Figure 11.95 Gunshot exit through the frontal, in the background, entrance through the occipital with the outline of the bullet (sideways).

Source: Photograph by the author.

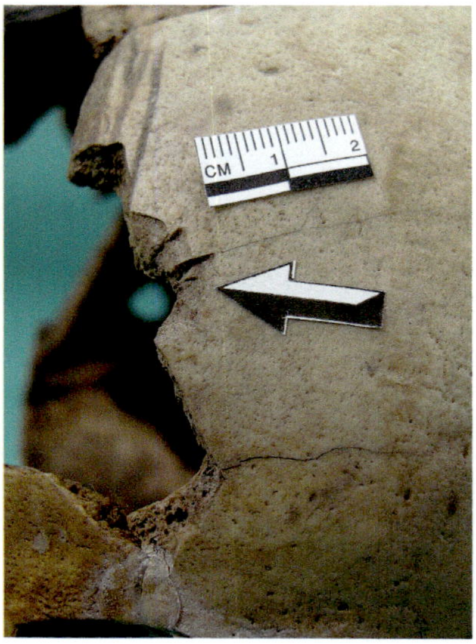

Figure 11.96 Gunshot exit through the skull. Beveling, indicated by the arrow. Entry visible in the background.

Source: Photograph by the author.

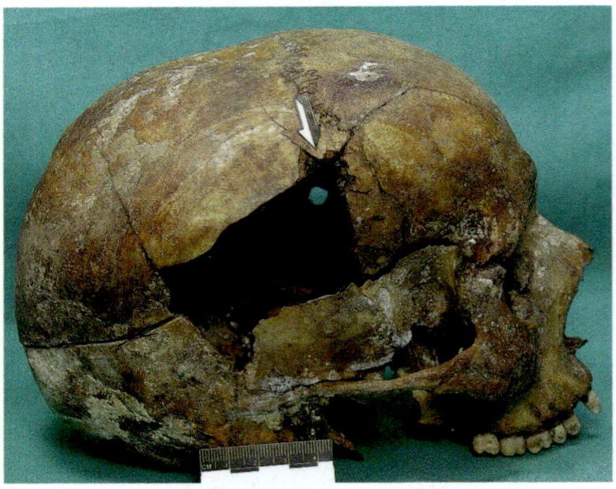

Figure 11.97 Gunshot exit through the right parietal. Beveling indicated by the arrow. Entry visible in the background.

Source: Photograph by the author.

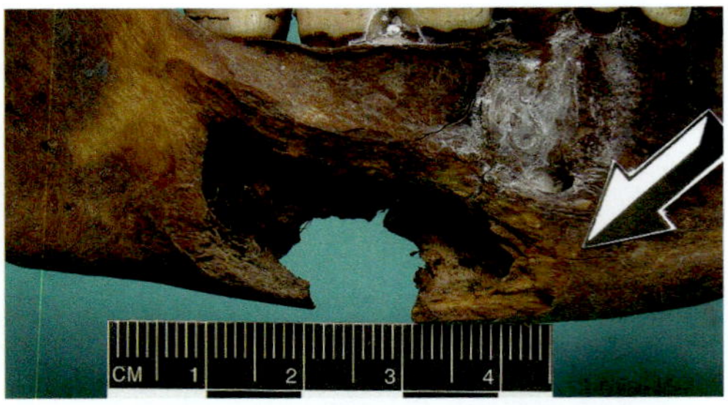

Figure 11.98 Gunshot exit through the mandibular body. Beveling indicated by the arrow. Entrance visible in the background.

Source: Photograph by the author.

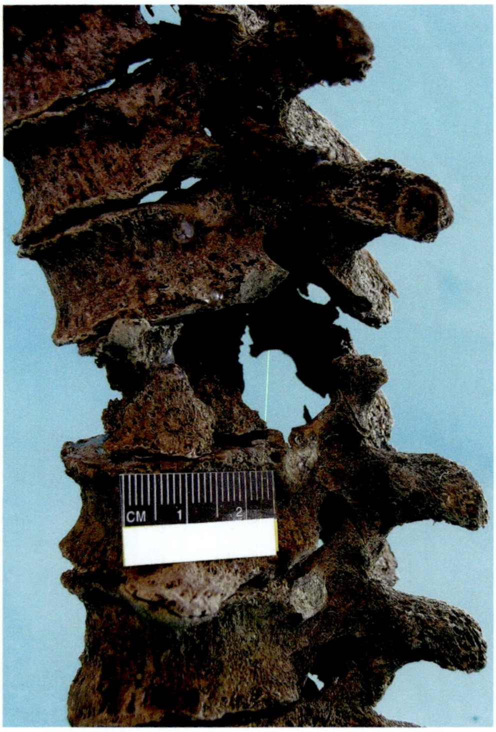

Figure 11.99 Gunshot exit through the thoracic vertebra body. Entrance visible in the background.

Source: Photograph by the author.

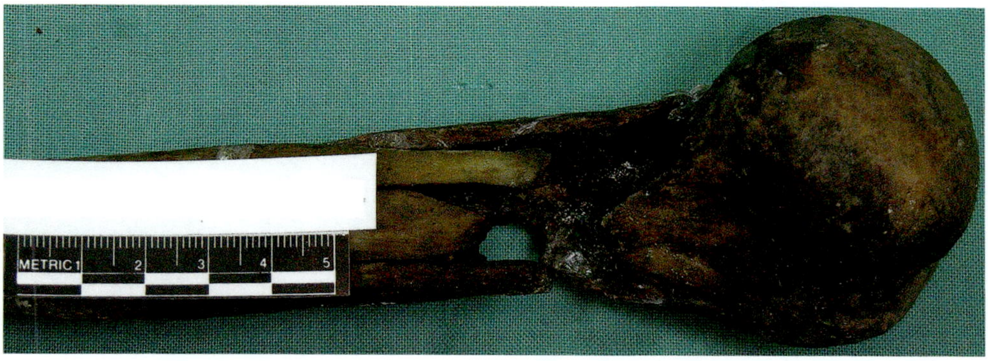

Figure 11.100 Gunshot through the humeral metaphysis. Entrance visible in the background.

Source: Photograph by the author.

Injuries Caused by Shotgun Pellets

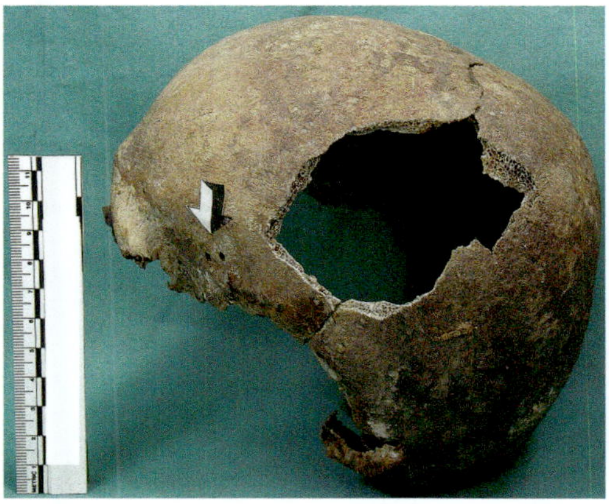

Figure 11.101 Two pellet entrances on the frontal bone indicated by the arrow.

Source: Photograph by the author.

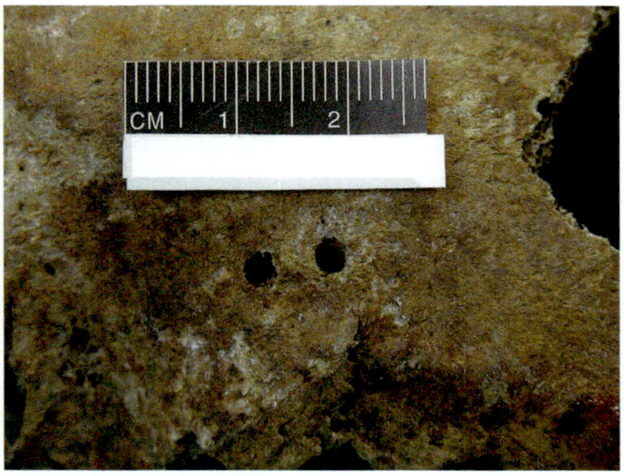

Figure 11.102 Details of the two pellets' entrance.

Source: Photograph by the author.

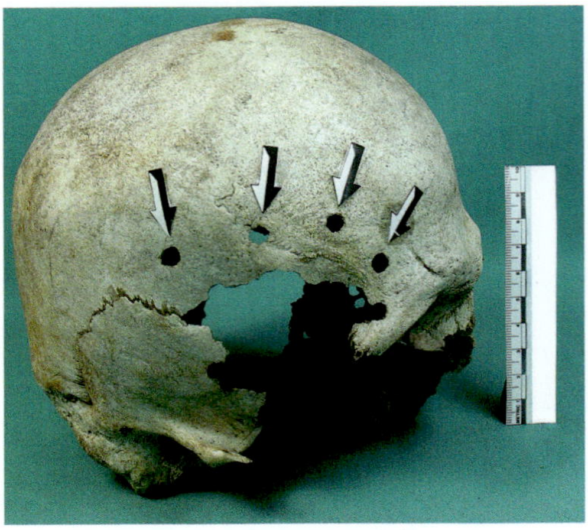

Figure 11.103 Entrance defects caused by pellets through the parietal region.

Source: Photograph by the author.

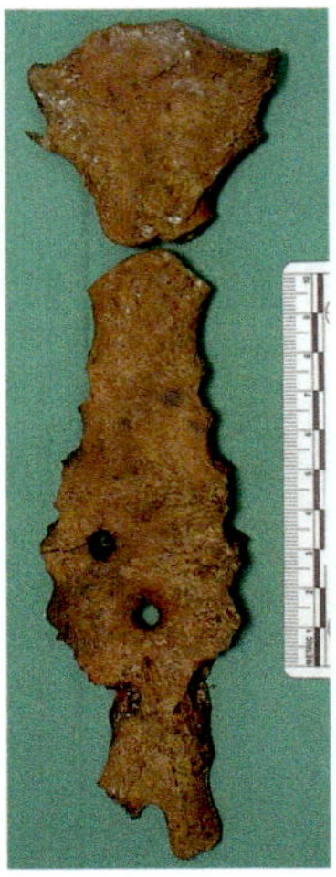

Figure 11.104 One entrance defect through the sternum caused by a pellet and congenital.

Source: Photograph by the author.

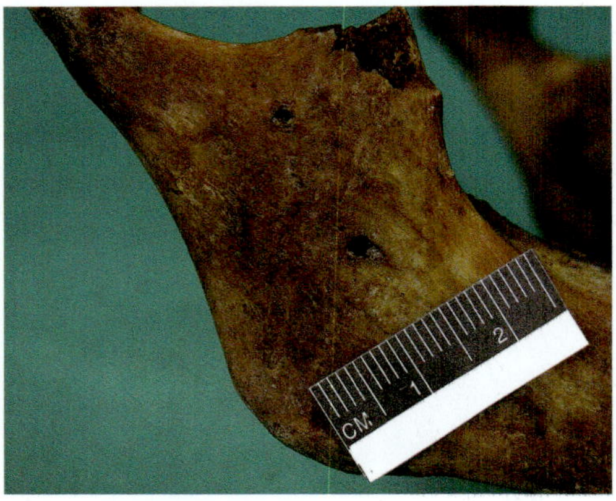

Figure 11.105 Two defects on the ascending ramus of the mandible caused by pellets

Source: Photograph by the author.

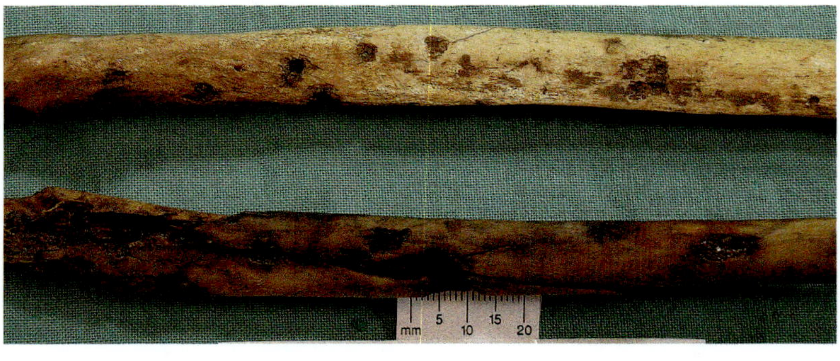

Figure 11.106 Ulna and radius with pellet injuries.

Source: Photograph by the author.

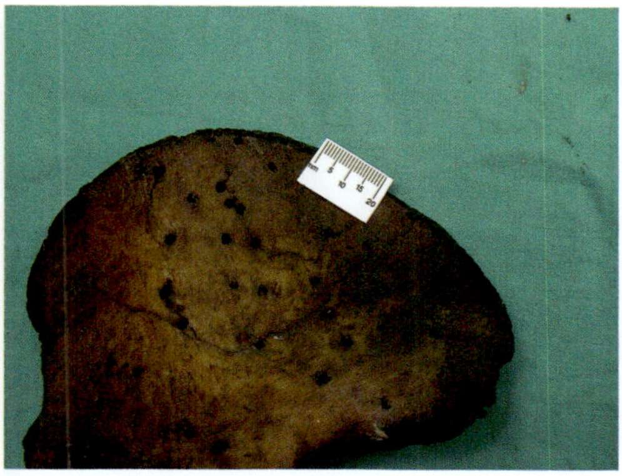

Figure 11.107 Posterior view of the ilium with several pellet injuries (entrance).

Source: Photograph by the author.

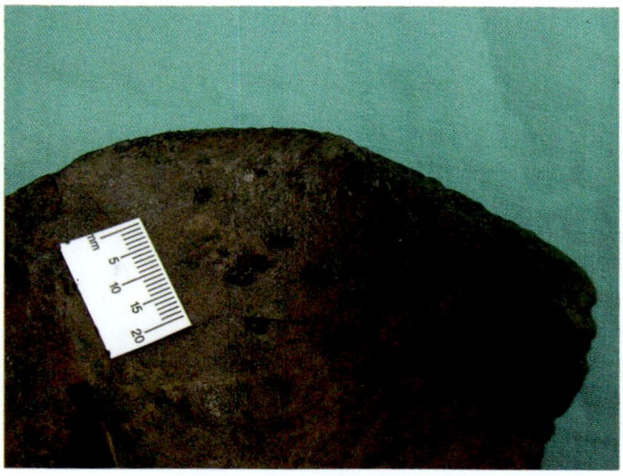

Figure 11.108 Anterior view of the ilium with several pellet injuries (exit).

Source: Photograph by the author.

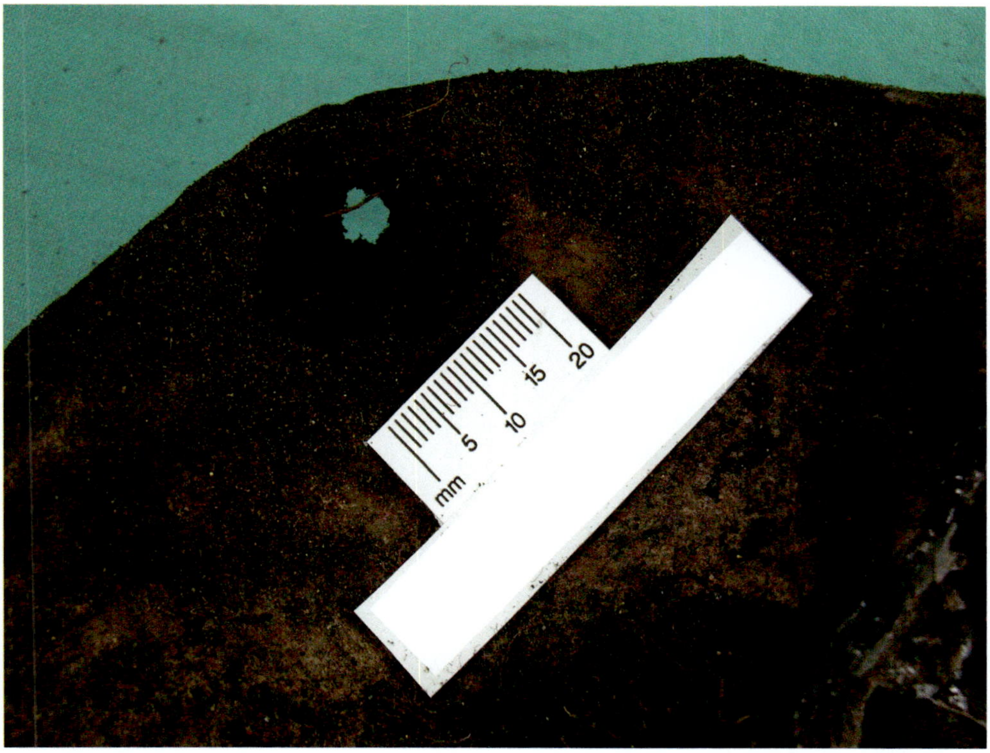

Figure 11.109 Another example of pellet exit through the ilium. Entrance visible in the background

Source: Photograph by the author.

Shrapnel or Bullet Embedded in Bone

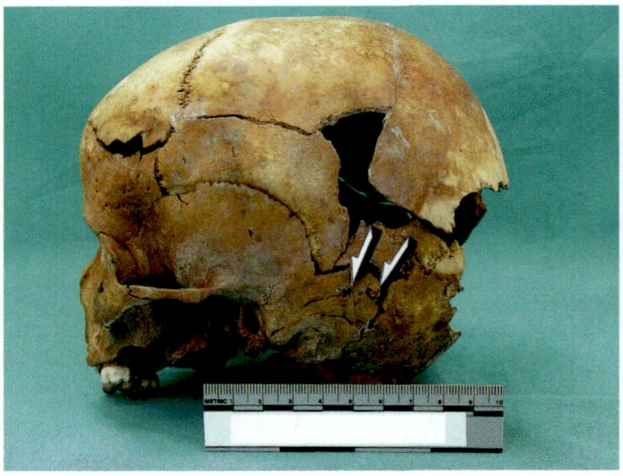

Figure 11.110 Arrows point to a defect and shrapnel fragments embedded in the occipital bone.

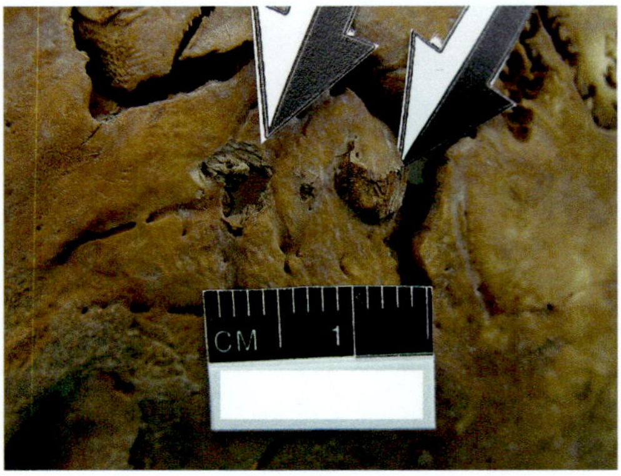

Figure 11.111 Details of the defect and the shrapnel fragment indicated by arrows.

Source: Photograph by the author.

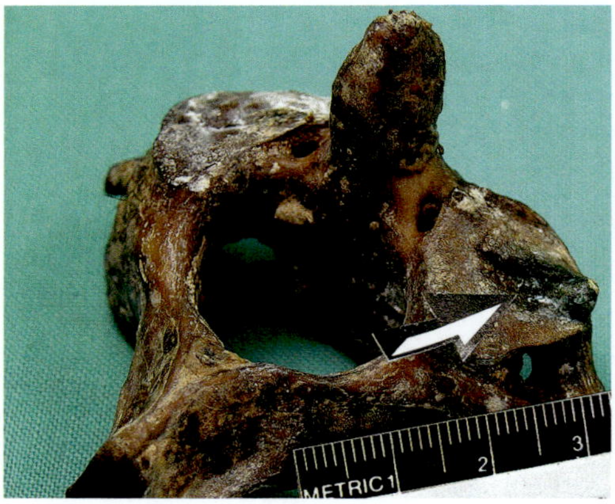

Figure 11.112 Bullet embedded in the superior articular facet of C2 indicated by the arrow.

Source: Photograph by the author.

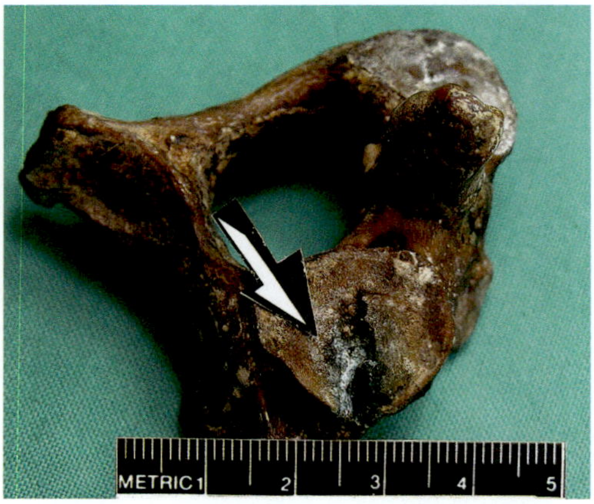

Figure 11.113 Bullet removed from the superior articular facet of C2, indicated by the arrow.

Source: Photograph by the author.

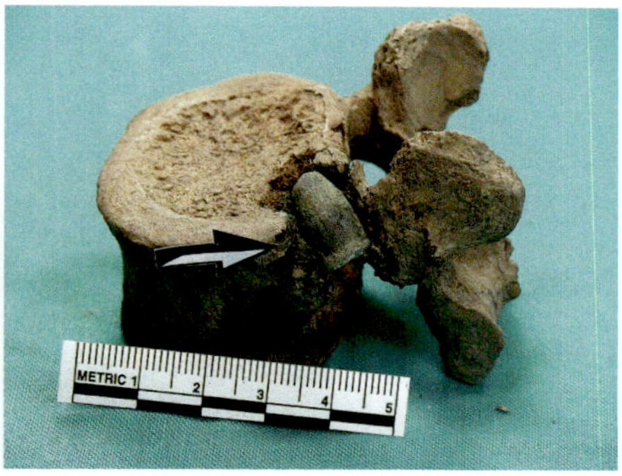

Figure 11.114 Bullet embedded in the body of a thoracic vertebra, indicated by the arrow.

Source: Photograph by the author.

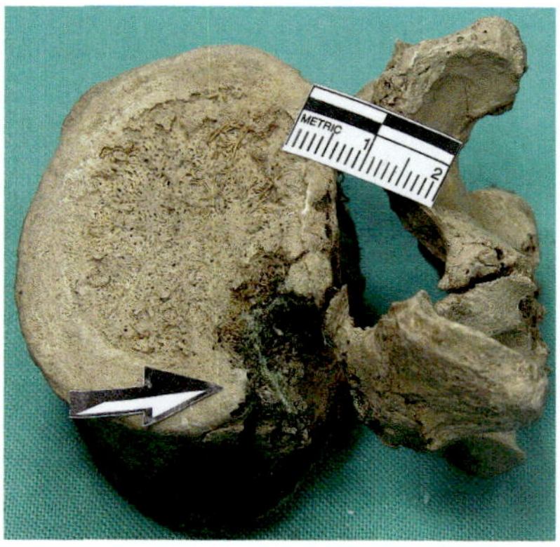

Figure 11.115 Bullet removed from the thoracic vertebra indicated by the arrow.

Source: Photograph by the author.

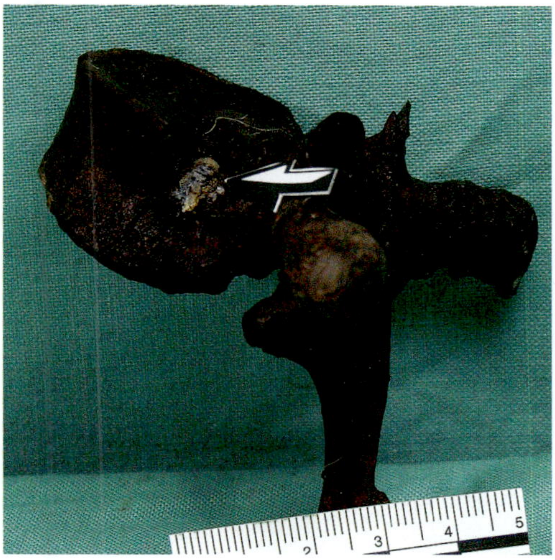

Figure 11.116 Bullet embedded in the vertebral body of T7, indicated by the arrow.

Source: Photograph by the author.

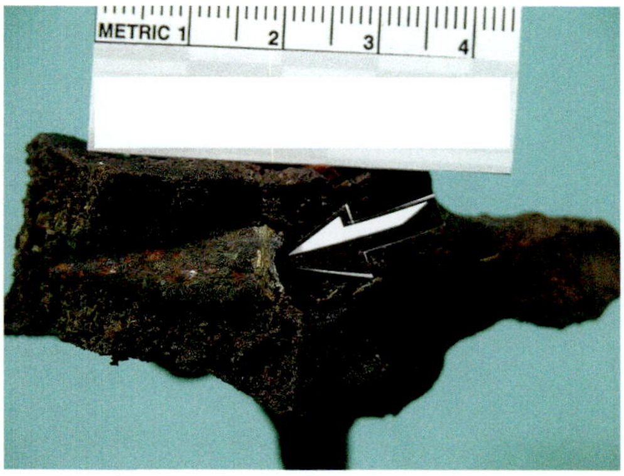

Figure 11.117 The bullet can be visible after sectioning the vertebral body.

Source: Photograph by the author.

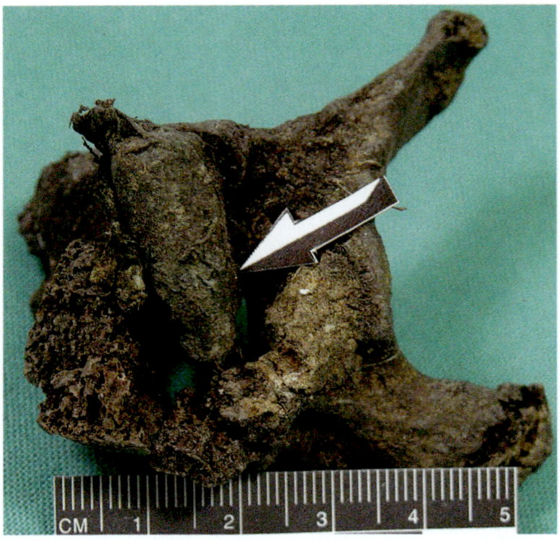

Figure 11.118 Bullet embedded and partially destroying vertebral body.

Source: Photograph by the author.

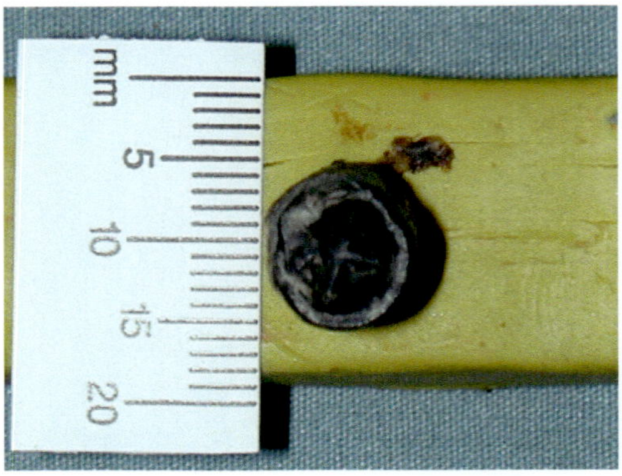

Figure 11.119 Bullet embedded in the rib body.

Source: Photograph by the author.

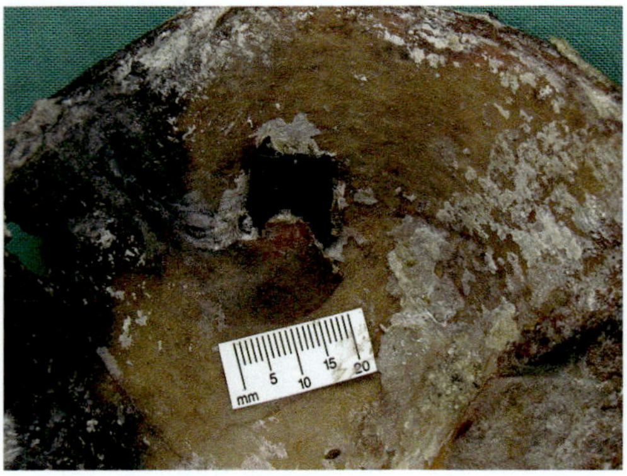

Figure 11.120 Detail of the embedded bullet in the ilium.

Source: Photograph by the author.

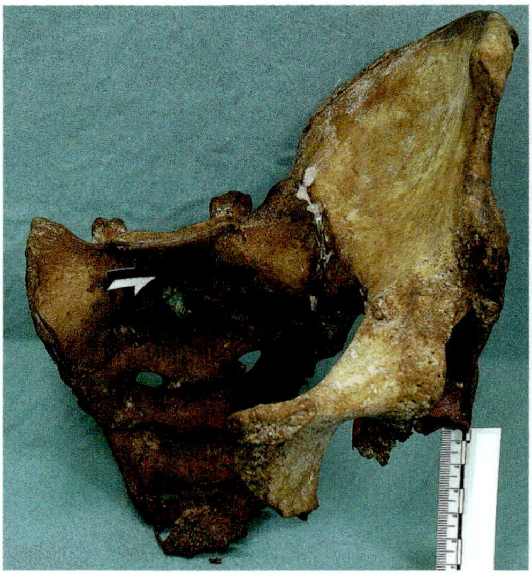

Figure 11.121 A general view of the sacrum, with a bullet embedded in S1.

Source: Photograph by the author.

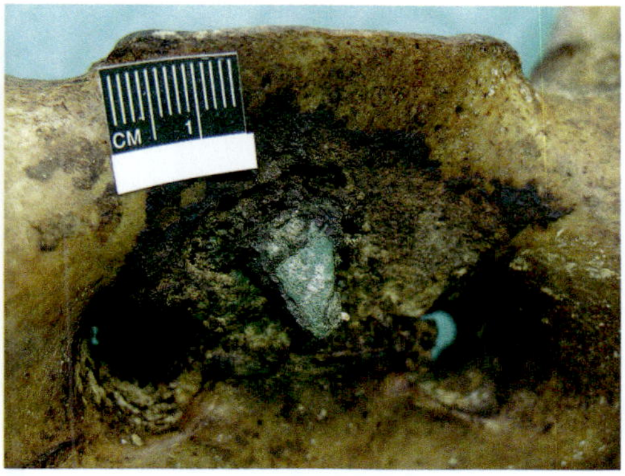

Figure 11.122 Detail of the bullet embedded in S1.

Source: Photograph by the author.

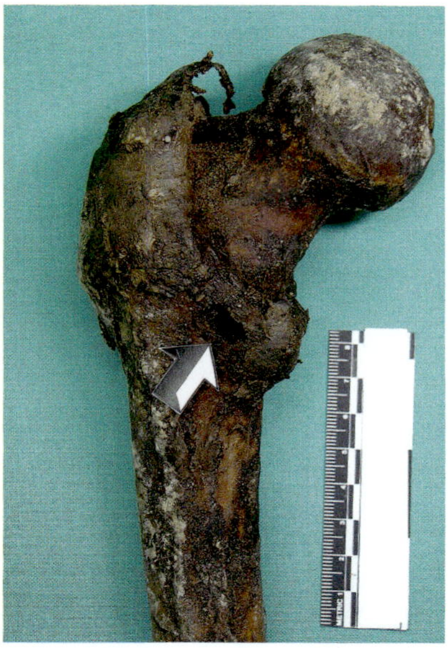

Figure 11.123 Gunshot entrance in the femur indicated by the arrow before sectioning.

Source: Photograph by the author.

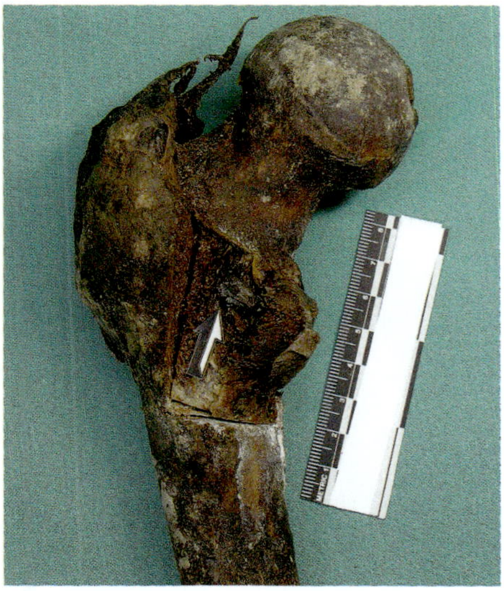

Figure 11.124 After the femur has been sectioned, the bullet can be visibly indicated by an arrow.

Source: Photograph by the author.

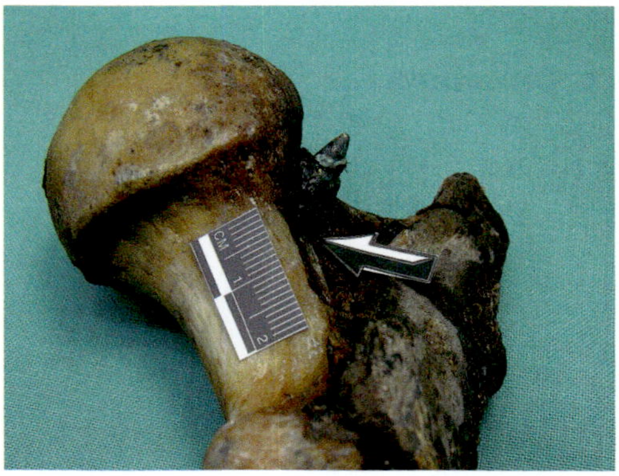

Figure 11.125 Bullet embedded in the neck of the femur indicated by the arrow. The bullet penetrated the bone base-first.

Source: Photograph by the author.

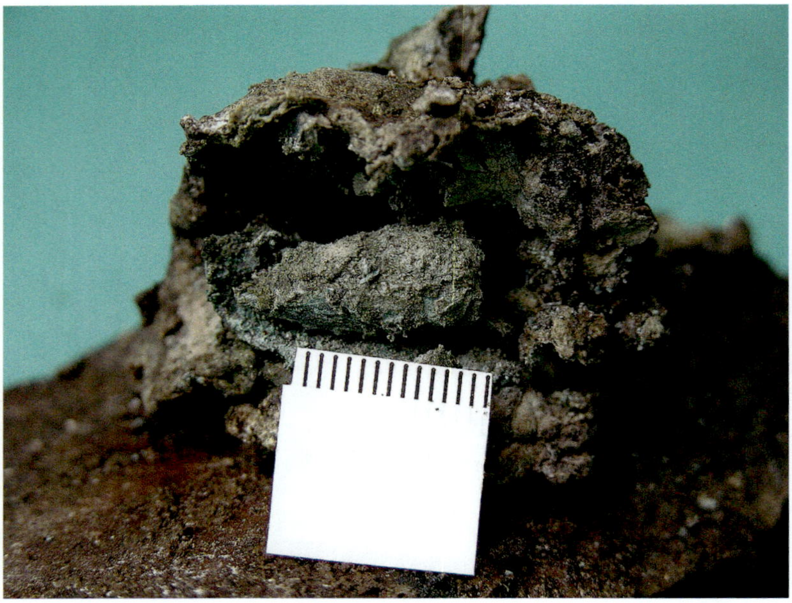

Figure 11.126 Bullet embedded in the femur.

Source: Photograph by the author.

Bullet Trajectory

The trajectory is used to interpret the direction followed by the projectile, from the entrance to the exit. A forensic rod and arrow are usually used to show the trajectory.

Different colors should be used to denote each bullet trajectory in circumstances where there are several trajectories. This will allow for a clear visualization of each individual trajectory and avoid misinterpretation.

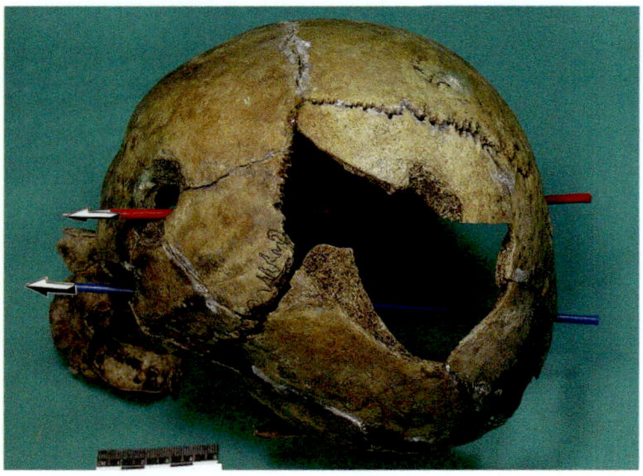

Figure 11.127 Skull with two gunshot trajectories from back (occipital) to front; the red one through the frontal bone, and the blue one through the maxilla.

Source: Photograph by the author.

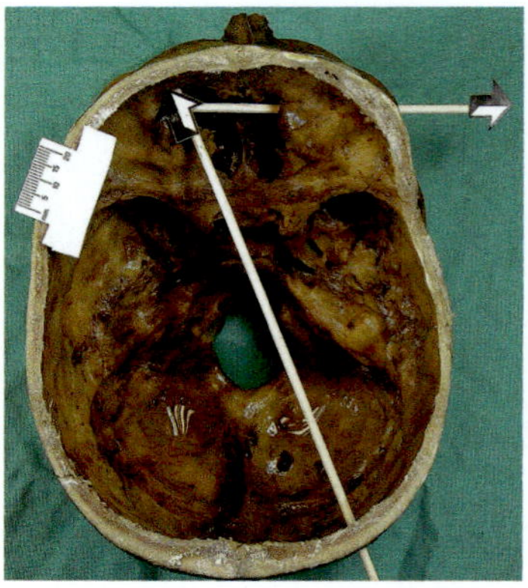

Figure 11.128 Endocranial view of the ricochet against the frontal bone. Entrance through the right parietal upon impact, the trajectory was redirected through the right orbit.

Source: Photograph by the author.

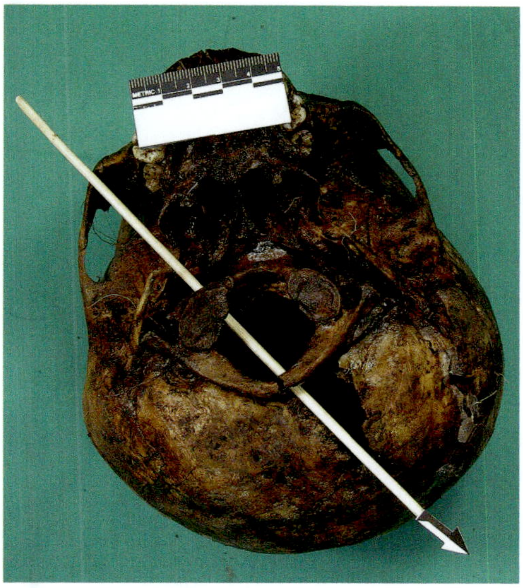

Figure 11.129 Gunshot trajectory from the right zygomatic through the occipital and C1.

Source: Photograph by the author.

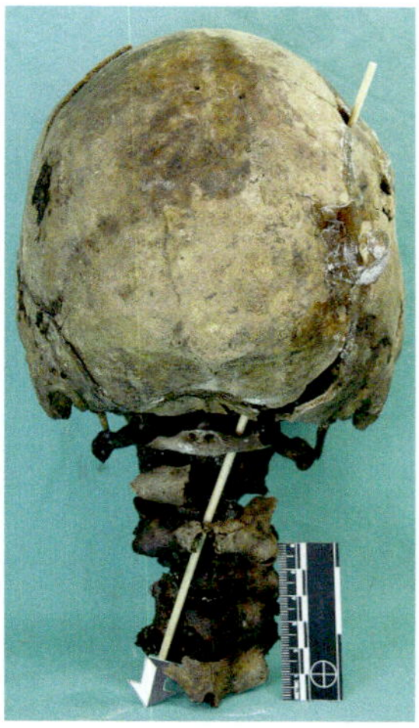

Figure 11.130 Downward trajectory through the right parietal, occipital, and cervical vertebrae.

Source: Photograph by the author.

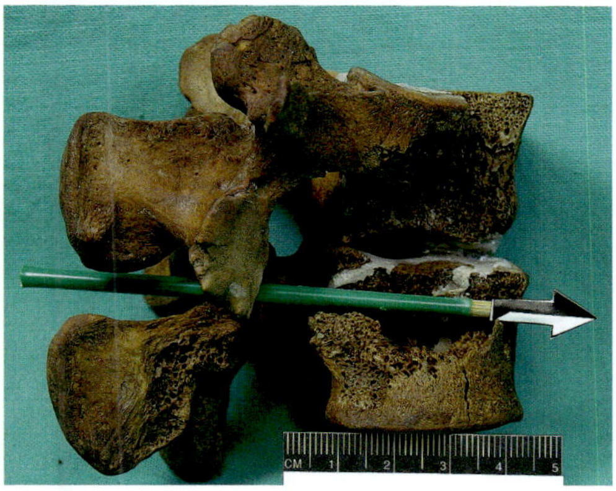

Figure 11.131 Gunshot trajectory through thoracic vertebrae, from back to front.

Source: Photograph by the author.

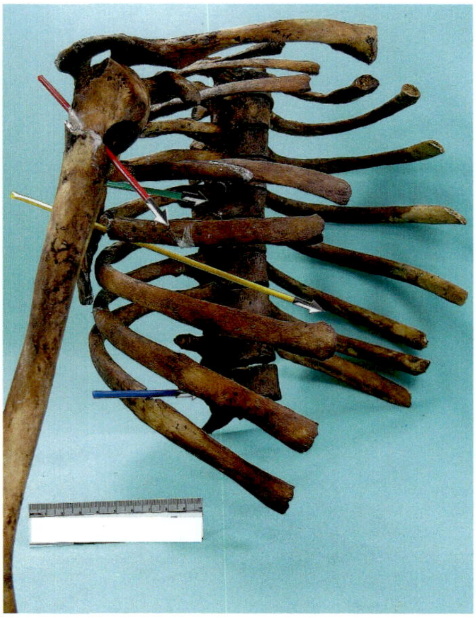

Figure 11.132 From back to front, multiple gunshot trajectories through the right side. Note: Colored rods were used to differentiate each trajectory.

Source: Photograph by the author.

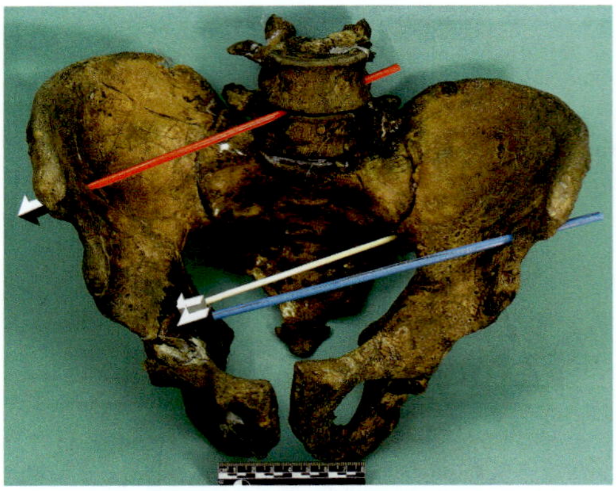

Figure 11.133 From left to right, trajectories of three bullets. Note: Colored rods were used to differentiate each trajectory.

Source: Photograph by the author.

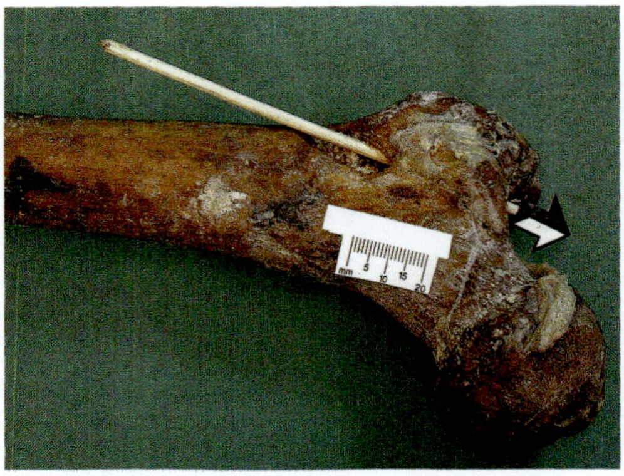

Figure 11.134 Gunshot trajectory through the greater trochanter of the femur.

Source: Photograph by the author.

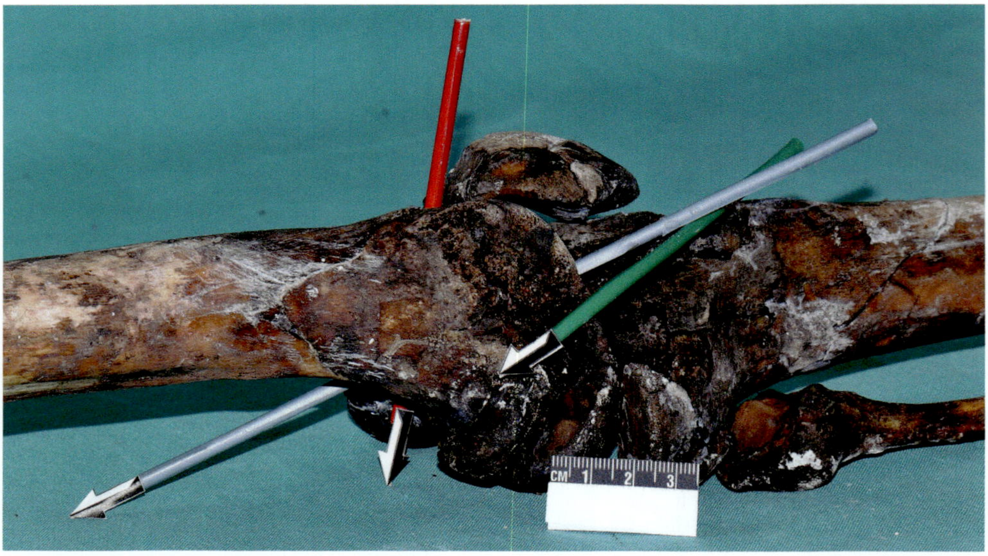

Figure 11.135 Multiple gunshot trajectories through the knee.

Note: Colored rods were used to differentiate each trajectory.

Source: Photograph by the author.

Injuries Caused by Sharp Instruments

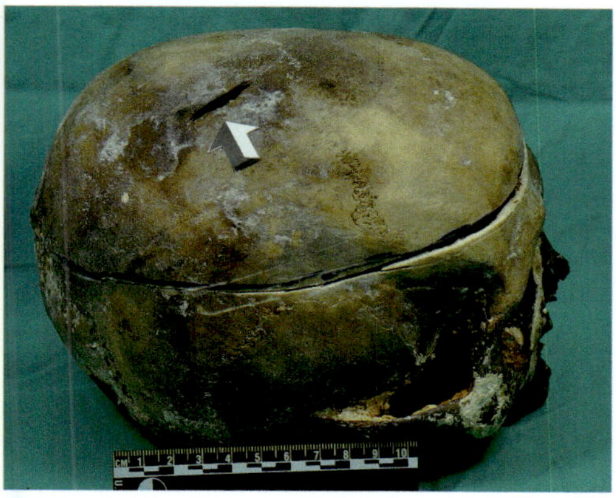

Figure 11.136 Arrow indicating a "slot machine" injury on the right parietal caused by a sharp object, indicated by arrow.

Source: Photograph by the author.

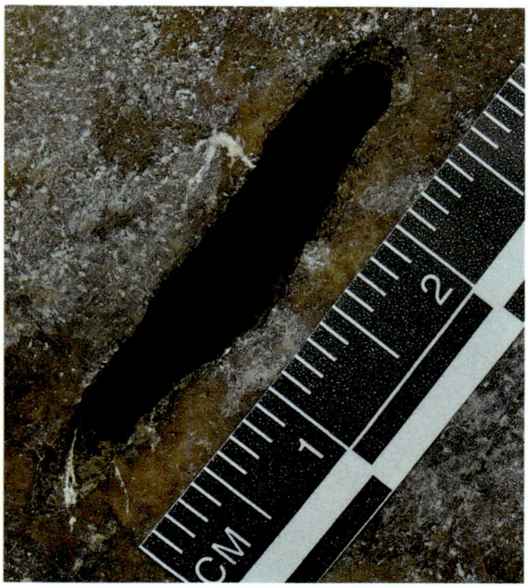

Figure 11.137 Detailed external view of the injury as shown in Figure 11.136

Source: Photograph by the author.

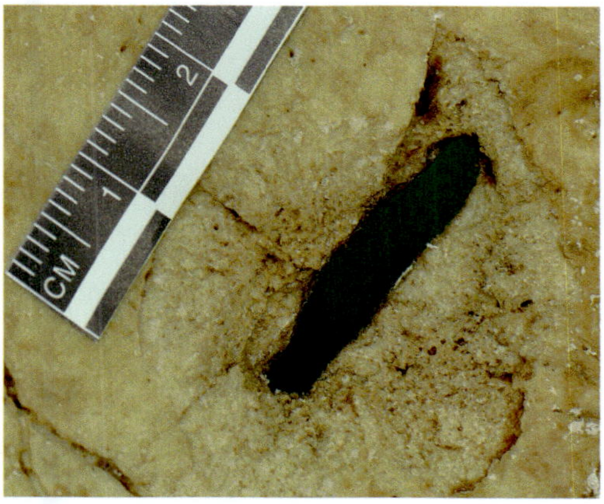

Figure 11.138 Detailed internal view of the injury as shown in Figure 11.136.

Source: Photograph by the author.

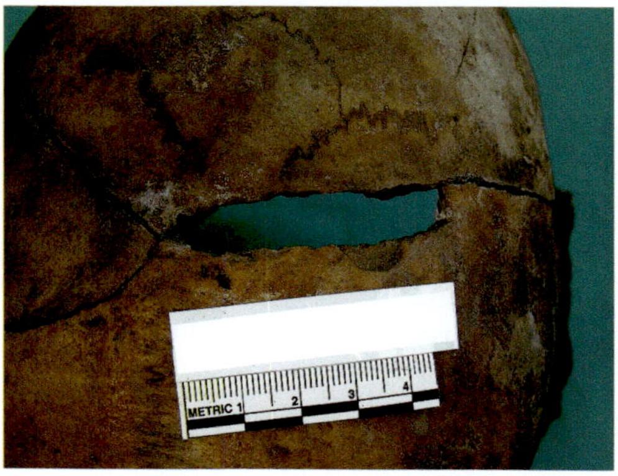

Figure 11.139 External view of a "slot machine" injury caused by a sharp object.

Source: Photograph by the author.

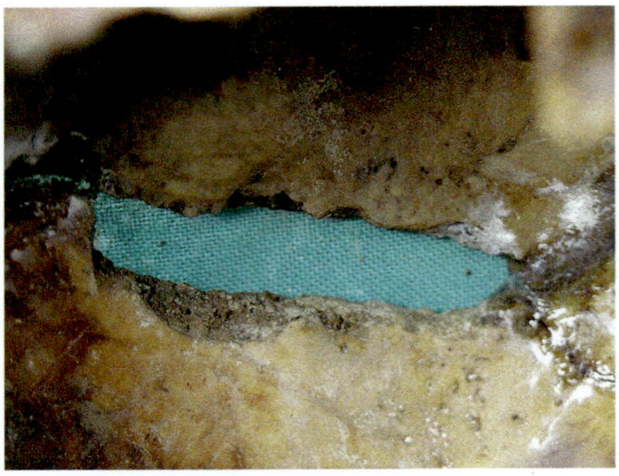

Figure 11.140 Internal view of the injury from iFigure 11.139.

Source: Photograph by the author.

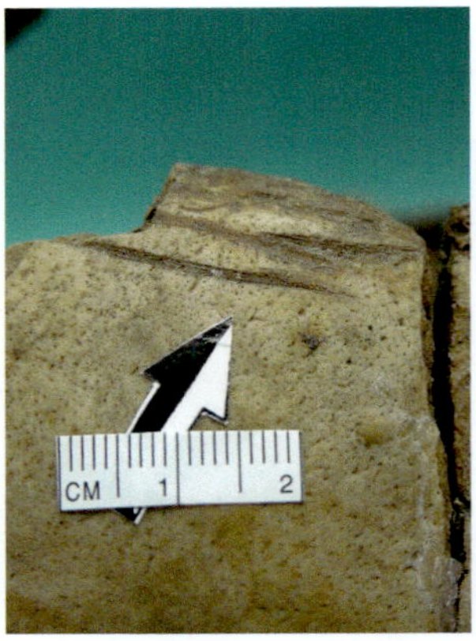

Figure 11.141 The arrow indicates the marks left on a piece of skull by a sharp object.

Source: Photograph by the author.

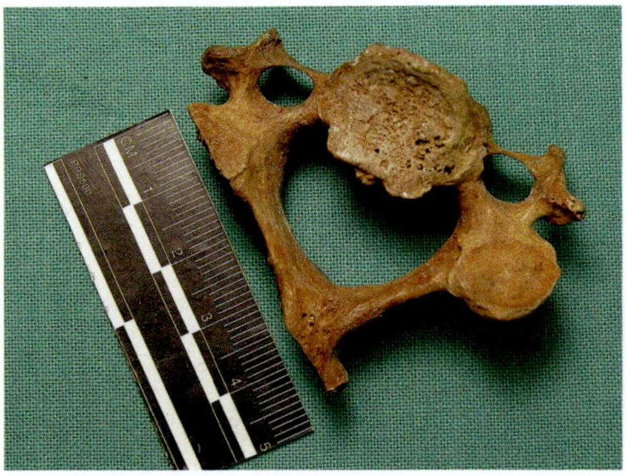

Figure 11.142 Chop of the spinous process of the cervical vertebra.

Source: Photograph by the author.

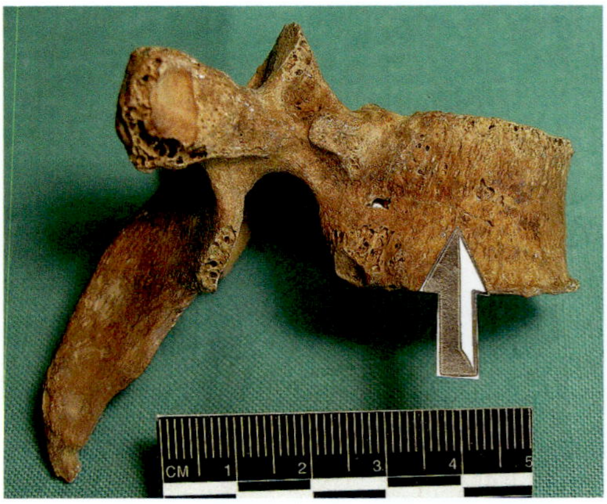

Figure 11.143 Lateral view of the thoracic body with an arrow pointing to a cut.

Source: Photograph by the author.

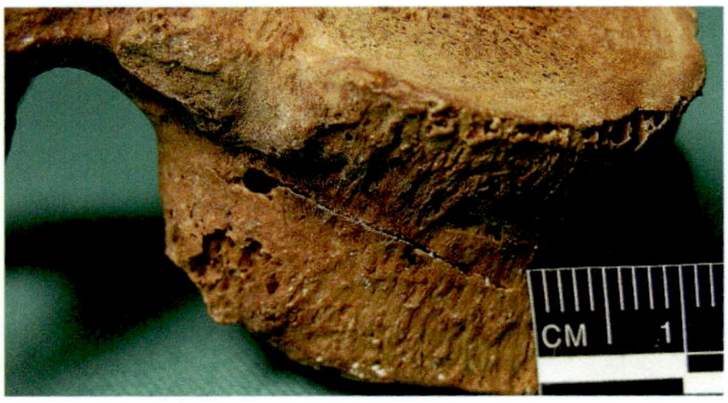

Figure 11.144 Close up of the cut from Figure 11.143.

Source: Photograph by the author.

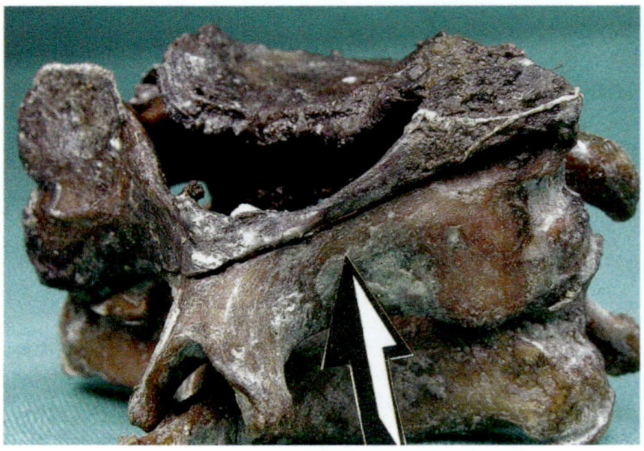

Figure 11.145 View of the cervical vertebrae with an arrow pointing to a chop.

Source: Photograph by the author.

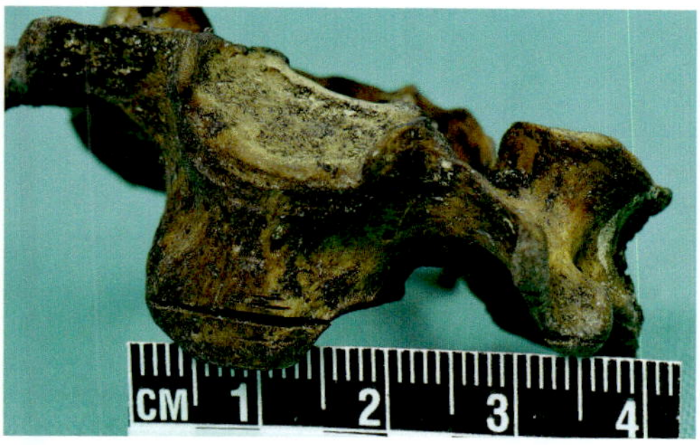

Figure 11.146 View of the vertebra, which has a shop wound and four minor incisions on its body.

Source: Photograph by the author.

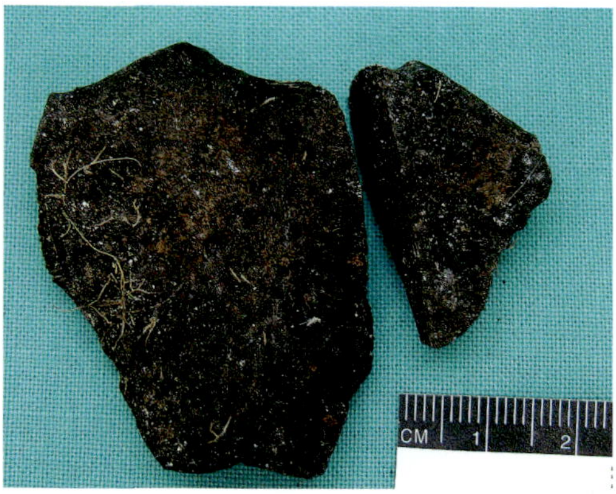

Figure 11.147 A shop sectioning the manubrium of the sternum.

Source: Photograph by the author.

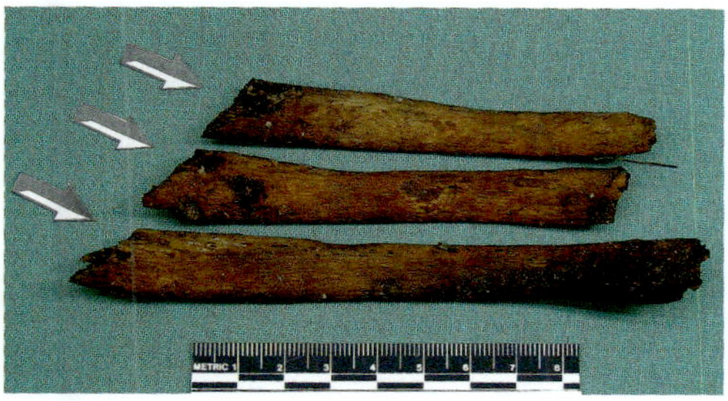

Figure 11.148 Sectioning of three consecutive ribs.

Source: Photograph by the author.

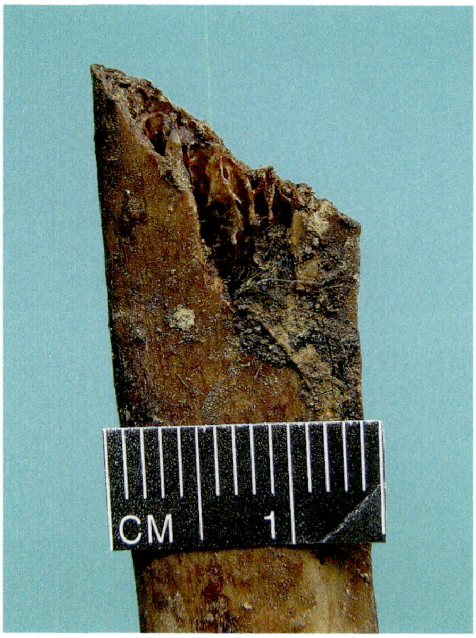

Figure 11.149 Close-up of one of the ribs, from Figure 11.148.

Source: Photograph by the author.

Dentition

12

Both the maxillary and the mandible should be examined from multiple perspectives, including the anterior (front), lateral, occlusal, and lingual aspects.

Take photographs of every facet of the teeth, including the type of occlusion and any dental treatment, such as fillings, crowns, prostheses, any broken or fractured teeth, as well as any other dental-related issues.

Several examples are presented in Figures 12.1 to 12.16.

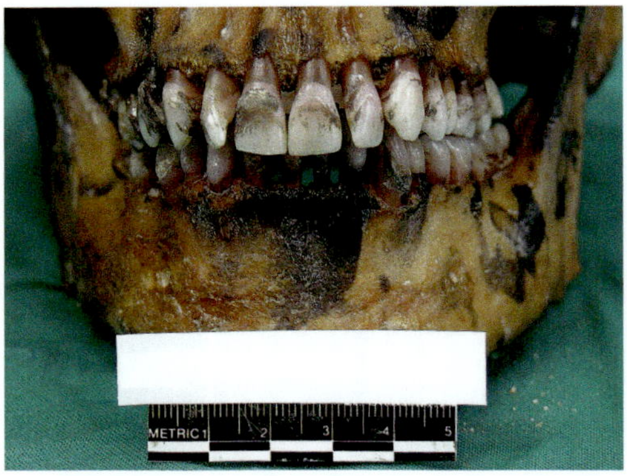

Figure 12.1 Anterior view of the articulated mandible and maxilla showing occlusion of the bone.

Source: Photograph by the author.

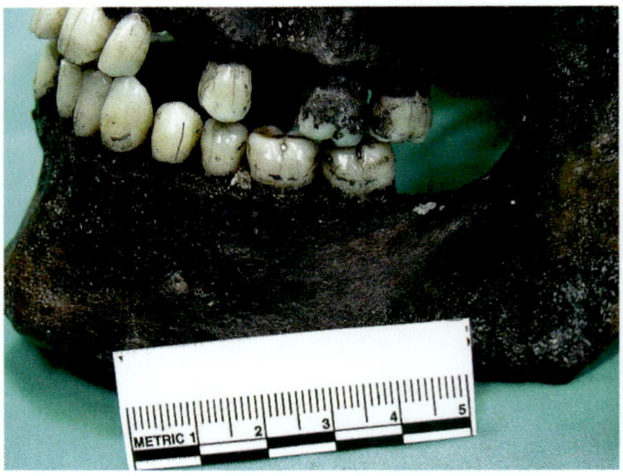

Figure 12.2 View of the left side of the mandible and the maxilla.

Source: Photograph by the author.

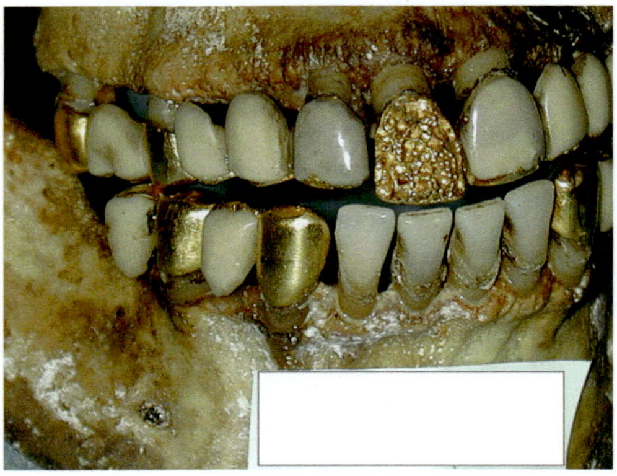

Figure 12.3 View from the right side of the mandible and the maxilla showing dental work.

Source: Photograph by the author.

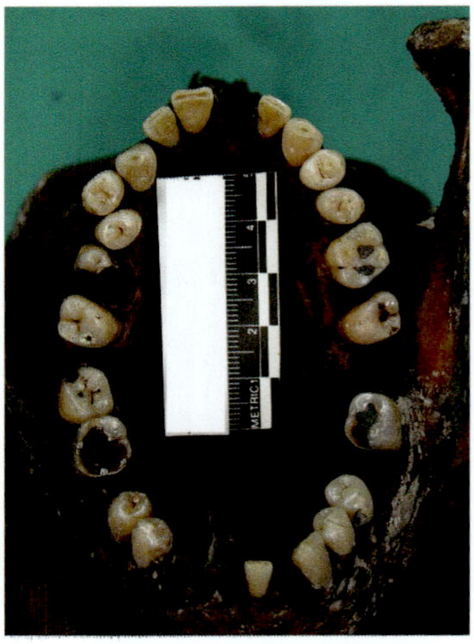

Figure 12.4 Occlusal view of the mandible and the maxilla.

Source: Photograph by the author.

DOI: 10.4324/9781003768838-15

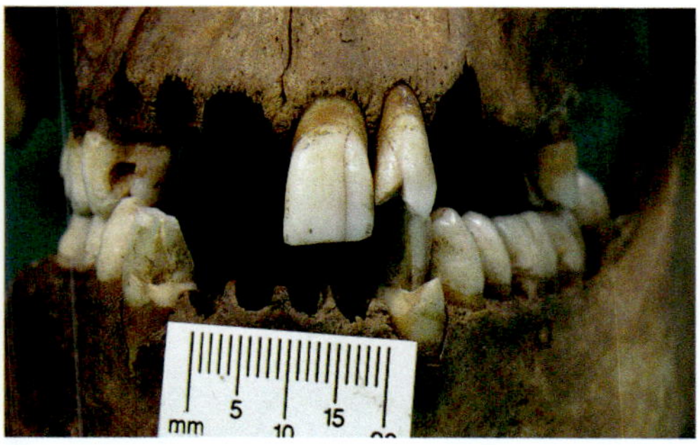

Figure 12.5 Detailed view of the fractured crown of the central incisor, as well as multiple shattered maxillary and mandibular teeth.

Source: Photograph by the author.

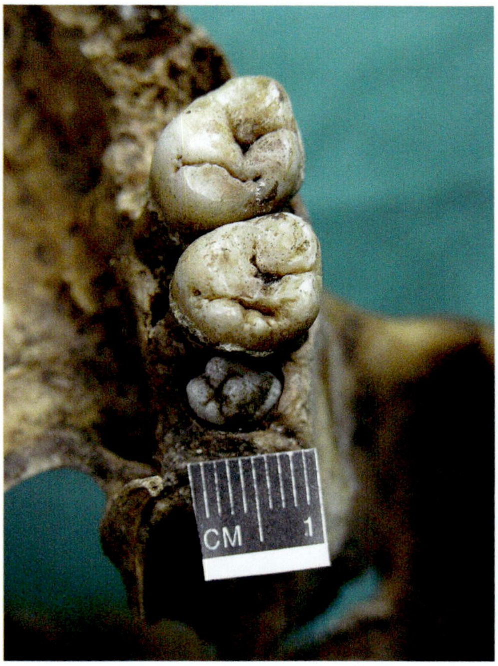

Figure 12.6 Detailed occlusal view of the third maxillary molar.

Source: Photograph by the author.

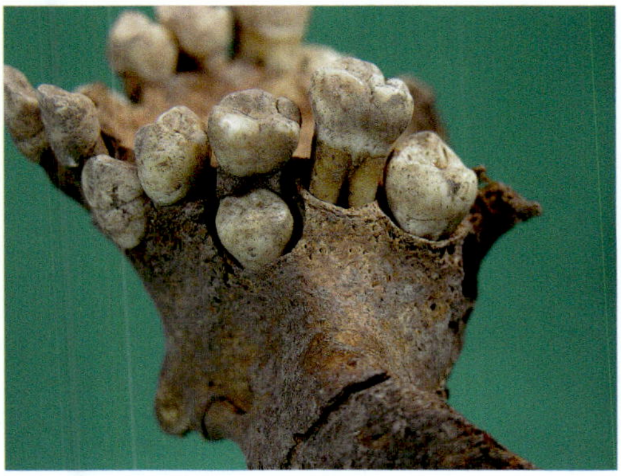

Figure 12.7 Detailed view of the third maxillary molar.

Source: Photograph by the author.

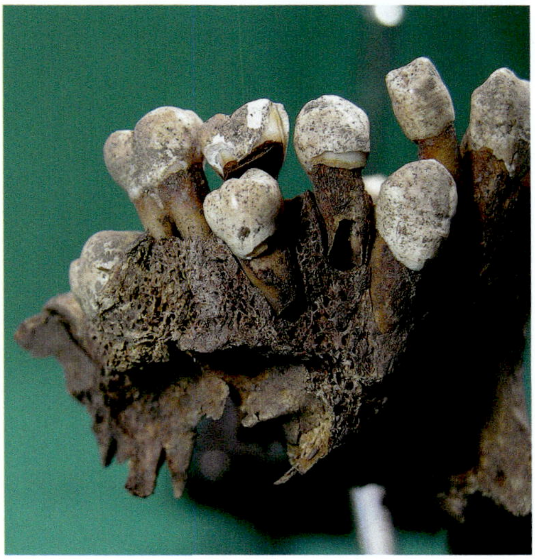

Figure 12.8 View of the third maxillary molar.

Source: Photograph by the author.

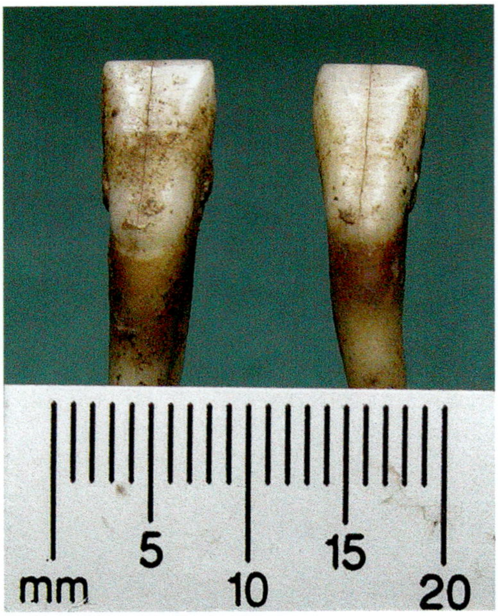

Figure 12.9 Close-up of the fractures on incisor crowns.

Source: Photograph by the author.

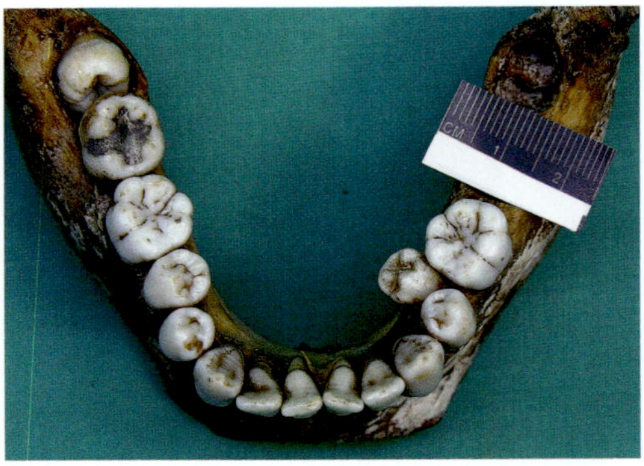

Figure 12.10 Occlusal view of the mandible with an impacted tooth.

Source: Photograph by the author.

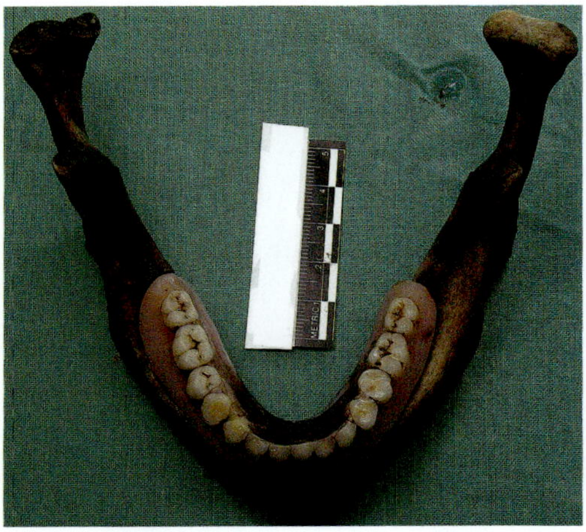

Figure 12.11 Occlusal view of the mandible with removable prosthesis (. /F) in situ.

Source: Photograph by the author.

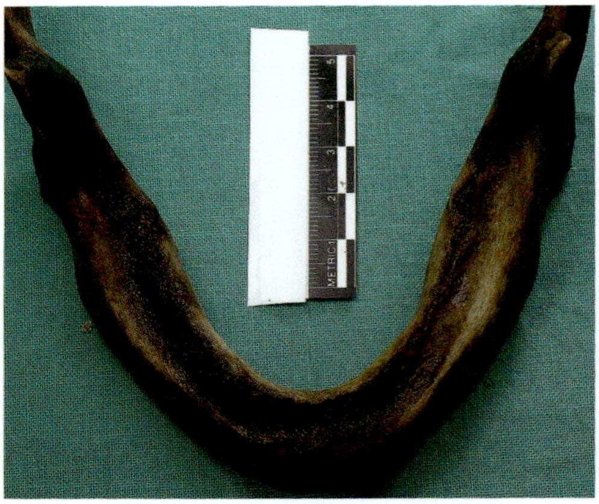

Figure 12.12 Occlusal view of the mandible without the removable prosthesis (. /F).

Source: Photograph by the author.

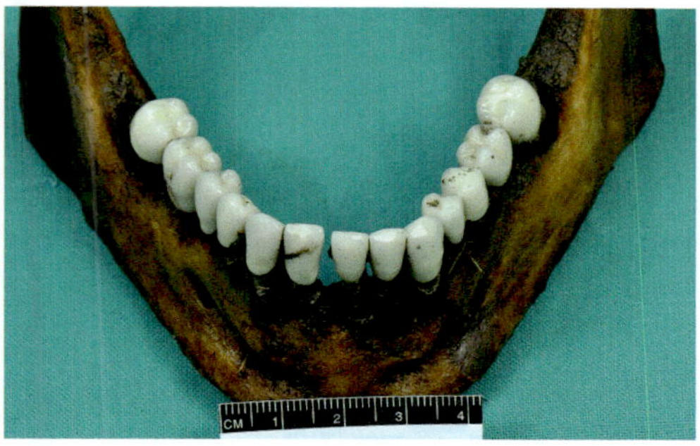

Figure 12.13 Occlusal view of the mandible, displaying artificial crowns.

Source: Photograph by the author.

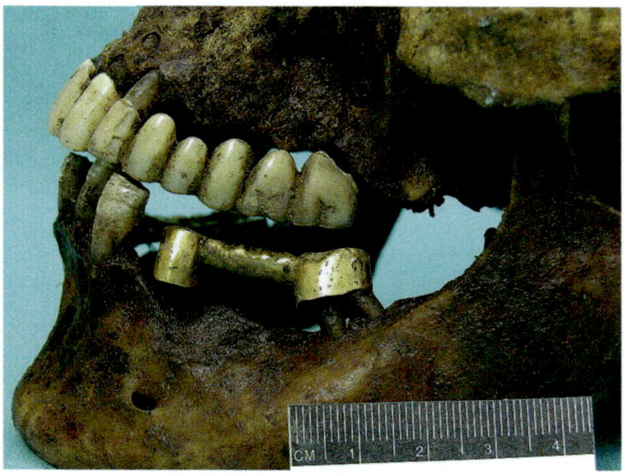

Figure 12.14 Several bridges are visible in this detail of the left side of the dentition.

Source: Photograph by the author.

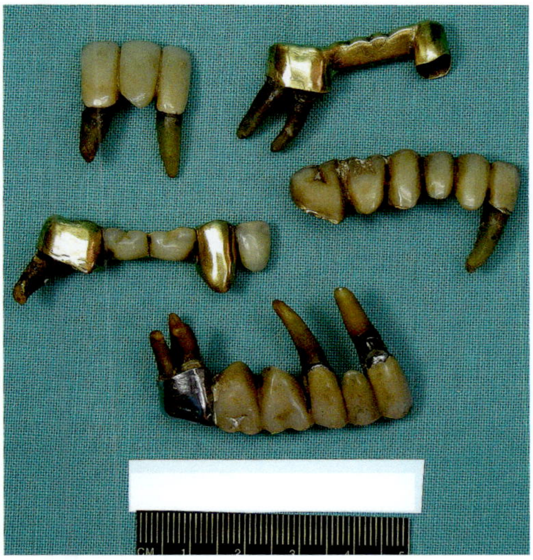

Figure 12.15 A general view of bridges from Figure 12.14.

Source: Photograph by the author.

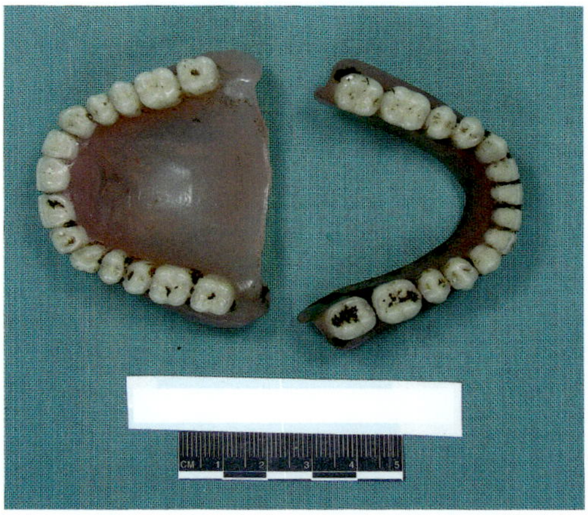

Figure 12.16 Occlusal view of a removable prosthesis (F/F).

Source: Photograph by the author.

Age

13

When estimating age from skeletal remains, experts typically examine key areas such as the skull, teeth, ribs, bone fusion, and pubic symphysis, depending on what is available.

To ensure this information is preserved for future analysis, always photograph the remains. Before taking photos, select the appropriate autofocus mode to capture clear, usable images.

Figures 13.1 and 13.2 illustrate two examples of this.

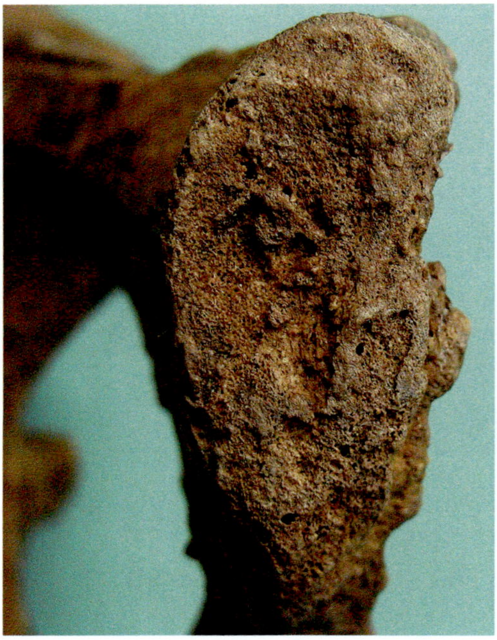

Figure 13.1 Detailed photograph of pubis use in age estimation.

Source: Photograph by the author.

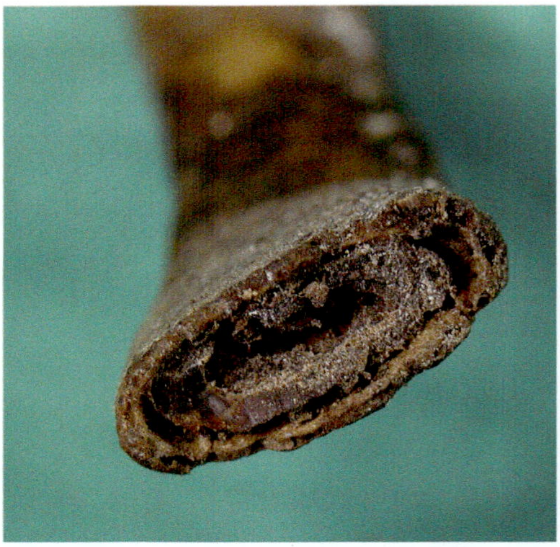

Figure 13.2 Detailed photograph of the sternal end of the rib for age estimation.

Source: Photograph by the author.

DOI: 10.4324/9781003768838-16

Artifact

14

Artifact (or evidence) refers to any item collected during legal proceedings to prove or disprove a fact, or to link suspects, victims, or crime scenes.

Each piece of evidence must be:

- Photographed clearly.
- Labeled with a unique identifier, such as a letter followed by a number (e.g., A1 for the evidence/artifact number) and the case number (e.g., 1234567).

Figures 14.1 to 14.9, presented below as examples, use the same evidence number despite originating from different cases.

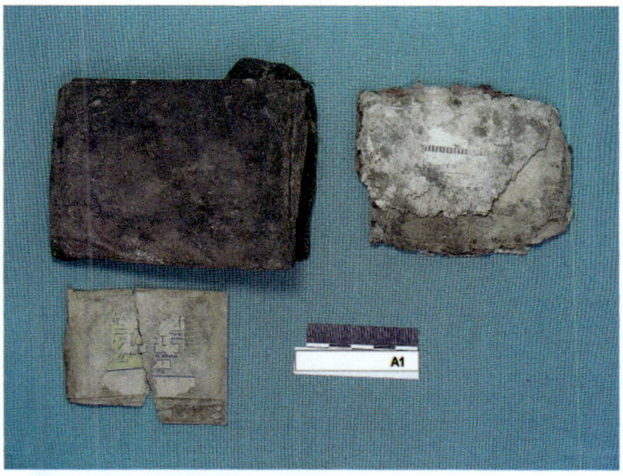

Figure 14.1 A1—Wallet and contents.

Source: Photograph by the author.

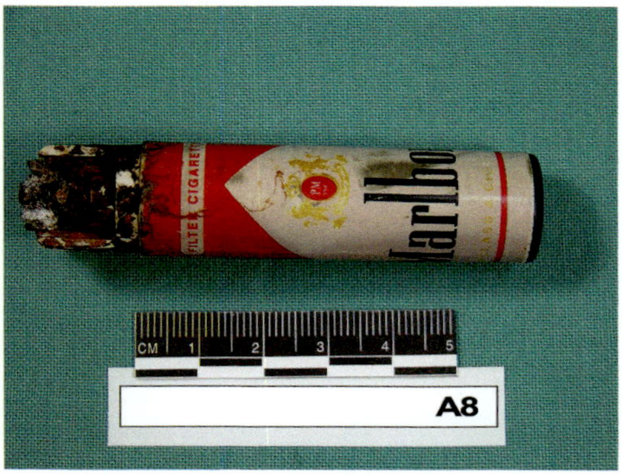

Figure 14.2 A8—Marlboro lighter.

Source: Photograph by the author.

DOI: 10.4324/9781003768838-17

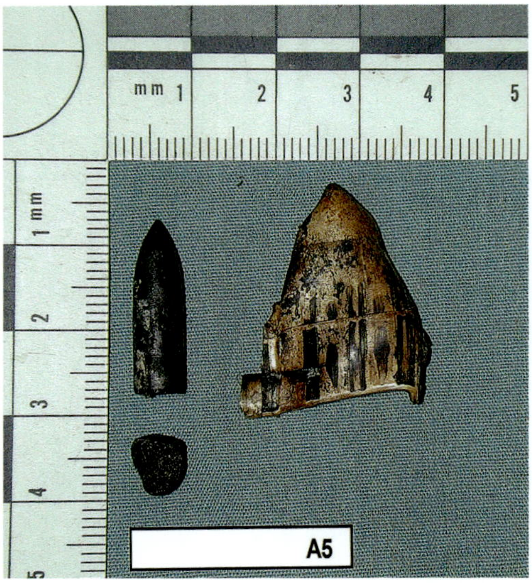

Figure 14.3 A5—Jacket and core.

Source: Photograph by the author.

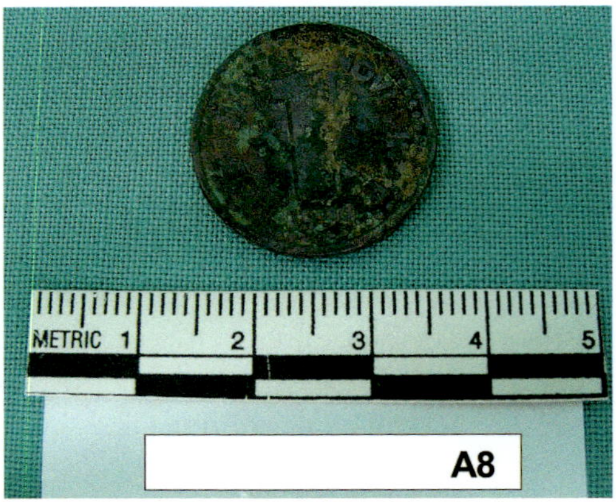

Figure 14.4 A8—Coin.

Source: Photograph by the author.

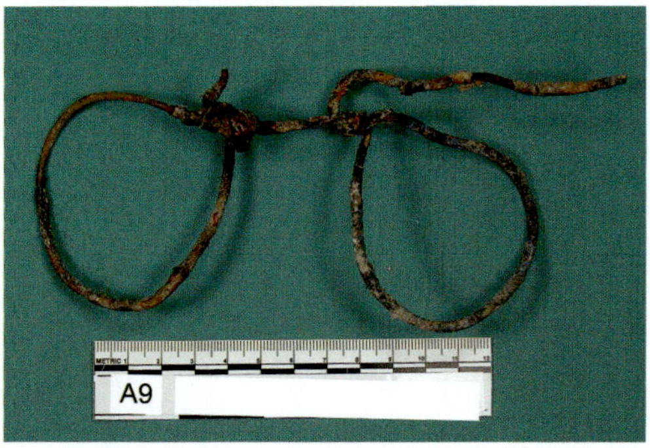

Figure 14.5 A9—Wire ligature.

Source: Photograph by the author.

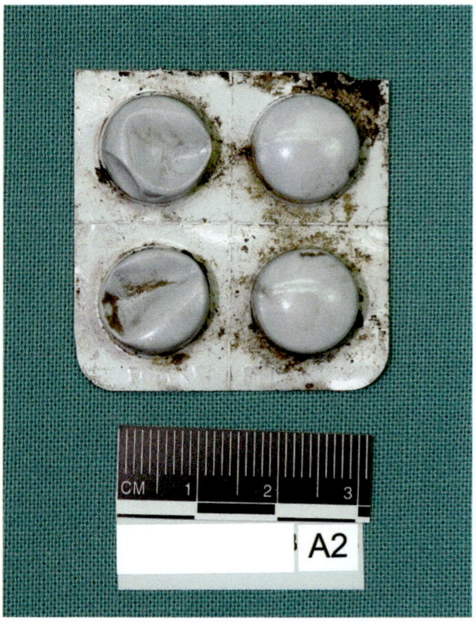

Figure 14.6 A2—Tablet medicine.

Source: Photograph by the author.

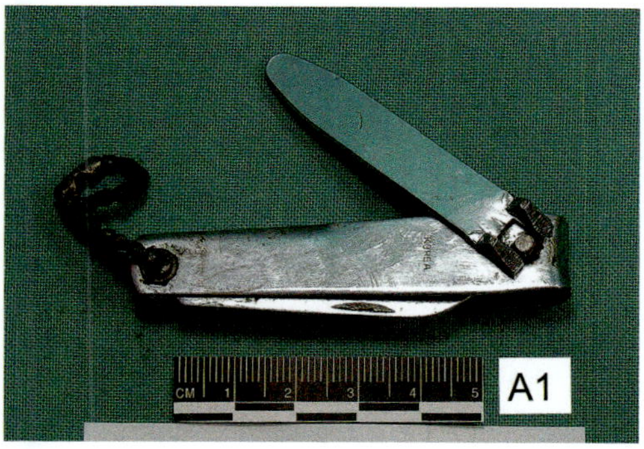

Figure 14.7 A1—Nail clippers.

Source: Photograph by the author.

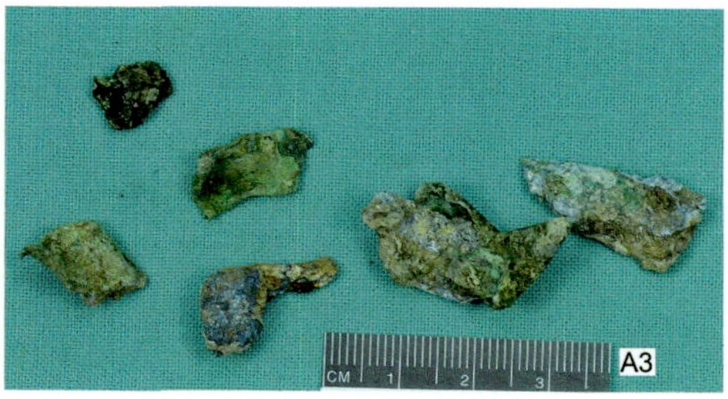

Figure 14.8 A3—Bullet fragment.

Source: Photograph by the author.

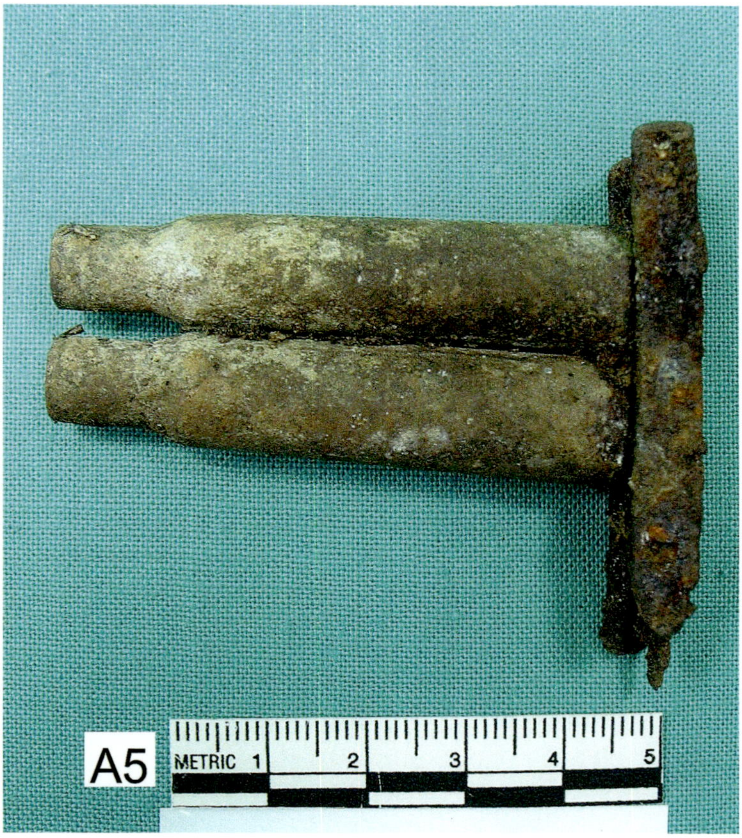

Figure 14.9 A5—Stripper Clip with two shell casings

Source: Photograph by the author.

X-ray

15

Whenever possible, photograph the evidence alongside its X-ray. This ensures a digital record is preserved in the case file and strengthens the documentation of the collected evidence.

Note: In Figures 15.1 to 15.6, case numbers have been removed from the X-ray images for confidentiality, as well as evidence numbers and rulers will not appear.

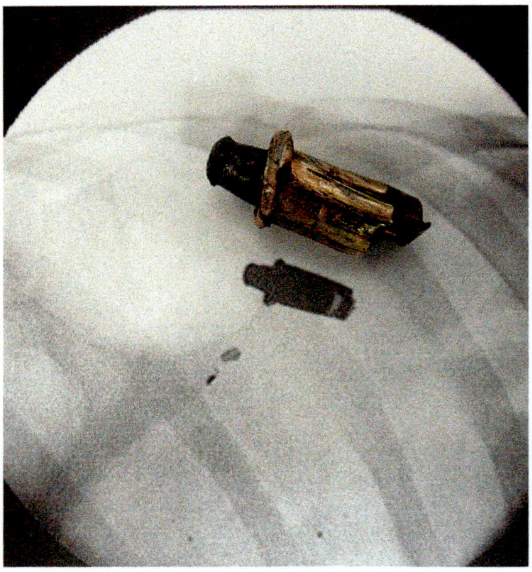

Figure 15.1 Bullet found in the rib cage.

Source: Photograph by the author.

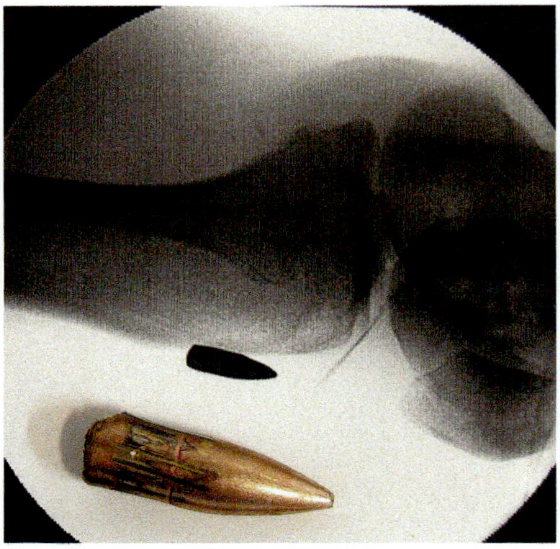

Figure 15.2 Bullet found in the tibia.

Source: Photograph by the author.

 DOI: 10.4324/9781003768838-18

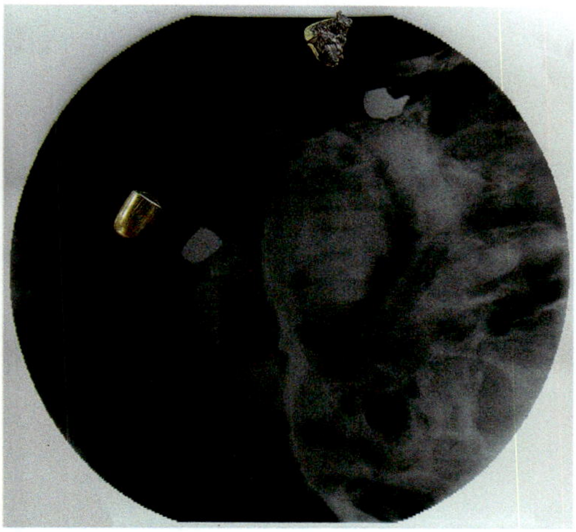

Figure 15.3 Bullet and a bullet fragment found in the pelvic area.

Source: Photograph by the author.

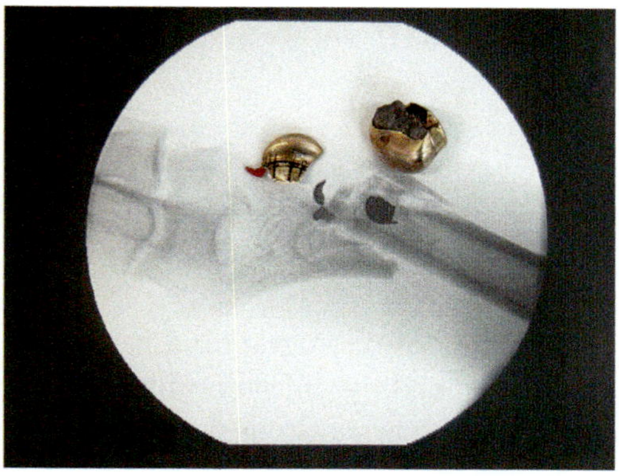

Figure 15.4 Bullet fragments found in the distal humerus.

Source: Photograph by the author.

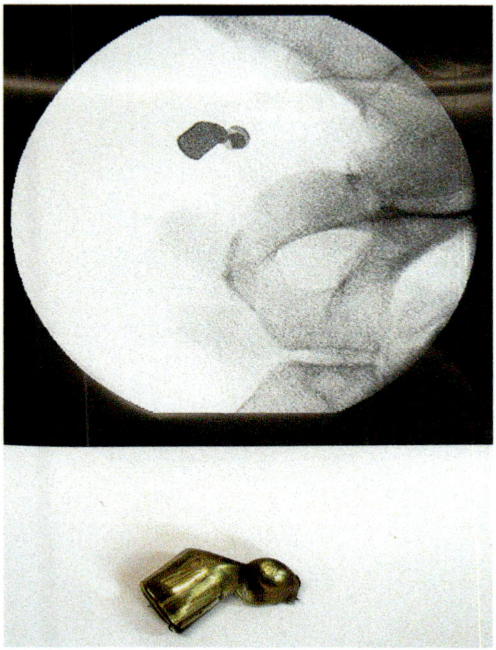

Figure 15.5 Bullet found in the pelvic area.

Source: Photograph by the author.

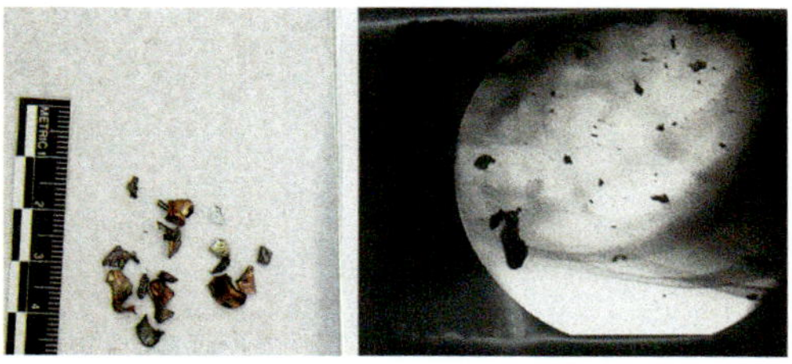

Figure 15.6 Metal fragments found in the rib cage.

Source: Photograph by the author.

Clothing

16

The process of photographing clothing begins with taking one or more general photographs, depending on the number of items of clothing. Figures 16.1 to 16.9 show several examples of how clothing should be photographed, depending on the type of event being documented.

Here is a step-by-step process:

1. General Overview: Start by taking one or more wide-angle photographs of all clothing items together, depending on the quantity.
2. Individual Items: Photograph each piece of clothing separately, capturing both the front and back views.
3. Detailed Shots (if needed): Take close-up images of specific features, such as size, labels, names, logos, or unique markings.

Annotating Injuries or Features

To highlight specific details:

- Use letters to label bodily injuries.
- Use arrows to point to relevant areas.

Purpose:

- Letters provide additional context or descriptions.
- Arrows visually indicate matches or areas of interest.

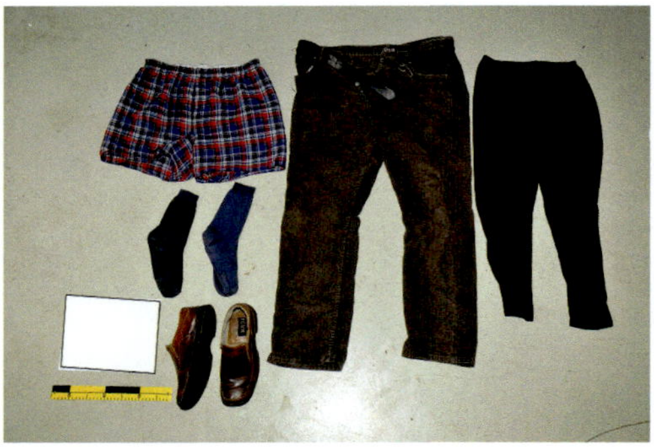

Figure 16.1 General view of the clothes.

Source: Photograph by the author.

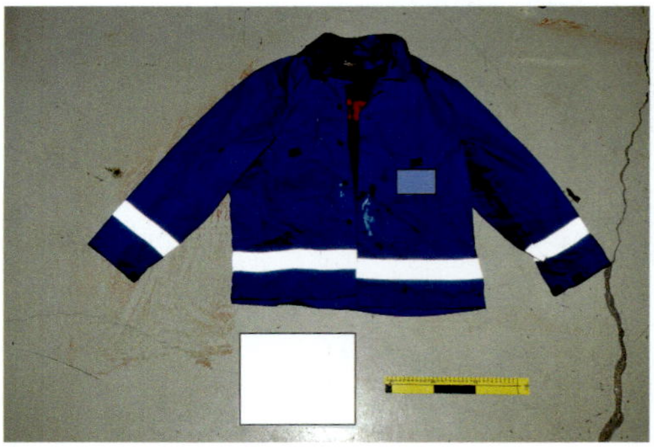

Figure 16.2 General view of the jacket.

Source: Photograph by the author.

DOI: 10.4324/9781003768838-19

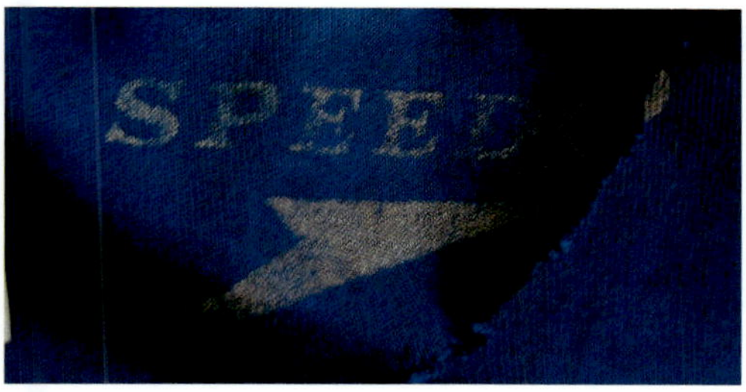

Figure 16.3 Close-up of the logo on the jacket.

Source: Photograph by the author.

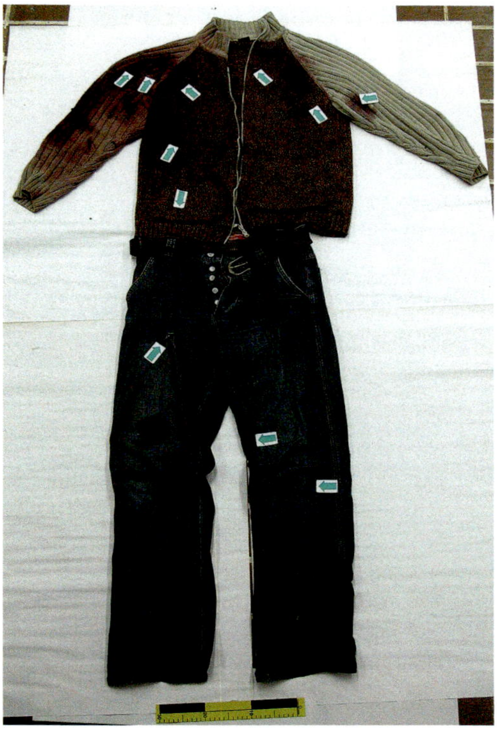

Figure 16.4 General view of the garments with gunshot defects marked by an arrow.

Source: Photograph by the author.

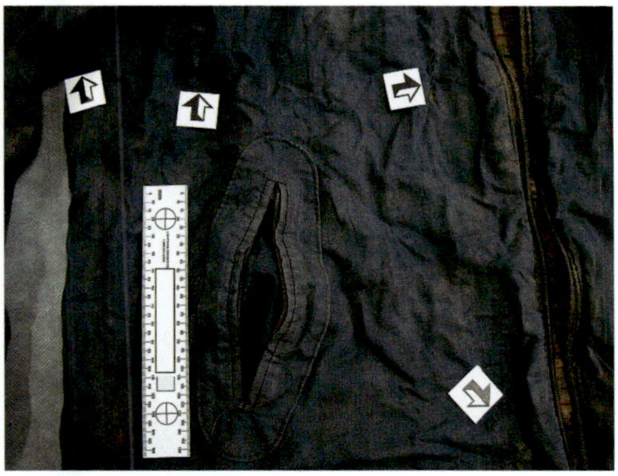

Figure 16.5 Mid-range view with a cluster of gunshot defects pointed by arrows.

Source: Photograph by the author.

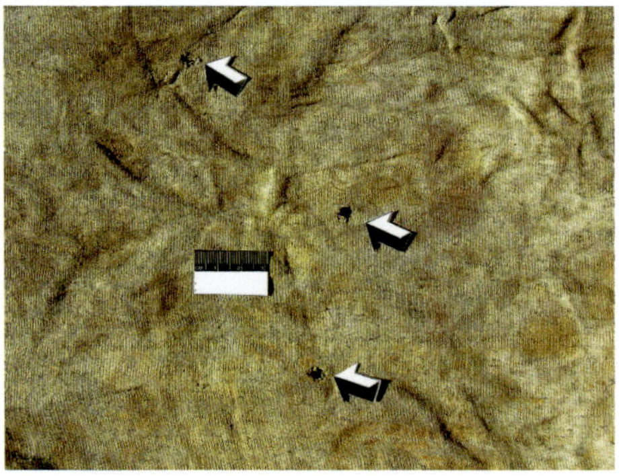

Figure 16.6 Another example of a mid-range view with a cluster of gunshot defects pointed by arrows.

Source: Photograph by the author.

To reconstruct and interpret bullet trajectories, you can use one of the following:

- A mannequin.
- A plastic skeleton.
- The victim's clothing.

Each method helps achieve a more precise analysis of the bullet's path.

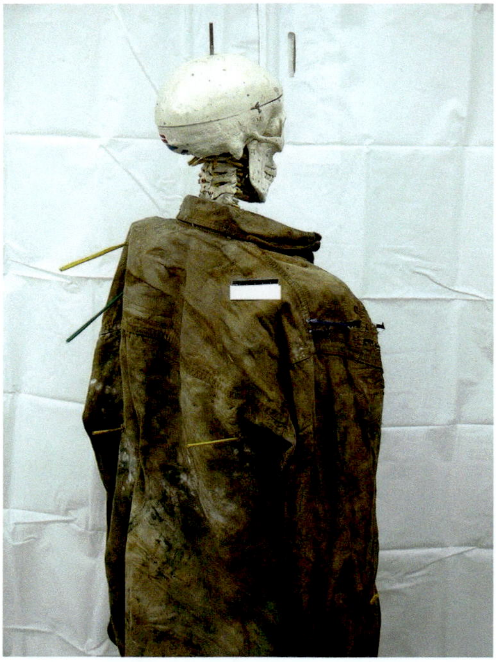

Figure 16.7 To illustrate the six different gunshot trajectories, a plastic skeleton and the victim's jacket were used.

Source: Photograph by the author.

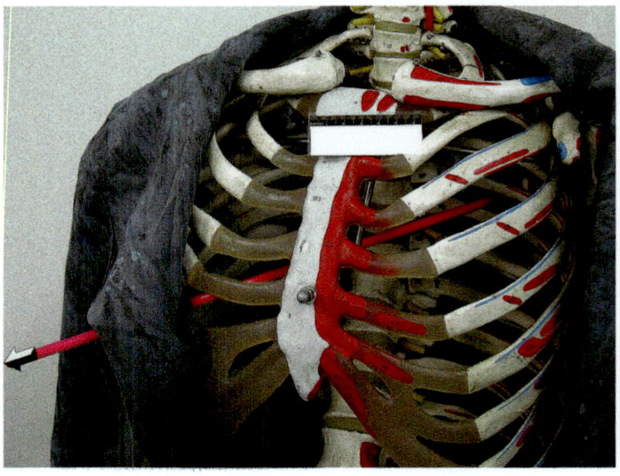

Figure 16.8 A plastic skeleton is useful to show the extent of damage caused to bones and organs in three dimensions to illustrate the harm done to the bones and organs by the trajectory.

Source: Photograph by the author.

Alternatively, you can combine the bones with the clothing for a more comprehensive analysis.

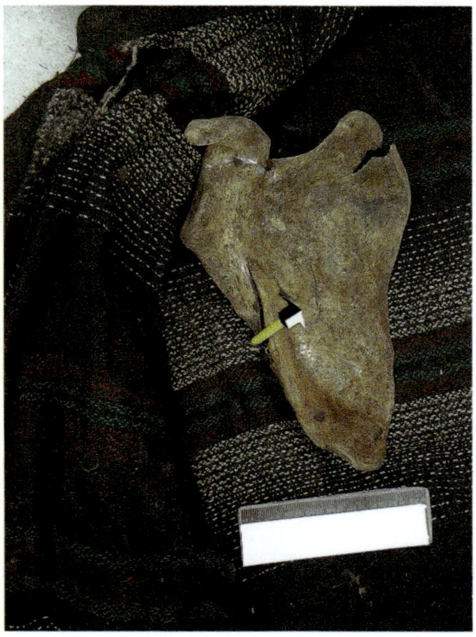

Figure 16.9 By analyzing the clothing alongside the bone, you can demonstrate a clear connection. For example, the bullet trajectory and scapula damage align with the hole found in the wool jacket, confirming the path of the injury.

Source: Photograph by the author.

Infrared Photography

17

A forensic photographer must capture all possible information that could aid in identification or evidence collection. Infrared photography is a powerful tool for revealing details invisible or nearly invisible to the naked eye.

With infrared, you can uncover:

- Identifying features (e.g., tattoos, old scars), depending on the body's condition.
- Hidden details in documents

Results may vary depending on the infrared camera or infrared filter used.

Examples: Figures 17.1 to 17.4 show infrared images taken with a Nikon D200 camera converted into infrared. These figures will demonstrate how infrared photography may discover information that the human eye is unable to see.

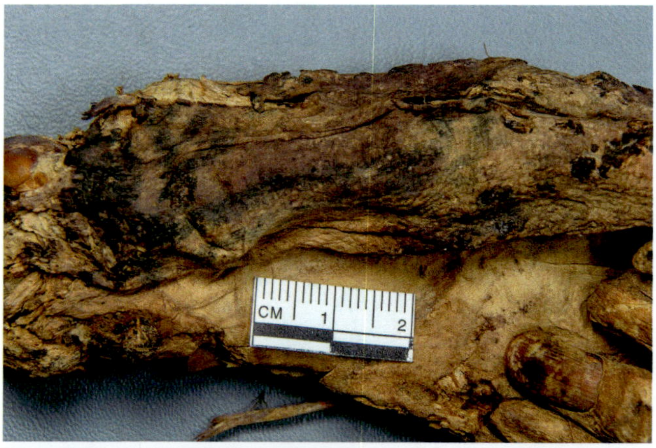

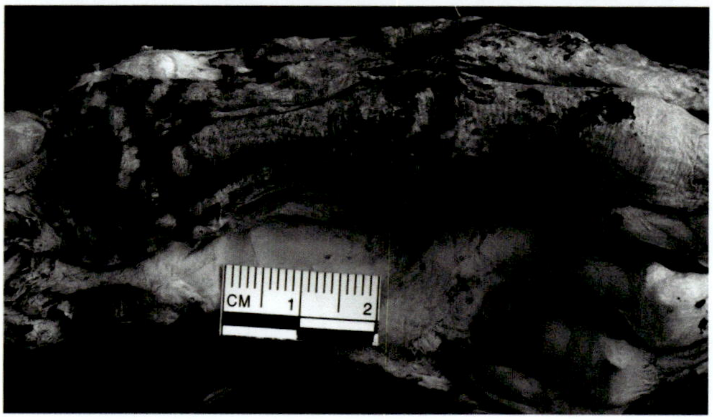

Figure 17.1 Tattoo on a mummy's hand (Pachacamac Museum in Peru).

Source: Photograph by the author.

DOI: 10.4324/9781003768838-20

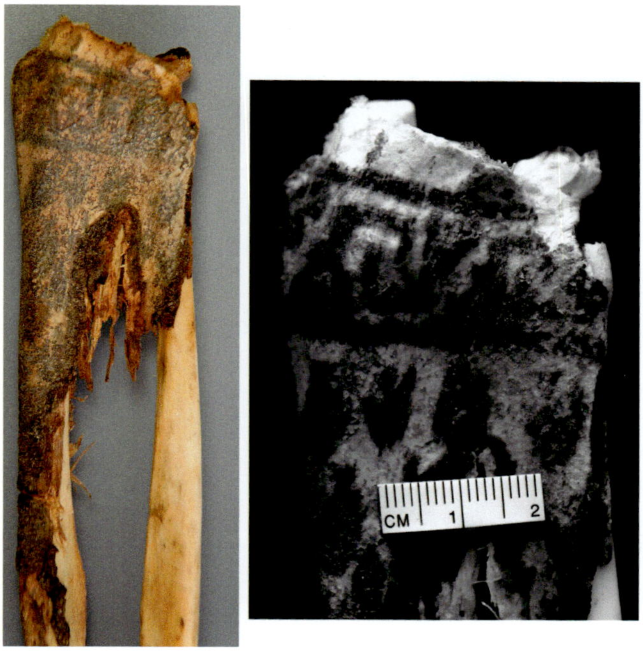

Figure 17.2 Another example. Tattoo on a mummy's forearm (Pachacamac Museum in Peru).

Source: Photograph by the author.

In the picture above, the design of the tattoo is difficult to discern. Picture taken with a traditional DSLR camera.

A better image and further details of the design are seen in this picture. Picture taken with a Nikon D200 converted to infrared.

Left, picture taken with a traditional DSLR camera.

Right, picture taken with a Nikon D200 converted to infrared.

The visibility of inks, stains, or damaged documents in infrared photography depends on the type of infrared equipment used. Results vary based on whether you use:

- An infrared camera.
- A filter with a specific wavelength (e.g., 550–850 nm).

Each method produces different outcomes, directly affecting what details can be revealed.

Figures 17.3 and 17.4 depict a printed page and an image with elements blacked out.

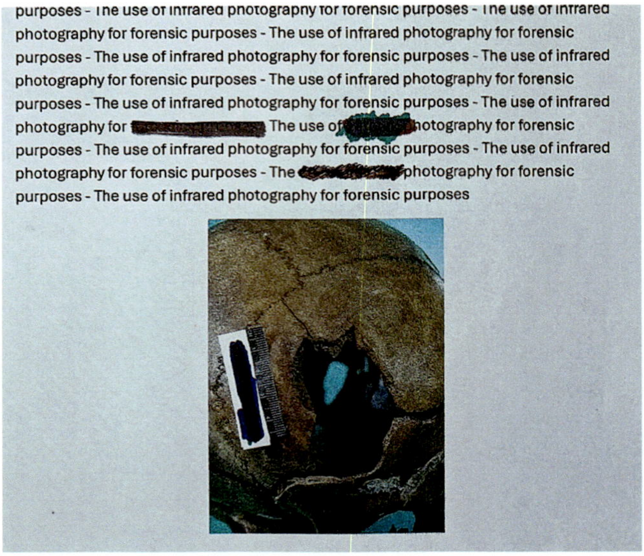

Figure 17.3 Photograph by the author.

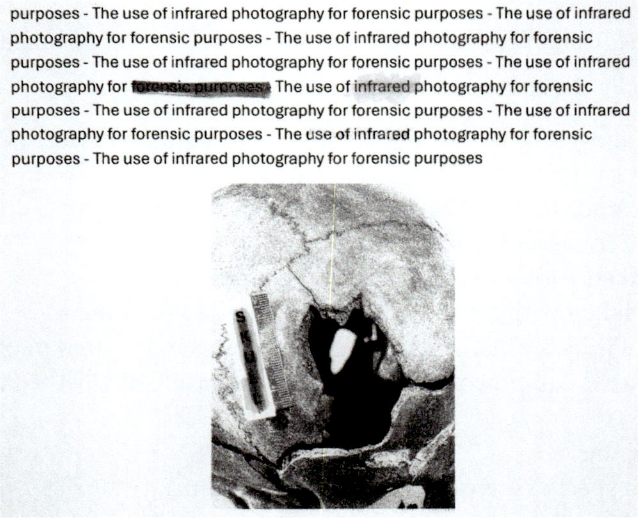

Figure 17.4 Photograph by the author.

To conceal particular words inside the document, a ballpoint pen, black, green, and red markers were used. Additionally, a black marker was utilized to conceal the label on the skull. Picture taken with a traditional DSLR camera.

Using an infrared camera, the words obscured by a marker were brought into view! An infrared camera is a great tool for uncovering concealed information.

Photography Guidelines That Can Be Used

18

Some Purpose in Forensic Photography

- To record and document injuries and evidence that cannot be preserved indefinitely or left untouched.
- To act as a future reference or aide-mémoire.
- To document minutiae and specific features of a given.
- To document injuries and record what they looked like before the autopsy.
- To show the condition of evidence or injuries at the time of examination.
- To illustrate and supplement the written medico-legal record.
- To corroborate the verbal description given by the pathologist.
- To prepare evidence that will be presented in court and confirm testimony.

Basic Material

- Camera.
- Lens.
- Flash.
- Case number.
- Different types of rulers.
- Arrow.
- Evidence number.
- Rods in a variety of colors, if possible.
- Photo Log.

Some Recommendations

1. **Documentation Requirements**

   Photograph every step of the autopsy process, including:
   - Opening and closing the body bag.
   - The body in anatomical position.
   - Clothing, evidence, and personal objects.
   - Ensure every discovery is clearly visible and confirmed in the photographs.
2. **Photographic Process**
   - Sequence: Photograph from skull to feet.
   - Perspectives: Capture general, mid-range, and close-up views.

DOI: 10.4324/9781003768838-21

- Take close-ups after mid-range shots.
- Clarity: Ensure all photographs are easy to understand and unambiguous.

3. **Technical Standards**
    - Use appropriate settings and autofocus for sharp, clear images.
    - Shoot in RAW format (if possible) to preserve an unaltered original file.
    - Include a ruler (scale) and file/evidence number in each photograph.
    Ensure the ruler and number are the following:
    - Proportional to the subject.
    - Not obscuring the subject.
    - Oriented toward the head (if applicable).
4. **Annotations and Reconstruction**
    - Use arrows (in mid-range or overview shots) to highlight points of interest.
    - Perform reconstruction (if applicable) to better understand injuries.
5. **Organization and Custody**
    - Never mix photographs from different cases in the same folder.
    - Use the same camera for each case and store images sequentially in the individual case folder.
    - Maintain exclusive custody of all photographs.
    - In a photo log, each photograph must be recorded along with its description.
    - Record any errors or observations in the "remarks" section of the photo log.

Example of an Autopsy Procedure

1. A picture of the closed body bag should be taken first, as in Figure 18.1 and then opened as in Figure 18.2.

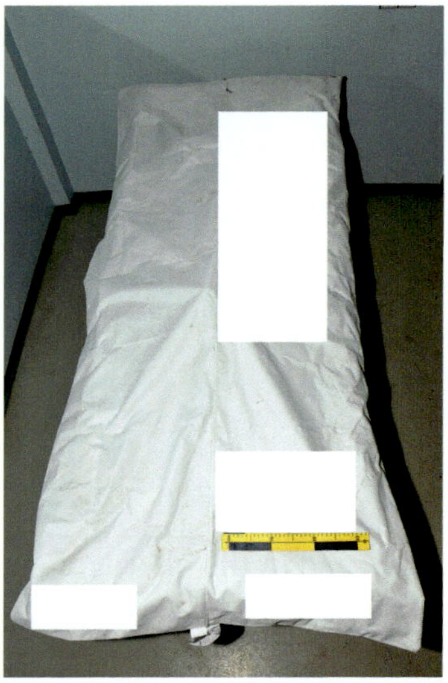

Figure 18.1 Photograph by the author.

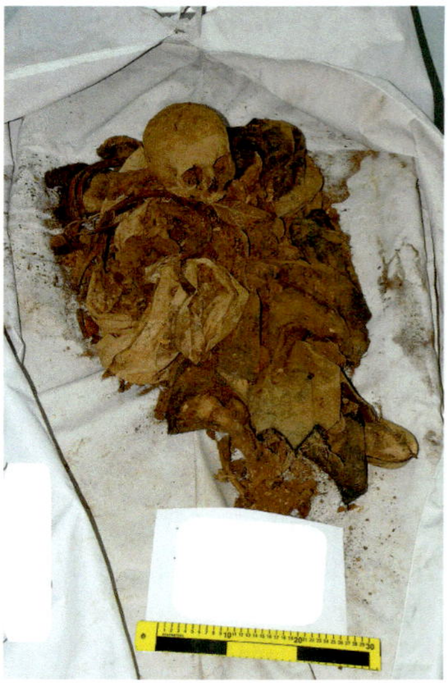

Figure 18.2 Photograph by the author.

2. If there are any artifacts associated with the human remains (bullets, ligatures, among others), a general picture, as in Figure 18.3, and a detailed picture, as in Figure 18.4, must be taken along with an evidence number before removing them. Before the photographs are taken, arrows will be used to indicate the points of interest.

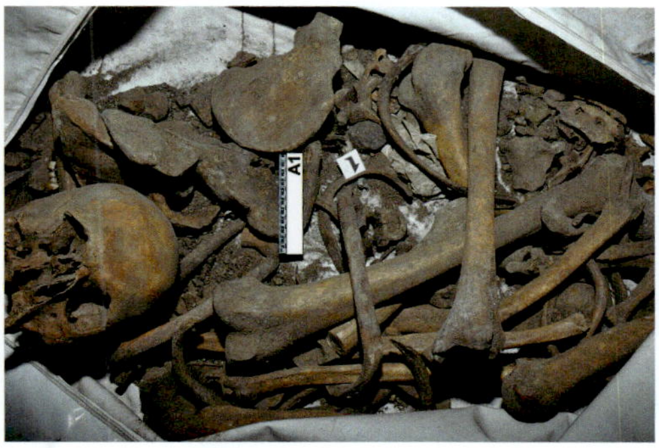

Figure 18.3 Photograph by the author.

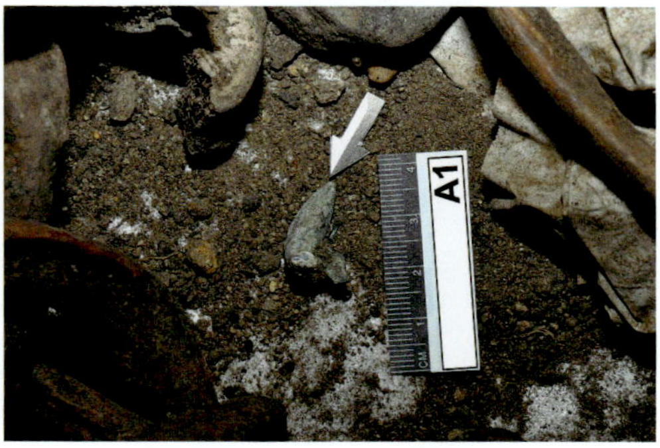

Figure 18.4 Photograph by the author.

3. Take a photograph in a correct anatomical position as in Figure 18.5.

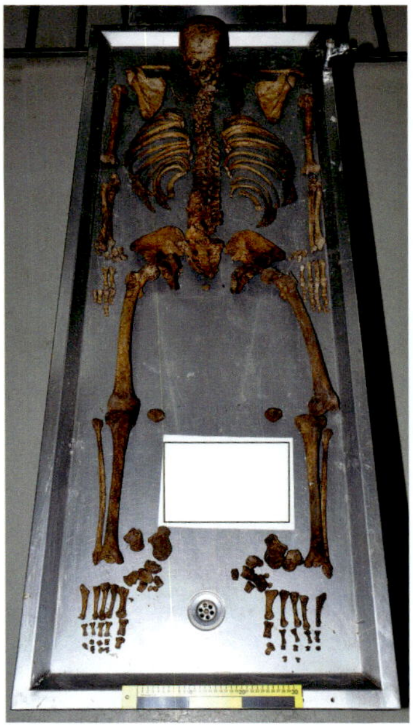

Figure 18.5 Photograph by the author.

4. Before shooting details, a general photograph should be taken showing all injuries indicated by arrows, as in Figure 18.6.

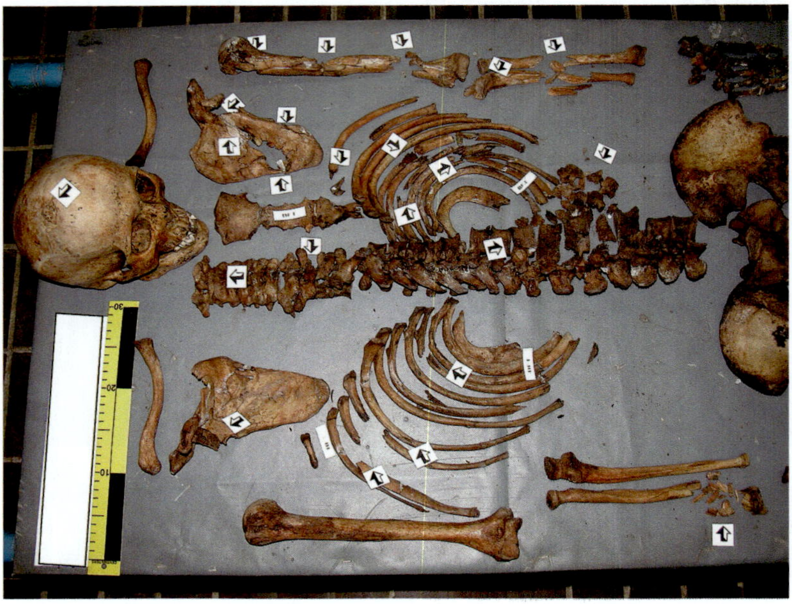

Figure 18.6 Photograph by the author.

5. Detailed pictures should start with the skull and work their way down to the feet. A general picture will always come before the close-up.
6. A photograph of every side of the cranium, including the front, left, back, right, top, and base, should be taken as shown in Figures 18.7 to 18.13. Any visible details per side will be documented as shown in Figure 18.9.

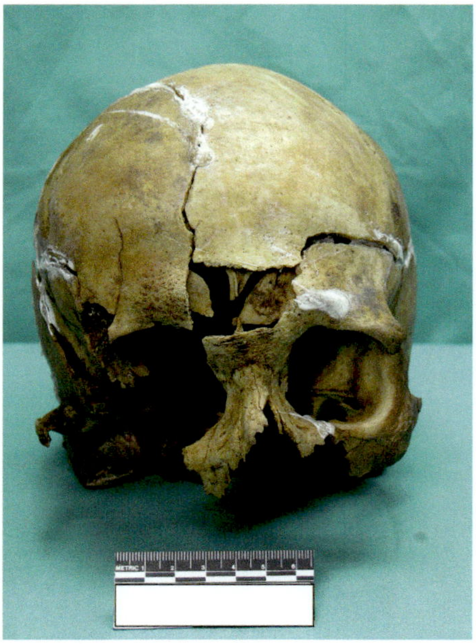

Figure 18.7 Photograph by the author.

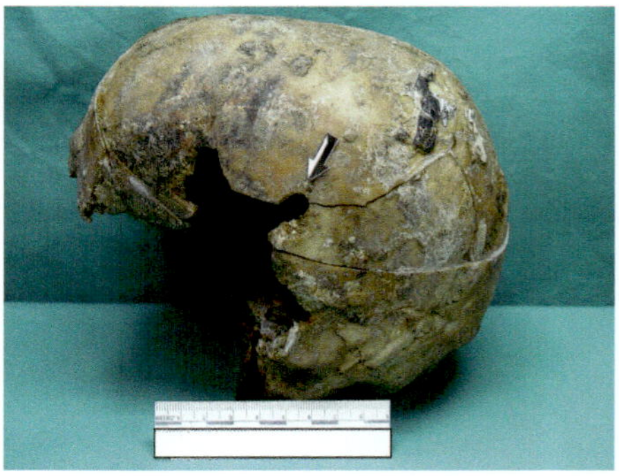

Figure 18.8 Photograph by the author.

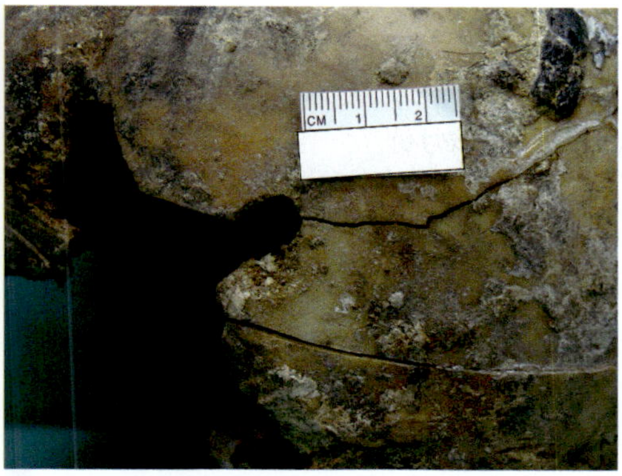

Figure 18.9 Photograph by the author.

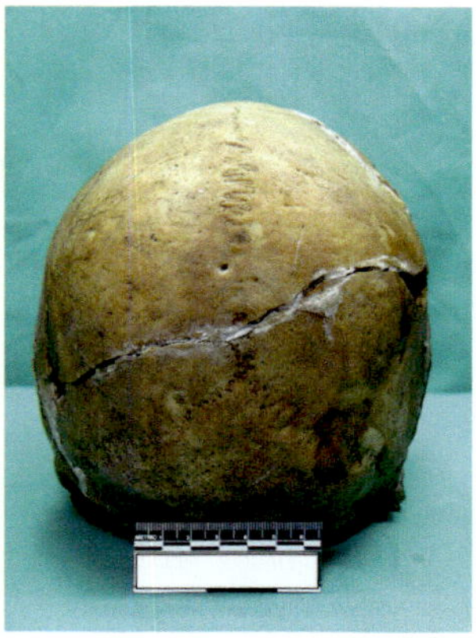

Figure 18.10 Photograph by the author.

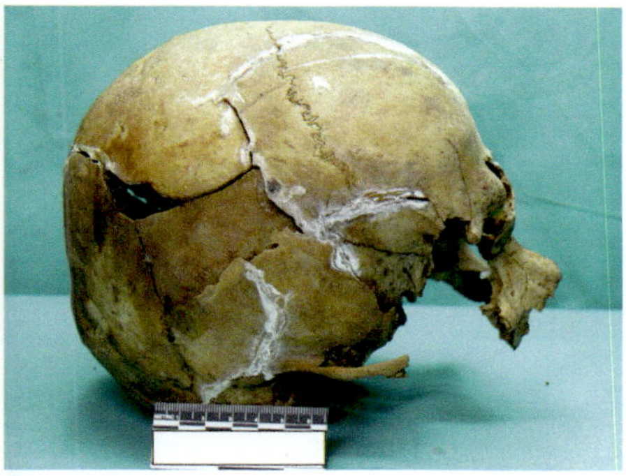

Figure 18.11 Photograph by the author.

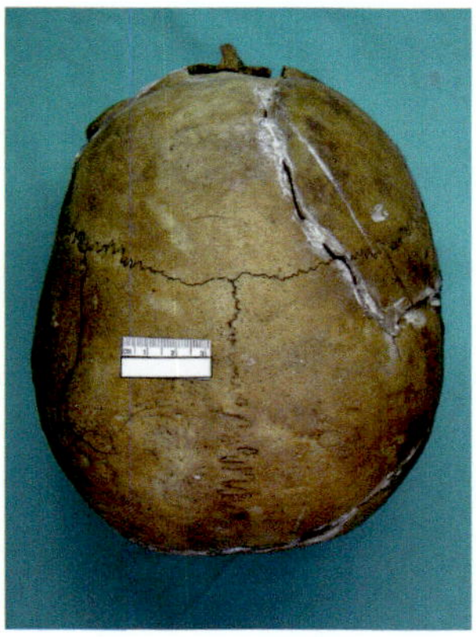

Figure 18.12 Photograph by the author.

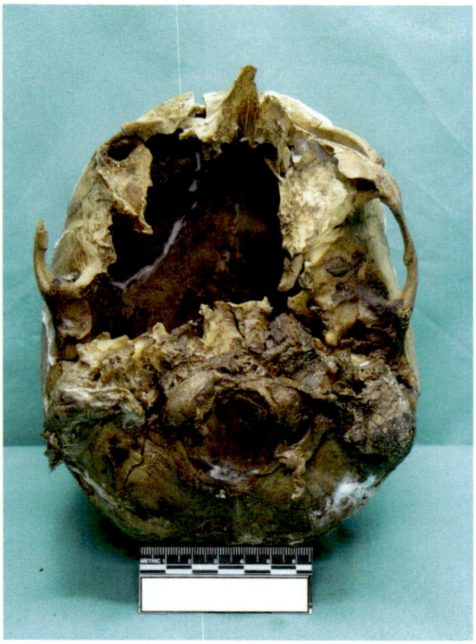

Figure 18.13 Photograph by the author.

7. Each side of the teeth must be photographed (front, left, right, and occlusal) as in Figures 18.14 to 18.17 without overlooking details as in Figures 18.18 to 18.21. This includes prostheses, bridges, and other similar elements.

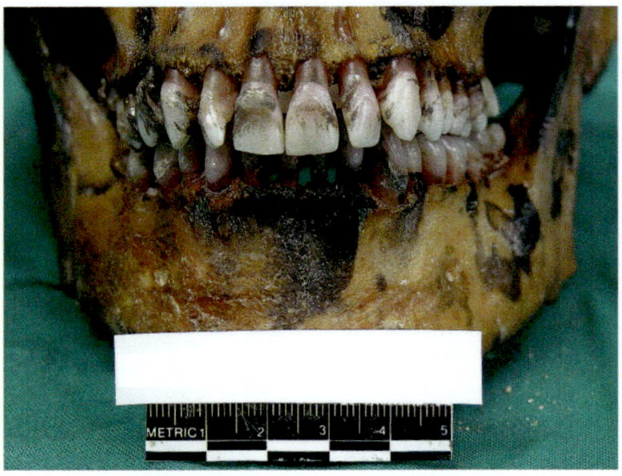

Figure 18.14 Photograph by the author.

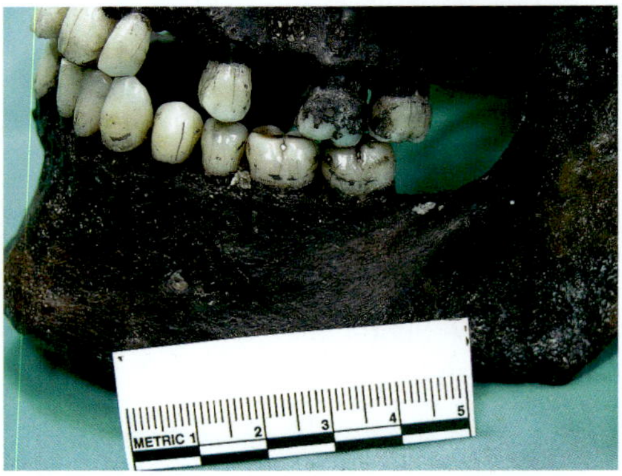

Figure 18.15 Photograph by the author.

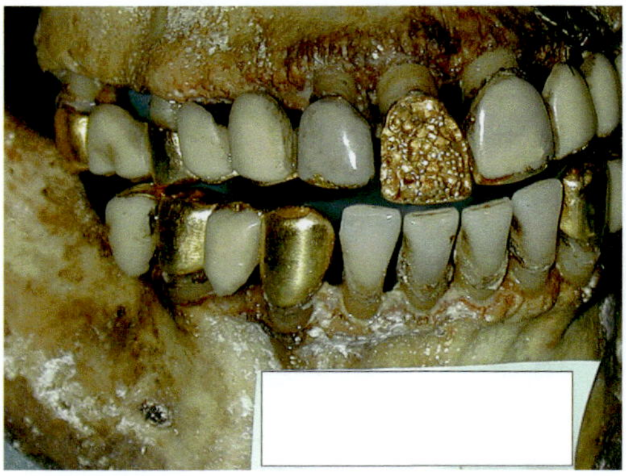

Figure 18.16 Photograph by the author.

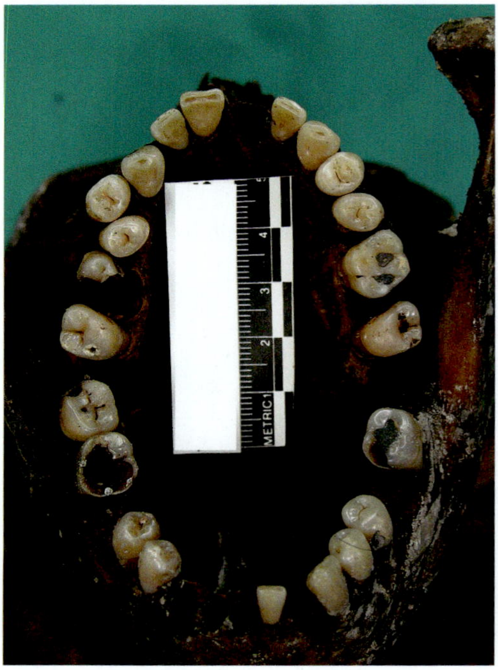

Figure 18.17 Photograph by the author.

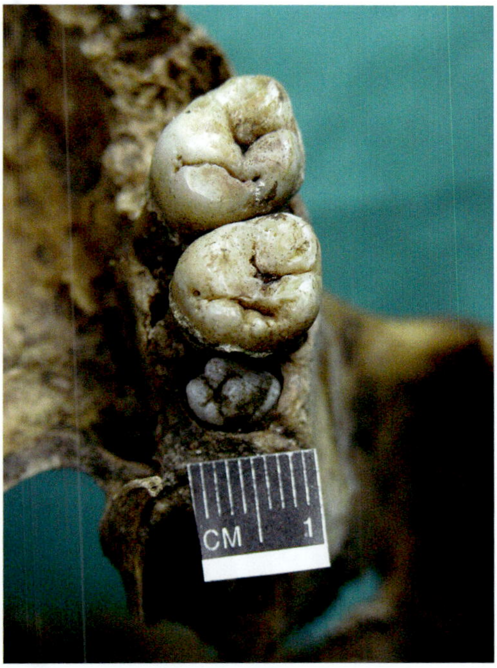

Figure 18.18 Photograph by the author.

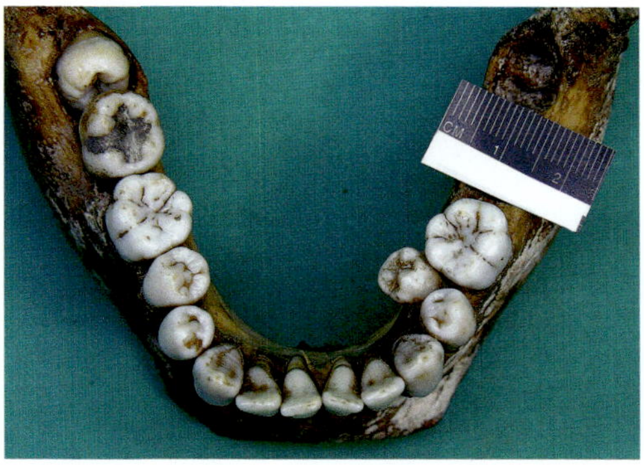

Figure 18.19 Photograph by the author.

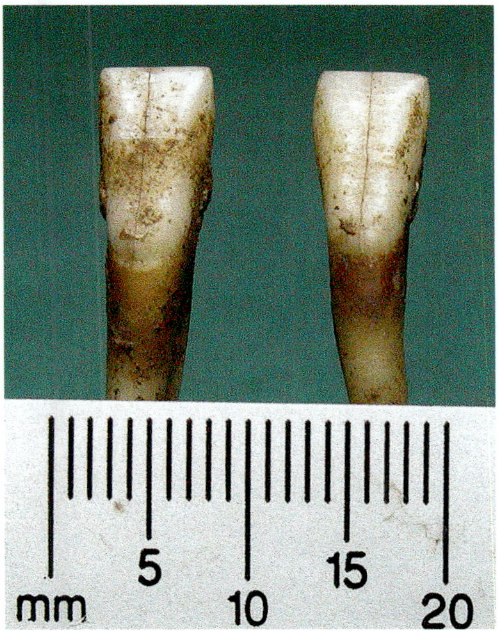

Figure 18.20 Photograph by the author.

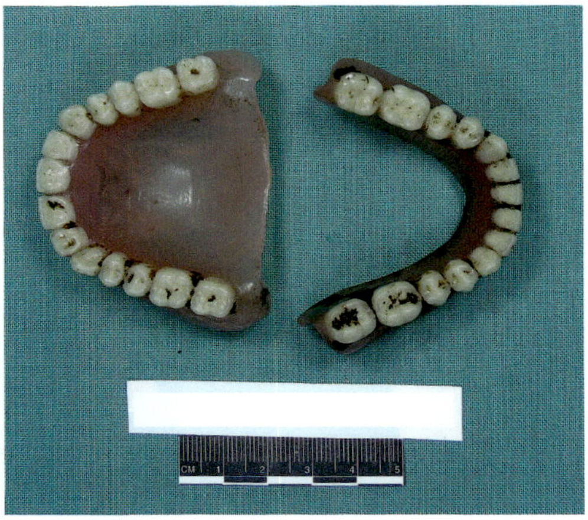

Figure 18.21 Photograph by the author.

8. Arrows are used to highlight the point of interest, whether an injury, an old fracture, or something else. Depending on the subject, to provide more information, a number will be added for the purpose of identification, as in Figures 18.22 to 18.24.

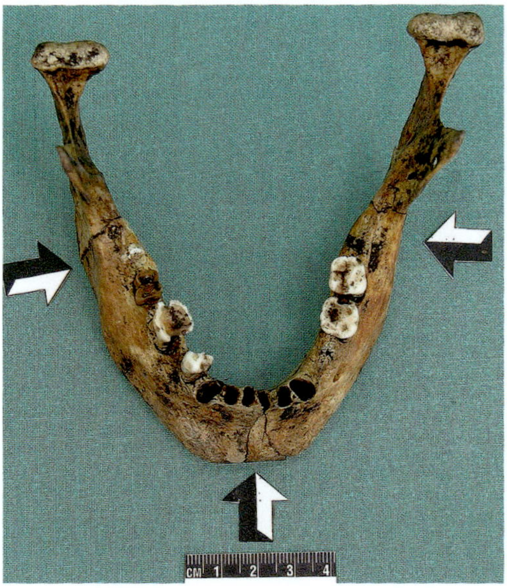

Figure 18.22 Photograph by the author.

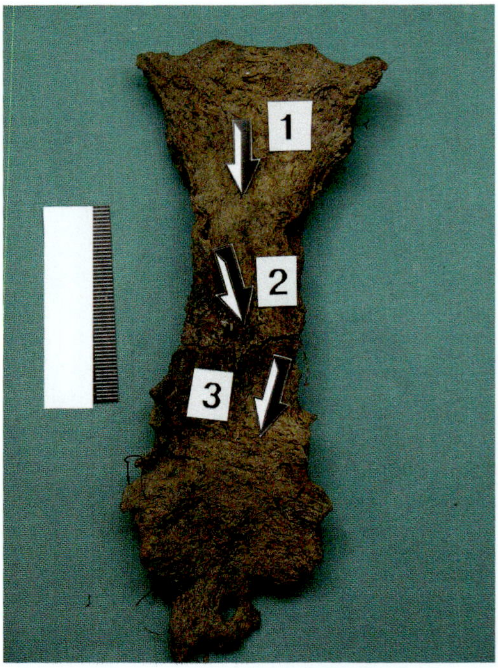

Figure 18.23 Photograph by the author.

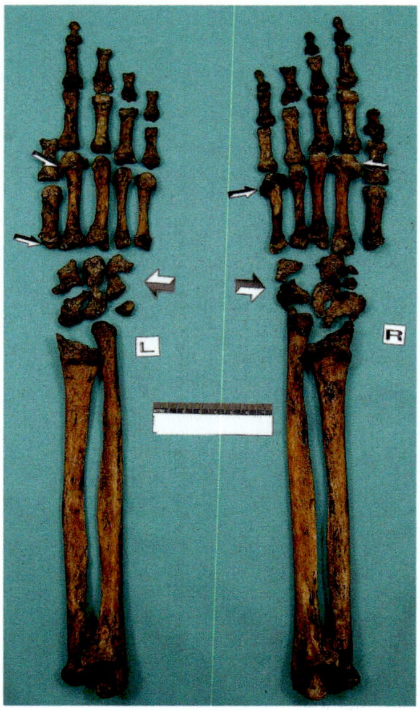

Figure 18.24 Photograph by the author.

9. When photographing the ribs, in anatomical position, a label should be included to identify the item as in Figure 18.25. The label might, for instance, read “R5” for right rib number five, as in Figure 18.26

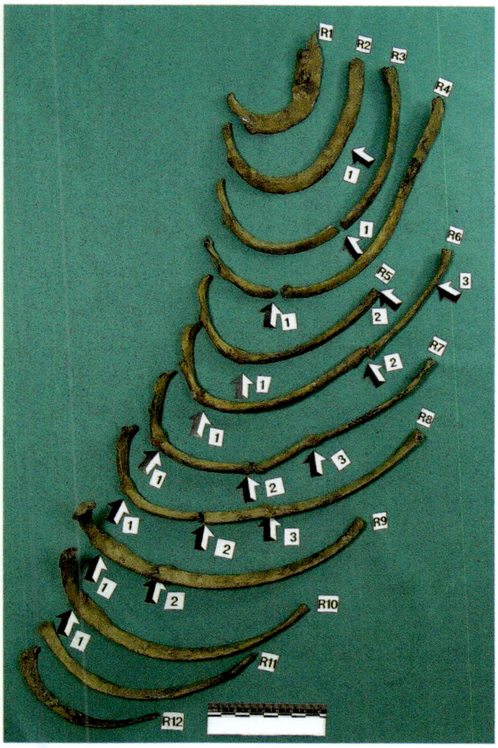

Figure 18.25 Photograph by the author.

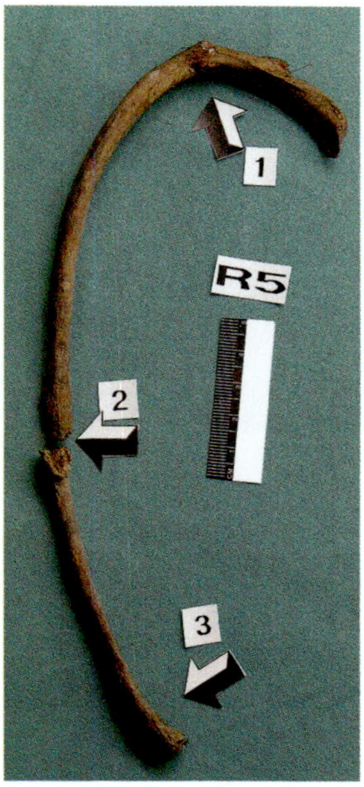

Figure 18.26 Photograph by the author.

10. It may be necessary to carry out a reconstruction to acquire a more comprehensive understanding of the type of fracture, as in Figure 18.27 and Figure 18.28, or gunshot trajectory as in Figures 18.29 and 18.30.

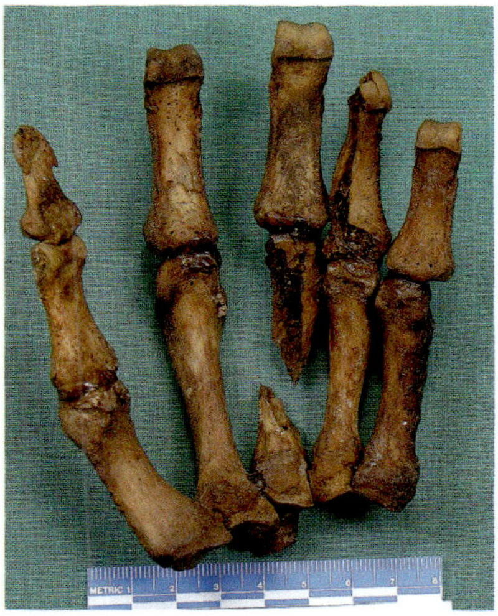

Figure 18.27 Photograph by the author.

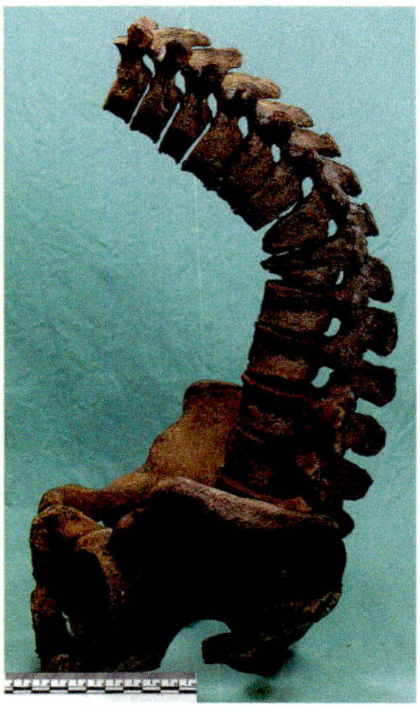

Figure 18.28 Photograph by the author.

For each gunshot trajectory, forensic rods (or similar) of varying colors (if possible) are used to identify a trajectory.

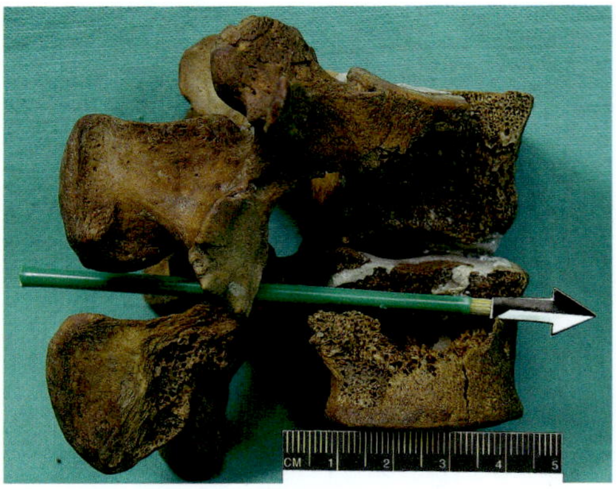

Figure 18.29 Photograph by the author.

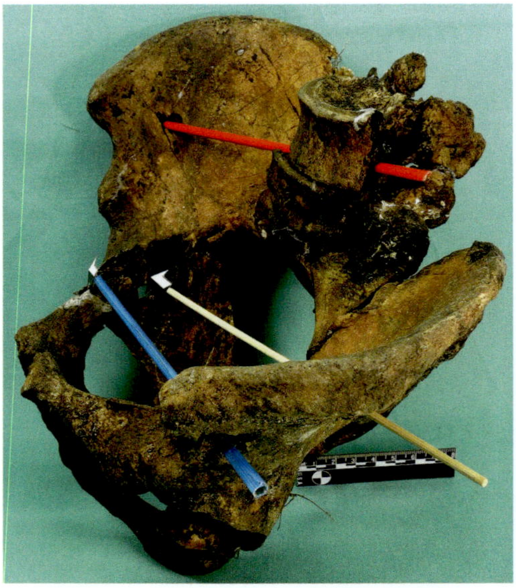

Figure 18.30 Photograph by the author.

11. To ensure that each piece of evidence or personal item is properly identified, it must be photographed and accompanied by a number, as in Figures 18.31 and 18.32.

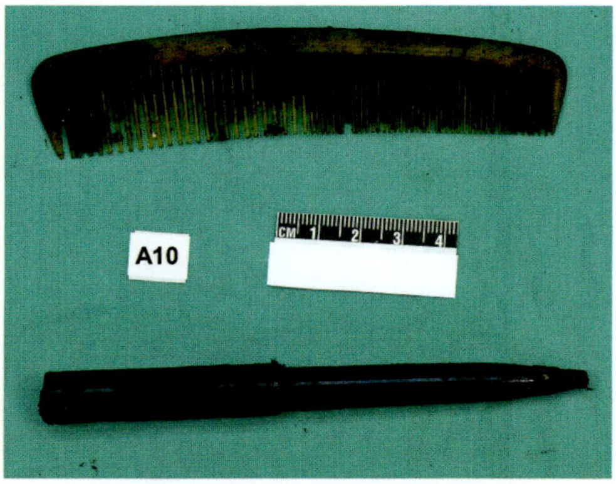

Figure 18.31 Photograph by the author.

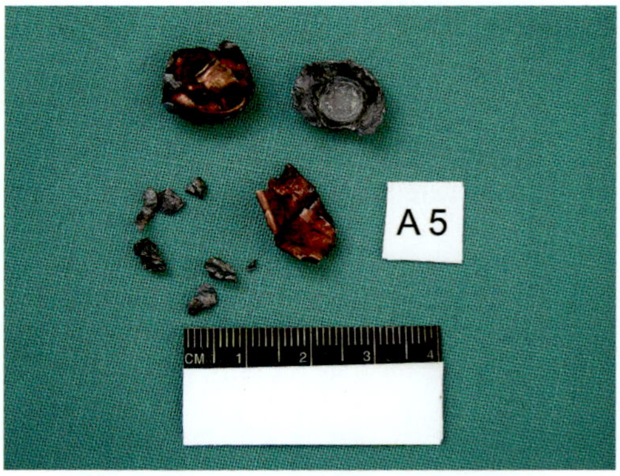

Figure 18.32 Photograph by the author.

12. General photos of the front and back of all garments should be taken whenever possible. These photos must cover the entire garment as in Figure 18.33. Then, for each garment individually, photos should be taken as in Figure 18.34, including additional information such as size, name, logo, as in Figure 18.35.

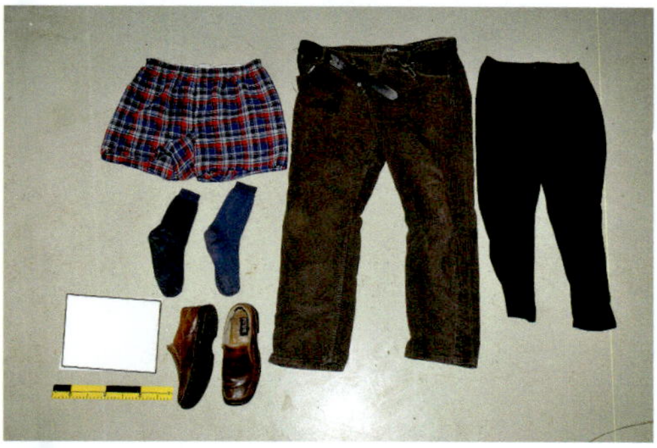

Figure 18.33 Photograph by the author.

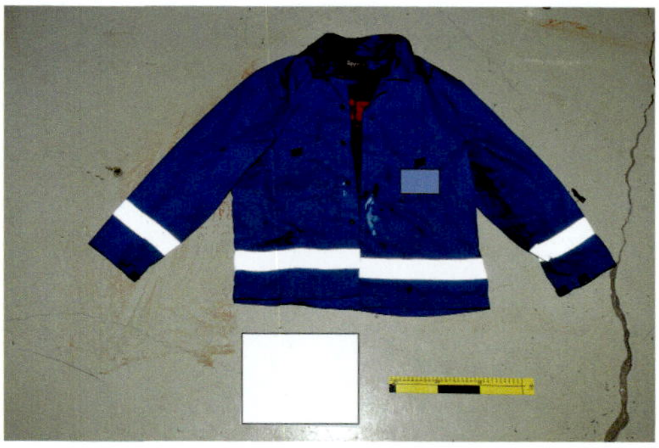

Figure 18.34 Photograph by the author.

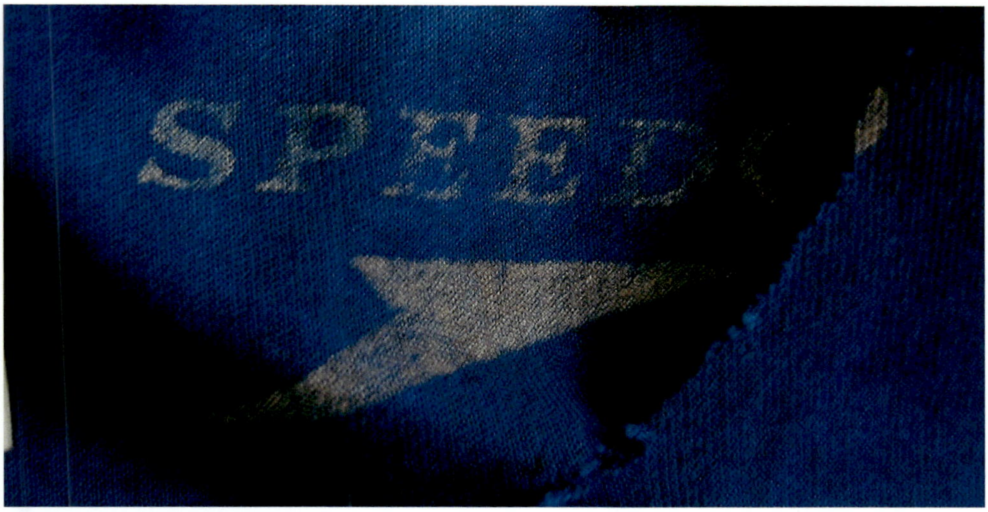

Figure 18.35 Photograph by the author.

Whenever there is evidence of a gunshot defect or any other type of damage, a general photograph will be taken, and arrows will be used to specify defects, as shown in Figure 18.36. This will be followed by taking a detailed photograph of the damage, as shown in Figure 18.37.

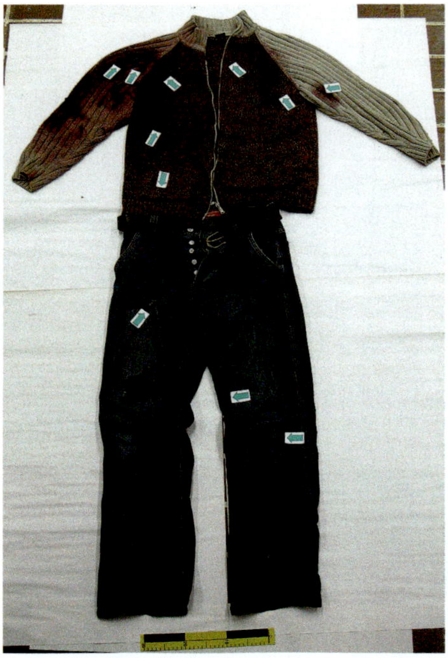

Figure 18.36 Photograph by the author.

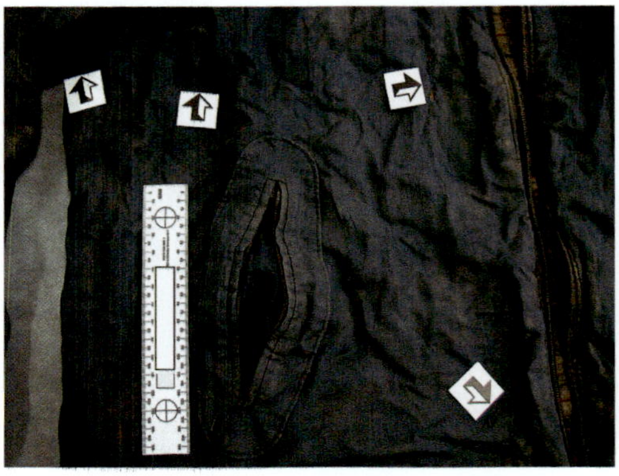

Figure 18.37 Photograph by the author.

13. To better understand and explain the injuries identified during the autopsy, it is advisable to take a photograph using a mannequin or a plastic skeleton, as in Figures 18.38 and 18.39.

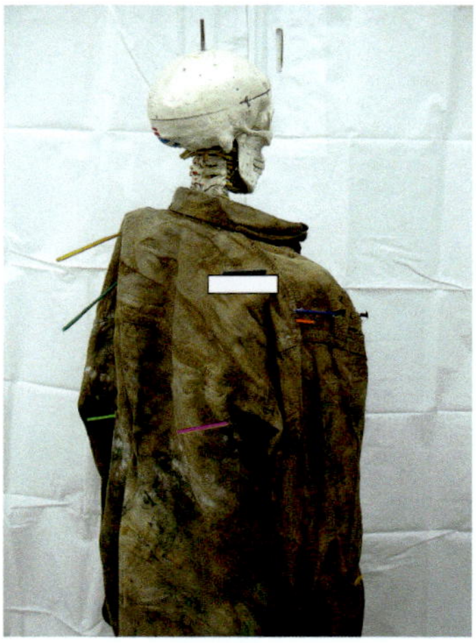

Figure 18.38 Photograph by the author.

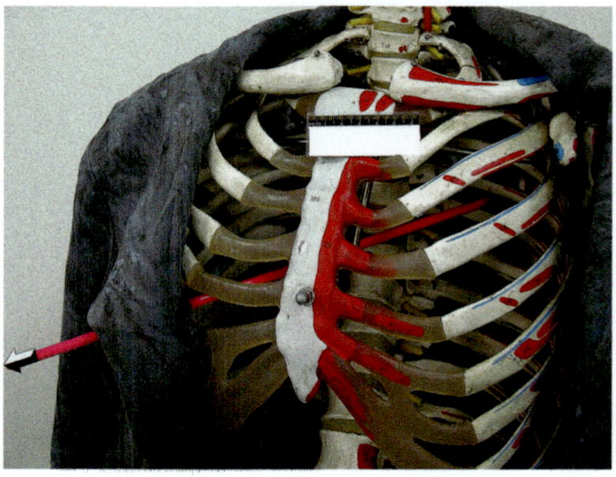

Figure 18.39 Photograph by the author.

14. Another option is to use the bone in conjunction with the associated garment as in Figure 18.40.

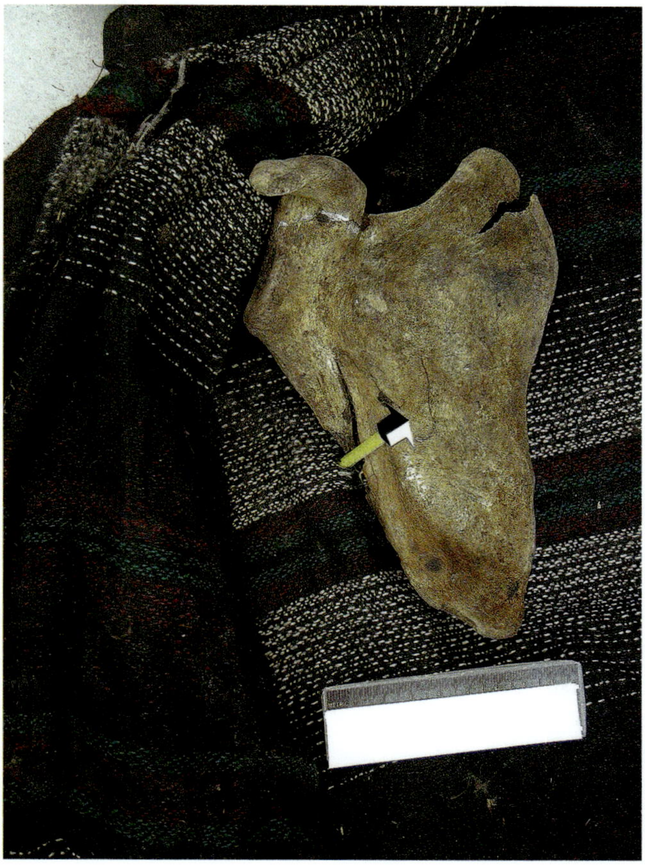

Figure 18.40 Photograph by the author.

Example for Identification as DVI or Other

In certain situations—such as train or plane accidents, tsunamis, or exhumations—examinations are conducted solely for identification. In these cases, photography is essential to support the identification process.

Photographic Process

1. General Overview: Start with a wide-angle photograph of the subject.
2. Detailed Shots: Mid-range followed by close-up images.

Technical Considerations

- Select the appropriate autofocus and camera settings for the subject.
- Avoid using flash on metallic objects to prevent glare.
- Position the camera for the best possible view.

Example and Limitations

An example of the photographic process for identification is provided below. However, depending on the condition of the body, some images may not be feasible to capture.

1. **Head**
   - Face and profile (front and side views).
   - Eye color.
   - Contact lenses (in situ and removed, if possible).
   - Glasses (in situ and removed, if possible).
2. **Dentition**
   - Tooth decay.
   - Prostheses, bridges, crowns.
   - Shark teeth, mixed dentition.
   - Other dental features.
3. **Body**
   - Old fractures, deformities, amputations.
   - Prosthetics (including surgical sutures, wires, staples, screws, plates, and serial numbers).
   - Birthmarks, scars, tattoos.
   - Other distinguishing features.
4. **Age Indicators**
   - Pubic symphysis.
   - Sternal rib ends.
   - Other age-related marker.
5. **Bone Reconstruction**
   - Compression, kyphosis.
   - Other structural factors.
6. **Clothing**
   - Document each item individually.
   - Brand, size, name, logo.
   - Other identifying details.
7. **Documents**
   - Insurance policies, car registration.
   - Wallet contents, personal letters.
   - Other relevant documents.
8. **Personal Items**
   - Keys, lighters, phones, glasses.
   - Any other items found with the body.
9. **Jewelry**
   - Piercings, earrings.
   - Medallions, bracelets, watches, rings.
   - Note: Record any inscriptions, maker's marks, names, dates, or other details.

Quiz 19

1. **If you are using a full-frame camera with a 50 mm lens, the relationship with a Nikon APS will be:**
   A: 50 mm
   B: 75 mm
   C: 80 mm
2. **When the aperture is set to f/4, what aperture allows twice as much light to enter?**
   A: f/1.4
   B: f/2.8
   C: f/5.6
3. **What is the depth of field?**
   A: The distance from the subject
   B: The area of focus in front of and behind the subject
   C: The coverage angle of the focal length used
   D: All the above
4. **What influences the depth of field?**
   A: Aperture
   B: Distance from the subject
   C: Focal length
   D: All the above
5. **Which of these apertures is the widest?**
   A: f/1.4
   B: f/5.6
   C: f/8
   D: f/16
6. **The exposure triangle is formed by three parameters; what are they?**
   1 –
   2 –
   3 –
7. JPEG is a type of file:
   A : Compressed
   B : Destructive
   C : Non-destructive
   D: A and B
   E: A and C
8. **Good exposure is the outcome of the following:**
   A: Speed, ISO, and aperture
   B: Light, aperture, and speed
   C: ISO, aperture, and light

DOI: 10.4324/9781003768838-22

9. **By having a high ISO, you will be able to:**
   A: Compensate for the lack of light with noise in the image
   B: Compensate for the lack of light without affecting the image
10. **Who determines the amount of light that is allowed to enter the camera?**
    A: ISO
    B: Speed
    C: Aperture
    D: Optical quality of the lens
    E: Speed and aperture
    F: Aperture and ISO
11. **Which of these settings will give you the maximum depth of field?**
    A: f/2.8
    B: f/11
    C: f/16
12. **Which aperture is accountable for the situations in which only a section of your shot is clear while the rest is blurred?**
    A: f/1.8
    B: f/8
    C: f/16

Answer 20

Camera

Photo 1: Canon G2—4 MP
Photo 2: Nikon 90—12.3 MP
Photo 3: Nikon D800—36 MP
Photo 4: Nikon Coolpix 5700—5 MP
Photo 5: Fujifilm S9100—9 MP
Photo 6: Nikon D200—0.2 MP

Quiz

Answer 1: B
Answer 2: B
Answer 3: B
Answer 4: D
Answer 5: A
Answer 6: Aperture, shutter speed, and ISO
Answer 7: D
Answer 8: A
Answer 9: A
Answer 10: E
Answer 11: C
Answer 12: A

DOI: 10.4324/9781003768838-23

Useful Resources 21

Exposure Simulation

This section presents a range of useful concepts and resources commonly employed in photography. These include exposure simulation, the exposure triangle, ISO, and shutter speed, all of which assist photographers in producing good quality images. A proper understanding and application of these principles contributes to effective photographic documentation and facilitates the accurate recording of visual information.

When given a particular set of camera settings, this application will attempt to create as close to an image as possible to the authentic final shot.

http://www.andersenimages.com/tutorials/exposure-simulator

With this program, you may achieve a balance that highlights underexposure and overexposure depending on the setting that you choose between ISO sensitivity, shutter speed, and aperture.

https://www.camerasim.com/exposure-contraption

Exposure Triangle

Using examples, this software will demonstrate how an exposure triangle operates. https://dima.fi/exposure

ISO

This web page will provide an explanation of how ISO operates, along with examples. https://exposuretherapy.ca/photography-guide/exposure-and-iso/

Shutter Speed

This web page will provide an explanation of how shutter speed operates, along with examples. https://10380663infostudies.wordpress.com/2012/09/21/week-2-basics-of-camera/

 DOI: 10.4324/9781003768838-24

Some Basic Glossaries

Aperture: Used to increase or decrease the amount of light coming into the camera.

Arrow: Arrows are used as visual indicators to highlight a specific element or draw attention to a point of interest. Additionally, they can be used to indicate the direction of a trajectory together with forensic rods.

Autofocus (AF): Allows you to automatically capture an object with sharpness.

Bracketing: Allows the camera to take three or more identical photos with different parameters in difficult conditions

Diaphragm: Made up of several metal blades that determine the aperture, which in turn controls the depth of field and the aperture.

Depth of Field: (DOF) The distance between the objects in a picture that appears to be in focus.

Exif: (Exchangeable Image File Format): Provided information about the images, including the date, time, aperture, speed, ISO, GPS, and other relevant details.

Exposure: The amount of light that hits the sensor, which will determine whether the photo is well-taken or not.

Forensic rods: Forensic rods come in various colors and are used in the process of reconstructing the trajectory of a bullet.

Histogram: A curve that illustrates the portions of a photograph that are bright and dark

ISO: (International Standards Organization): Allows adjustment of the amount of light when this is insufficient

JPEG: (Joint Photographic Experts Group): Standard format with image compression.

Noise: An unwanted component in photographs that can be caused by a high ISO, extended exposure times, or other variables.

Overexposure: The result of an image having an excessive amount of light.

RAW: Unlike JPEG, a format that does not compress photos but is heavier and contains more data.

Sensor: Captures the light transmitted by the lens and then transmits this data to create a digital image

Underexposure: The reverse of overexposure; photographs are darker, with insufficient light for appropriate exposure.

White balance: A process that involves adjusting a digital photograph to make the colors appear more real.

Some Bibliographic Resources

Fotografía forense aplicada a la antropología forense y bioarqueología, Alain Wittmann, 2014, ISBN: 9786120016152.

Handbook of Forensic Photography, Sanford Weiss, CRC Press Taylor & Francis 2022, ISBN: 9781003047964.

Human Osteology, Tim D. White, Michael T. Black, Pieter A. Folkens, Academic Press, 2011, ISBN: 9780123741349.

Human Osteology, Timothy D. White, Academic Press, 1991, ISBN: 9780127466101.

Revista de la Asociación Latinoamericana de Antropología Forense, diciembre 2025, alafforense.org/revista.

Skeletal Trauma, Identification of Injuries Resulting from Human Rights Abuse and Armed Conflict, Erin H. Kimmerle, José Pablo Baraybar, CRC Press Taylor & Francis 2008, ISBN: 9780849392696.

Traumatismos óseos: identificación de las lesiones resultantes de las violaciones de los derechos humanos y conflictos armados, Erin H. Kimmerle, José Pablo Baraybar, ISBN: 6124610108, 9786124610103.

Index